APPLIED ASSEMBLY LANGUAGE ON THE BBC MICROCOMPUTER

Edward Ball

Dept. of Elelctronic and Electrical Engineering, University of Salford

Prentice/Hall PHI International

Englewood Cliffs, New Jersey   London   New Dehli   Rio de Janeiro
Singapore   Sydney   Tokyo   Toronto   Wellington

British Library Cataloguing in Publication Data

Ball, Edward
  Applied Assembly language on the BBC
  Microcomputer.
  1. BBC Microcomputer – Programming
  2. Assembling (Electronic computers)
  I. Title
  001.64'2   QA76.8.B35

  ISBN 0-13-039389-4

ISBN 0-13-048992-1
ISBN 0-13-049008-3 (CASSETTE)

PRENTICE-HALL INTERNATIONAL INC., London
PRENTICE-HALL OF AUSTRALIA PTY., LTD., Sydney
PRENTICE-HALL CANADA, INC., Toronto
PRENTICE-HALL OF INDIA PRIVATE LIMITED, New Delhi
PRENTICE-HALL OF JAPAN, INC., Tokyo
PRENTICE-HALL OF SOUTHEAST ASIA PTE., LTD., Singapore
PRENTICE-HALL INC., Englewood Cliffs, New Jersey
PRENTICE-HALL DO BRASIL LTDA., Rio de Janeiro
WHITEHALL BOOKS LIMITED, Wellington, New Zealand

Printed in Great Britain by A. Wheaton & Co. Ltd., Exeter

10 9 8 7 6 5 4 3 2 1

To Helen and Elizabeth

Contents

Preface

Preface

This is a book on applying assembly language. Books on assembly language are often dry texts on computer science, mainly concentrating on the topic of arithmetic. This often puts readers off assembly language as arithmetic is one of the more difficult areas and in any case there is often little point in just being able to carry out quick arithmetic. The reader really wants a book which shows how to apply assembly language to the problems where it has real advantages.

The aim of the author has been to write such a book which makes assembly language attractive to those starting programming and, at the same time, shows how to use the strengths of assembly language in typical problems. The basic techniques are introduced gradually and then developed so that the reader is shown how to apply assembly language to write larger more interesting programs. The popular applications of assembly language graphics and a simple word processor have been chosen to demonstrate the techniques. The application of assembly language to interfacing the computer is also discussed and a simple electronic interface board is described.

A cassette tape is available separately containing software which takes the mystery and difficulty out of learning to program in assembly language. This software, called Monitor,

helps the beginner by providing assembly programming in a very
user-friendly form and it has been used to teach many hundreds
of beginners to program in assembly language. Monitor looks
after the reader through the early chapters of the book and
the ideas of assembly language are introduced gradually so
that, starting from a simple base, the more complex ideas are
developed. A listing of the program is given in appendix B
for readers who may not wish to purchase the tape.

Although the main emphasis of the book is not on arithmetic, a
book on assembly language would be incomplete without a study
of the subject. An introduction is given in chapter 5 and the
subject developed further in chapter 7.

In addition to Monitor the tape contains other programs
demonstrating animated graphics and a simple word processor,
both written in assembly language.

MACHINE REQUIREMENTS

The Monitor software has been designed for a model B BBC
microcomputer. A model A microcomputer may be used provided
it has been upgraded so that it has 32K of memory. The
software and book are suitable for all versions of the
operating system but the assembly language programmer will get
much more from the BBC computer if it has the more modern
version of the operating system (1.0 or higher). Early
machines may have the operating system 0.1 but these can be
converted at modest cost to the later version by ACORN dealers
and this is recommended as it gives access to many more
features of the machine.

APPLIED ASSEMBLY LANGUAGE
ON THE BBC MICROCOMPUTER

1

Introduction

WHY ASSEMBLY LANGUAGE AND MACHINE CODE?

Why bother with assembly language when BASIC is so good? BASIC is easy to program, it allows a very good level of access to most of the computers facilities, and it is much less complex than assembly language. In fact BASIC and the other high level languages have been developed for the very reason that they make the power of the computer available in an easily usable way.

Unfortunately the ease of use is bought at a price. One problem is that the computer needs to use a lot of its computing time in interpreting the high level statements and converting them into binary instructions. This makes languages like BASIC slow in operation. Another problem is that BASIC has been designed to simplify programming and although this is good, a simplified language necessarily restricts the programmer to that which can be expressed in BASIC.

For most programs these restrictions of lack of speed and flexibility are a small price to pay for the great convenience of a language which is easy to use. From time to time, however, problems occur which cannot be solved using a high level language and it is here that assembly language programming comes into its own.

There are two other good reasons for studying assembly language. It is very educational as it gives great insight into the detailed working of the computer chips and of course it can be a fascinating hobby. If you are tired of BASIC and are looking for a new stimulating direction what better than mastering the natural language of the computer?

Computer languages arouse strong feelings among programmers and some programmers dogmatically advocate the use of either BASIC or assembly language exclusively. It is more useful to take a balanced view and to recognise the strengths and weaknesses of each and to solve problems using the most appropriate language. With many microcomputers a choice has to be made between BASIC and assembly language but it is fortunate that the BBC computer in particular allows the programmer to mix BASIC and assembly language programs. The clever programmer then uses a mixture of the two languages, to obtain the advantages of each to solve problems that would be difficult or impossible using either language alone.

It is of some interest to look at the relationships between the different types of computer language so that an overall perspective can be gained.

The most fundamental form of instruction that the computer obeys is binary code i.e. a sequence of 0 and 1 digits, and the program consists of a list of code. Although unintelligible to people this code is the natural language of the computer. The direct use of binary code provides the most fundamental type of program but unfortunately it is very difficult for programmers to use. Binary codes are hard to remember and the consequent number of mistakes makes the development of programs a time consuming business.

A great deal of help in this "low level" programming using binary codes is available to the programmer through the use of ASSEMBLY LANGUAGE which gives access to the complete range of binary instruction codes through an intermediate easily remembered language. Even using this assembly language, however, it still takes a long time to develop programs.

Comparatively simple tasks are composed of long sequences of
assembly language. Mistakes are easily made due to the
complex internal structure of the computer.

For this reason the "high level languages" such as BASIC have
been devised. When using such languages the programs are
written in a form which is much easier to understand (usually
a mixture of statements very much like the standard
mathematical equations already learned from school and simple
words taken from everyday English language). The high level
language must be converted into the binary codes before the
computer can obey the program. This takes time and often uses
large amounts of memory. Two methods can be used: COMPILATION
and INTERPRETATION. The compiler takes the text of the program
and converts all of it into an equivalent set of binary codes
which are then stored. This complete binary program may then
be run at a later time.

An interpreter, however, operates quite differently. The text
of the high level language is taken in small sections and only
converted into binary instructions as the program is actually
run. This mixing of the text conversion and the running of
the binary codes makes the process slow. Interpreters are not
all bad, however, as the ability to run small sections of
program, with the immediate indication of errors, is very
useful when developing programs.

Compilers produce binary code which runs quite quickly but
they use large amounts of memory and take a long time to do
the actual compilation. For this reason interpreters are much
more common on microcomputers and the BASIC on the BBC
microcomputer is run by an interpreter.

Good though compilers and interpreters are, however, the
results of both are inferior in two ways to assembly
language. High level language versions of program frequently
occupy much more memory than assembly language programs and
take longer to run.

In general the advantages of using a high level language (ease
of use and speed of program development) greatly outweigh
these disadvantages, and most programs are therefore written
in high level languages. High level languages fall down,

however, when a program needs to run at the fastest possible speed or if the amount of computer memory is critical. A good example of this is the computer game. If a game is written in BASIC the movement of objects on the screen is limited by the speed of operation of the BASIC and in consequence jerky flickering images result. The use of assembly language, however, greatly speeds up the animation of objects and smooth motion is possible.

In conclusion BASIC (or other high level languages) are usually used in preference to assembly language due to the ease of programming. Assembly language is used when BASIC is too slow or does not give enough access to the internal structure of the computer.

NUMBERS

Before we can progress with a study of assembly language we need to look at how the computer deals with numbers. We need to know how numbers are stored in the computer and the details of how arithmetic and data manipulations are performed.

In everyday life the numbers that we use belong to the decimal system and we use the rules of arithmetic learned in the early years of life. The computer uses many of the same techniques that we are familiar with for adding, subtracting, multiplying and dividing numbers. The natural number system for modern computers, however, is the binary system (due to the ease of representing binary numbers electronically) and this has both advantages and disadvantages for the programmer and designer of computer systems. The first major disadvantage of course is that we are not familiar with binary numbers. It is difficult, even after many years of programming experience, to get a "feel" for the size of binary numbers and very difficult to carry out even simple mental arithmetic in binary. The seeming contradiction is that the rules of binary arithmetic are much simpler than those of the decimal system and the memorisation of long multiplication, division, addition and subtraction tables is not necessary. The human difficulty with binary is due to the fact that although the arithmetic rules are very simple, the numbers themselves are long monotonous sequences of "0"s and "1"s and are easy to forget.

Decimal

Before we progress to the binary numbers let us first return
to the early days of school work and revise the operation and
meaning of the decimal system. In the decimal system the
number ten is said to be the BASE or RADIX of the number
system and there are ten different symbols or digits
0,1,2,3,4,5,6,7,8 and 9 which represent the numbers less than
ten. Numbers of ten and over are represented by a sequence of
digits, for example the number 1275.863 is a short hand way of
saying that this number is the sum of:

```
  1   x ten x ten x ten
 +2   x ten x ten
 +7   x ten
 +5
      .
 +8   x 1/ten
 +6   x 1/(ten x ten)
 +3   x 1/(ten x ten x ten)
```

The point is known as the DECIMAL POINT.

Binary

The computer works in the binary system which has the radix 2
and there are two symbols 0 and 1 to stand for the numbers
less than two. Numbers greater than 1 are represented by a
sequence of digits as before. For example the binary number
1011.3101 which is interpreted as the sum:

```
  1   x two x two x two
 +0   x two x two
 +1   x two
 +1
      .
 +1   x 1/two
 +0   x 1/(two x two)
 +1   x 1/(two x two x two)
```

The point is known as the <u>BINARY POINT</u>.

Thus the binary number 1011.101 is equivalent to the decimal
number (1 x 8 + 0 x 4 + 1 x 2 + 1 x 1 + 1 x 1/2 + 0 x 1/4 + 1
x 1/8) .

This is equal to (8 + 0 + 2 + 1 + 0.5 + 0 + 0.125) = 11.625
decimal.

Integers

Numbers that have no fractional part are known as integers and
are the simplest type of number.   Fractional binary numbers
are left until Chapter 7 for further consideration.   For the
moment it is convenient to consider only integers.

Bits and Bytes

The BBC computer, in common with many other microcomputers
works with binary numbers that have a fixed length of eight
digits, commonly called 8 BIT binary numbers (a BIT is a
single binary digit). The name BYTE is given to such 8 bit
binary numbers. The structure of the byte is shown in Figure
1.1.

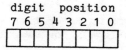

Figure 1.1

Digit position 0 is known as the least significant bit and
digit postion 7 as the most significant bit.

Some examples of bytes and their decimal equivalents are given
below:

```
00010110   decimal 22
11111111   decimal 255
           (the largest possible byte)

00000000   decimal 0 (the smallest)
10000000   decimal 128
```

Hexadecimal (HEX)

As it is so difficult to mentally picture or remember binary numbers it is often useful to work in a number system which is closely related to binary but has easily remembered numbers. Such number systems have a radix which is itself a power of two and the systems in common use are OCTAL (base eight) and HEXADECIMAL (base sixteen).

The hexadecimal system (usually called HEX for convenience) has been employed as the standard for the BBC microcomputer. In hex, as the radix is sixteen, there are sixteen symbols used to represent the numbers less than sixteen. They are: 0,1,2,3,4,5,6,7,8,9,A,B,C,D,E and F. The letters A to F are used for the numbers greater than 9. Numbers greater than F are written as a sequence of digits representing the sum:

```
 1    x sixteen x sixteen x sixteen
+7    x sixteen x sixteen
+A    x sixteen
+F
```

The hex number 17AF is thus equivalent to the decimal number (1 x 4096 + 7 x 256 + 10 x 16 + 15 x 1) = 6063 decimal.

The close relationship with binary means that it is very easy to convert from hex to binary and vice versa. Each hex digit is exactly equivalent to a group of four bits and conversion merely consists of exchanging them according to the following table:

HEX	BINARY	HEX	BINARY
0	0000	8	1000
1	0001	9	1001
2	0010	A	1010
3	0011	B	1011
4	0100	C	1100
5	0101	D	1101
6	0110	E	1110
7	0111	F	1111

To convert from hex to binary e.g. the hex number B2 we look up from the table that B is 1011 and 2 is 0010 and put the groups together to obtain 10110010. To convert from binary to hex e.g. 11010110 we perform the opposite process i.e. look up from the table that 1101 is D and 0110 is 6 and thus obtain the hex number D6.

Hex and Decimal Numbers in the Computer

The BBC microcomputer has the power both to read and print hex numbers as well as the more usual decimal. The method used on input is to precede the hex number with the & symbol e.g. &7621. The printing out of a number in the hex form is via a slightly modified form of the BASIC PRINT statement. The ~ symbol is placed directly in front of the number or expression to be printed e.g. PRINT ~X will print the number contained in X as a hex number.

These facilities are actually very useful as they enable very quick simple conversions of decimal and hex numbers to be performed. For example to convert from decimal to hex we just type PRINT ~ ddddd where ddddd is the decimal number to be converted. To convert from hex to decimal just type PRINT &hhhh where hhhh is the hex number to be converted.

It is possible to do the conversions without using the computer and a method is given in the appendix but it is mainly of academic interest as the user will usually rely on the PRINT statement as above.

THE INTERNAL STRUCTURE OF THE COMPUTER

We have already seen that the basic unit or size of number on
the BBC microcomputer is the 8 bit binary number or byte. The
computer has two main sections for working with these bytes:
the MEMORY which is a set of storage locations for remembering
bytes of program or data and the CENTRAL PROCESSING UNIT (CPU)
which performs all the arithmetic and control of the
computer. The memory is simply a list of storage locations
containing bytes. The position in the list of a particular
location is known as the ADDRESS of that location. The BBC
microcomputer uses a 16 bit (2 byte) binary number to specify
the address of stores. Thus the address of the first store is
0000000000000000 = &0000 and the address of the last store is
1111111111111111 = &FFFF (65535 decimal). Expressed in
decimal there are thus 65536 different locations.

It is interesting to have a brief look at the electronics of
this. The CPU is a single electronic unit (the 6502 chip
itself) and the 16 bit address is output on 16 separate wires
known as the ADDRESS BUS. It uses 8 separate wires to actually
transfer data and these wires are known as the DATA BUS.

In reading a memory location the 6502 outputs an address on
the address bus and generates a control signal to the memory.
The memory then places the contents of the specified address
onto the data bus for the 6502 CPU to read. Similarly to
write data into the memory the CPU outputs the required
address but this time it puts the data to be written onto the
data bus. A different control signal is sent to the memory to
cause the data to be written into the required address.

We can thus regard the data bus as a channel that the CPU uses
to communicate with the memory and the address bus as
specifying the source or destination of the data.

Figure 1.2 is an illustration of this.

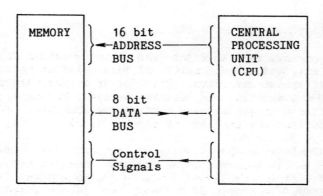

Figure 1.2

THE MEMORY

The storage locations may be of various types depending on the type of electronic components used to make them.   The   common types are:

Read Only Memory (ROM)

The values contained in this type of memory cannot be changed by the   computer   i.e.   the computer can only read from these locations and not write to them.   This   type of memory is used for storing fixed programs and data,   for   example   the   BASIC interpreter and the machine operating system.

Random Access Memory (RAM)

The bytes in this type of memory can both   be   read   from   and written to by the computer.   The   model   A   microcomputer   has 16384 (or &4000) bytes of RAM and the model B 32768 (or &8000) bytes. For convenience, the above numbers are often referred to as 16K and 32K (K is the symbol often used to denote thousands).   The model A is thus said to have 16K of RAM and the model B 32K.

Input/Output Devices

The computer has various input and output devices so that it can both read and output digital signals, also control various digital electronic circuits. The sort of things involved here are the chips that control the screen, keyboard, discs, printer, the analogue voltage reading system and the "user port" (used for the transfer of digital data).

In the BBC microcomputer the input/output devices are given locations in the memory and the computer communicates with the devices using the normal memory reading and writing instructions. This method is known as memory mapped input/output.

Paging

The total address range of the computer (65 536 locations) is subdivided into smaller groups of 256 locations, known as pages. The first 256 locations (addresses 0 to 255) are known as the zero page of memory, the next 256 as page 1 etc. The zero page of memory is of great importance to the assembly language programmer as many of the CPU functions have been optimised to work quicker in the zero page of memory. It is also important as it is used by the indirect operations.

Page 1 of the memory (addresses 256 to 511) is used by the computer for specialised CPU functions (subroutines and stack operations, Chapter 3).

CENTRAL PROCESSING UNIT (CPU)

The memory itself is only able to store data and programs, it is not capable of adding, subtracting or operating in any way on the data it contains. This function is carried out by the central processing unit or CPU, which, under the control of a program (a list of binary instruction codes stored in the memory), reads information from the memory, operates on it in some way and then usually stores the result back into the memory.

Registers

The CPU contains structures known as REGISTERS which are similar to stores in that they contain or store binary data. Unlike stores, which can only be read or written to, registers can perform more advanced functions on the data they contain. The CPU on the BBC microcomputer has several such registers and each has its own particular uses and range of functions. The most important is the A register (sometimes called the ACCUMULATOR) which is used for the majority of the arithmetic, logic and data transfers occurring in the CPU. Two other lesser used registers are the X and Y registers (sometimes called the INDEX registers) which are used for various counting operations (e.g. for program loops) and also in more advanced methods of referring to memory locations (INDEXED ADDRESSING MODES).

The CPU uses a 16 bit register called the PROGRAM COUNTER or PC to step through the instructions stored in the memory as programs are obeyed.

A special storage structure known as the STACK is contained in the memory. It is used for storing and retrieving information in a way such that the next item retrieved is the last item stored. This is useful in many assembly language programs and is dealt with more fully later (pages 54, 58). The CPU contains an 8 bit register called the STACK POINTER which is used to control this special data structure.

Finally the CPU also contains an 8 bit register called the STATUS register (sometimes called the P register). This is simply a collection of bits (called flags) that the CPU uses to control the detail of its arithmetic and logic operations, grouped together for convenience as a single byte. The internal CPU structure is illustrated in Figure 1.3

```
┌─────────────────────────┐        ┌─────────────────────────┐
│ ACCUMULATOR             │        │ PROGRAM COUNTER         │
│ (A register)            │        │ (PC) (16 bit)           │
│ (8 bit)                 │        │                         │
└─────────────────────────┘        └─────────────────────────┘

┌─────────────────────────┐        ┌─────────────────────────┐
│ INDEX REGISTER X        │        │ STACK POINTER           │
│ (8 bit)                 │        │ (SP) (8 bit)            │
└─────────────────────────┘        └─────────────────────────┘

┌─────────────────────────┐        ┌─────────────────────────┐
│ INDEX REGISTER Y        │        │ STATUS REGISTER         │
│ (8 bit)                 │        │ (P or flag              │
│                         │        │ register)               │
│                         │        │ (8 bit)                 │
└─────────────────────────┘        └─────────────────────────┘
```

CPU REGISTERS

Figure 1.3

PROGRAMS

The CPU can perform many types of operation on the memory
contents. It is instructed to carry out a particular
operation by a binary instruction code (called OP code). This
code is a single byte but, depending on the particular
function required it may be followed by another one or two
bytes specifying data or an address. A program consists of a
list of such instructions stored in the memory. The CPU
normally obeys each instruction in simple order, one after the
other, using the program counter to keep track of the list of
program instructions. The simple order can be changed by
certain specialised instructions (jumps, branches and
subroutines) but the detail of this is left until later.

A Simple Binary Program

The following sequence of binary codes is a program which,
when obeyed, causes the contents of memory location 01110000
to be copied into location 01110001. It does this by first
copying the contents of 01110000 into the A register and then
storing the A register into location 01110001.

Program:

                        10100101
                        01110000
                        10000101
                        01110001

The same program may be written in hex to make it a little easier to read.

Program:

                            A5
                            70
                            85
                            71

This fundamental level of programming is called MACHINE CODE PROGRAMMING as the program is written in the code that the computer actually obeys.

Mnemonics and Assembly Language

The above simple program written in hex is easier to remember than the binary form but it is still far from ideal. To understand the program we have to remember the meaning of the numbers A5 etc. Given the large number of possible codes and the fallibility of human memory we have a recipe for many errors. For this reason MNEMONICS and ASSEMBLY LANGUAGE have been devised to help the human memory to cope with the problem. A mnemonic is a collection of letters which is easy to remember as being associated with a particular CPU function and assembly language is the method of using these mnemonics to form a computer program. It is best illustrated by showing how the above program could be written in assembly language:

Program:

                        LDA &70
                        STA &71

The first mnemonic represents the instruction to load the A register (thus LoaD A) with the contents of the location &70 and the second to store the contents of A (thus STore A) into location &71.

It is obvious that the assembly language is easier to remember and understand than the binary or hex versions of the same program.

ASSEMBLERS AND DISASSEMBLERS

By its very nature the computer can only obey the binary instructions and cannot obey the text form of the assembly language. The assembly language must first be converted into the binary codes that the computer can execute and this process, called ASSEMBLY, is carried out by an ASSEMBLER. The assembler may take many forms but it is usually a computer program itself (or part of a program). It reads the program stored in text form in one part of the computer memory and converts it into binary in another part of the memory.

Occasionally we would like to operate the process in reverse to help to decipher the meaning of binary codes stored in the memory. This reverse process is known as DISASSEMBLY and it is carried out by a DISASSEMBLER. It is particularly useful when examining the operation of software written by others, when the text assembly language form (often called the SOURCE text) of the program is not available. For example the ACORN BASIC and MACHINE OPERATING SYSTEM can be inspected using a disassembler.

SUMMARY

Computers operate using binary numbers and instructions, which are often expressed in hexadecimal to make them easy to read and remember. The computer stores the numbers and instructions in the memory and carries out all its processing using the central processing unit (CPU). Assembly language is the natural language to program the CPU and is used for the applications where speed of operation is critical.

AAL-B

2

Getting Started

The BBC computer provides an assembler; access to this assembler is normally carried out through the BASIC interpreter. The system is very powerful, allowing programmers to operate in a mixture of assembly language and BASIC. It is not, however, particularly "user friendly" and does not contain built-in features to enable the programmer to easily learn assembly language or to "trouble shoot" sections of program which do not work. Assembly language programs often do not run the first time and then need extensive modification and development.

Monitor

The tape available as a supplement to this book helps to overcome these problems. It contains software called Monitor which is a simple but useful aid to the development of assembly language programs.

Monitor is a program written in a mixture of BASIC and assembly language (illustrating the author's belief in mixing languages to use the strengths of both) and may be listed, printed or modified by the user as for any other BASIC program. A listing of Monitor is given in the appendix.

Monitor is first loaded into the computer from the tape
recorder by the usual method i.e. CHAIN "Monitor" and then
the user interacts with the Monitor software to develop the
assembly language programs.

Numbers may be input to Monitor in either hex (using the &
prefix) or in decimal (no prefix).

ALL numbers displayed by Monitor are in hex.

If at any time you make a mistake when using Monitor it is
always safe to press the ESCAPE or BREAK keys. You can in
fact press the BREAK key when you get stuck or can't remember
the Monitor commands. The menu of commands will then be
displayed. The H command will also cause the menu to be
printed on the screen.

The simplest function or command that Monitor has is the D
command, which allows the contents of the computer memory to
be displayed on the screen in hexadecimal number format. When
D is pressed Monitor first asks for the start address of the
section of memory to be displayed and then for the number of
bytes that are to be displayed. It then prints in hex the
block of memory specified.

Addresses are printed on the left, at the start of each line
and then the contents of that location and the following eight
locations are printed along the line. If you try to display
more than 1 screen full of memory the computer stops after it
has output a screen and waits until the user presses the SHIFT
key.

Exercise:

Use the D command to display the contents of memory location
&70 and the following 20 bytes.

Changing the Memory Contents

The command M is used to change the contents of memory
locations. In response to the M command Monitor requests the
start address of the first location to be changed and then it

displays the address, and the data that it currently contains,
as hex numbers. If a change in the   contents   is   desired the
new contents are simply typed in,   either as a decimal number
(in the range 0 to 255) or as a 2 digit hex number
(remembering the & prefix of course). The RETURN key is then
pressed to step onto the next location. If no change in the
memory contents is wanted the RETURN key is pressed without
typing in new data.   Mistakes may be corrected using the
DELETE key, up until the point that the   RETURN   key has been
pressed. If you want to go back to a previous location enter
^ and then press the RETURN key. When you have finished using
the M command   just press the ESCAPE (or BREAK) key to return
to the COMMAND mode.

If Monitor detects an obviously incorrect number it informs
the user and returns with the prompt.

Although we will not study the use of text until Chapter 3,
for completeness it is pointed out that text may be stored in
memory using the M command. For further details see page 50.

Exercise:

Use the M command to set the contents of memory locations &70
onwards to the decimal numbers 0 1 2 3 4 etc up to 16, such
that &70 contains the number 0, &71 contains the number 1 and
so on until &80 contains the decimal number 16. Use the D
command to display this block of memory and notice that it is
displayed in hex.

Although we have not covered the use of names within assembly
language programs it is useful to know, for later use, that
the M command, in common with all Monitor commands, will
recognise such names as standing for their numerical values
and we can thus also refer to addresses and data by name.

Entering a Program

Programs are entered in text form using the E command which
causes Monitor to enter the Edit mode of operation. This mode
uses the built in BASIC and most of the BBC BASIC facilities
are available.   The notable exception is the RENUMBER command

which does not work with Monitor programs. If you need to
renumber a program then this may be carried out using the N
command of Monitor. DO NOT use BASIC RENUMBER as it will
renumber the Monitor program and you will need to load it in
again from tape. The familiar BASIC system of entering
programs is used and text is entered, with a preceding line
number, in the same way as for a BASIC program. This line
number should be in the range 10 to 10000. Line numbers less
than 10 are simply ignored by Monitor but line numbers larger
than 10000 should not be used as they will overwrite Monitor
itself and you will then need to reload Monitor from the tape
recorder.

Program statements are conveniently entered one per line but
more than one may be put onto a line if necessary. They are
then separated by a : exactly as for BASIC programs. As the
action of assembly language programs is often complex and
difficult to follow it is sometimes useful to include comments
along with the program text. Comments are inserted into
assembly language programs with a preceding \ character,(which
is printed in teletext mode 7 as a 1/2), and anything
following this character is ignored by the assembler until
either a : is encountered or a new line is started. This
differs from the computer's way of treating comments in BASIC
where following a REM statement all the remainder of the line
is ignored.

Exercise:

Enter the edit mode by pressing the E key from the Monitor
prompt COMMAND?.

Clear any previous program by pressing the function key f9.

Enter the following program (program 1) by typing

```
10 LDA &70
20 STA &71
```

pressing the RETURN key at the end of each line.

The red function key f1 will list your program on the screen.

Key f9 erases any program so that a new program may be entered.

Key f2 may be used to automatically enter a new program. It first erases any existing program and then automatically invokes the BASIC AUTO function. The ESCAPE key is used to leave the effect of f2.

The DELETE key may be used in the usual way to correct typing errors. As with BASIC if it is desired to change a line already typed in, the replacement line is simply typed in with its line number and it replaces the old.

Most readers will be familiar with the use of the BASIC editing keys (at the top right of the keyboard) and their use in conjunction with the COPY key. All the usual features of these keys are available in Monitor and may be used as desired.

When you are satisfied with the program and wish to use the facilities of Monitor press either the BREAK key or the function key f0.

Assembling a Program

Leave the E command by using the BREAK key and assemble the program by using the A command. The assembler converts the text into binary instructions, checking it for errors, and gives a description on the screen. This description contains several parts. The addresses used to contain the binary instructions and the instructions are printed out on the left of the screen with the mnemonic form of the instructions on the right. At the start of the program the rather mysterious message OPT#Z is printed. For the moment we may ignore this as it is concerned with the more involved details of the assembler. A description is given in chapter 4. Note that the assembler has decided itself where to store the binary program. By default it chooses a safe place to store the program but you may override this feature (using the S command).

Errors found by the assembler are reported on the screen.

Running a Program

The R command will cause the computer to run the last binary program produced by the assembler. At the end of running the program a jump back into Monitor is made and the contents of the CPU registers printed on the screen together with the address of the next location following the program. This address is known as the BREAK ADDRESS as it is the point at which the computer broke off running your program and resumed running the Monitor program.

Exercise:

Use the M command to set the contents of locations &70 and &71 to two different values and run the program using the R command.

Check, using the D command, that the program has run successfully : &71 should have been set to the number contained in &70.

Note that the contents of the CPU A, X and Y registers are printed on the screen after the program has been run together with the microprocessor FLAGS.

Flags

The flags are simple 1 bit stores inside the CPU whose values are changed by various arithmetic and logic operations. For example, the Z flag records if the result of certain operations is zero, and if it is the Z flag is set to the value 1. If the result is not zero, however, the Z flag is set to the value 0. (It seems the wrong way round to me too but that's how it works!)

The C flag is used to record if a previous arithmetic operation had a result that was too big to fit into an 8 bit binary number.

The other flags displayed are the N, V, B, I and D flags. The

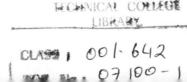

description of these will be left until later.

The individual flags are contained in a special register known as the STATUS or P register and this is printed out after the program is run. Note that bit 5 of the STATUS register is not used as there are only 7 flags and the order of the flag bits is NV?BDIZC, where ? stands for the missing bit 5.

When it Doesn't Work

The above simple program probably will work correctly first time but often assembly language programs do not initially. It then becomes very useful to know the status of the CPU at other points in the program than the end.   For example, although trivial in the simple case above, we could wish to check that the instruction LDA &70 really was loading A with the correct value.

Monitor provides two kinds of instruction to provide the answer to this type of question: the BREAKPOINT and the TRACE. The TRACE is used to step through a program, one instruction at a time, and the BREAKPOINT is used to to check the CPU status at a single point in the program.

Stepping through a Program (TRACE)

It is sometimes useful when developing programs to obey them one instruction at a time so that the detailed CPU operation may be followed through a program. This single stepping, or tracing, of program operation is provided in Monitor by the use of the Trace (T) command. This runs a previously assembled program one instruction at a time and gives a display on the screen of CPU status, before the program is run and then after each instruction is obeyed. It also gives the mnemonic form of each instruction for reference. The space bar on the keyboard may be used to control the stepping though the program, as each time the space bar is pressed another instruction is obeyed. This can be repeated as many times as needed until the end of the program is reached. Try the effect of using the T command, following assembly of the above program. Press the space bar until the end of the program is

reached. The command actually then single steps through a JSR
instruction which is the instruction which causes a return to
Monitor.

The ESCAPE or BREAK keys may be used to return to the Monitor
command mode at any time while single stepping.

Although not needed at this point it is useful to note that
if, instead of pressing the space bar to step   though
instructions, the S key is used instead it is possible to skip
over tracing instructions and only start the trace at a
specified address. This feature is very useful when longer
programs are being developed and the area of interest is at
the end of the program. Using S means that you can skip over
sections of program which work correctly and not be forced to
single step through the whole program every time.

Breakpoints

An alternative to stepping through every instruction in the
program, until the area of investigation is reached, is to let
the program run in the normal way until a specified address is
reached and then provide a print out of CPU status. This is
done by using the B command to set a BREAKPOINT on the address
at which the CPU status is required.   The program is then run
using the R command and, when the CPU encounters the address
at which the breakpoint is set, a print out of the CPU status
is given, the breakpoint is reset and further Monitor commands
may be given.

Exercise:

Assemble the above program 1 using the A command. A listing,
in hex, of the program's addresses is given on the left of the
screen. Use the B command to set a breakpoint on the address
at the start of the line with the STA &71 instruction, (do not
forget to put the & prefix in front of the hex address when
you enter the break address), and then run the program using
the R instruction. The program will then stop running just
before the STA &71 instruction and the CPU status will be put
on the screen.

AAL-B*

Note that breakpoints should only be set to addresses which
are the start of an instruction. These addresses are always
printed on the left of the screen by the assembler. The
reason for this is that the process is realised by Monitor in
a fashion which can only be effected at the start of an
instruction. Actually the instruction at the break address is
temporarily replaced by a jump into Monitor for a print out of
the status.

Further Breakpoints

Only one breakpoint is allowed at a time but following a break
it may be reset to a later point in the program again using B.
The program may then be restarted following the break by the
use of the U (resUme) command. This lets the program continue
from the break until the new break address, or the end of the
program, is reached.

The B and U commands may be used as many times as required to
step through a program.

Exercise:

Assemble the program and again set a breakpoint on the address
of the STA &71 instruction. Run the program and when the
break is encountered use the U command to resume the running
of the program.

Saving and Loading Programs

This is accomplished by the use of the BBC operating system
*SPOOL and *EXEC commands. To write to a file it is first
opened by issuing the *SPOOL nnnn command in the Edit mode of
Monitor, where nnnn is the desired file name. Following this
everything listed on the screen is also stored in the file
named in the *SPOOL command. When the file writing is
finished the user issues a *SPOOL command with no file name
and this closes the file.

For example, remembering that the users Monitor program
resides in line numbers 10 to 10000, the following program

lines will save the users program in a file called PROG1.

```
*SPOOL PROG1
LIST 10,10000
*SPOOL
```

The program is read back into Monitor by using *EXEC PROG1 which takes PROG1 and reads it in as if it were keyboard input. This has the effect of loading the saved program back into Monitor. Note that, as the program is loaded back in, the computer generates some error messages. These can be ignored as they do not effect the program read in. They are simply due to the fact that, *SPOOL has saved, along with the desired program lines, the lines >LIST 10,10000 and >*SPOOL and when these lines are read back in error messages result. This unfortunate fact is a property of the way that *SPOOL operates and applies equally to programs written in normal BASIC.

This method works for tape and disc filing systems but not the ECONET level 1 file server. The level 2 file server should remedy the problem.

SOME BUILDING BLOCKS

We now introduce some of the basic techniques used in constructing assembly language programs. The methods of specifying data are studied first and then a study of program loops and decision making is made followed by a look at some of the more advanced features of Monitor.

ADDRESSING MODES

We have so far seen only one instruction for loading the A register with a number and this is the LDA &70 instruction for loading A with the contents of memory location &70. There are many other types of instruction for loading the A register. Many have the LDA mnemonic but the information which follows the LDA is different and specifies a different source of data from which A will be loaded. The term ADDRESSING MODE is used to describe the different methods of addressing the data source. The modes will now be described in turn.

Immediate Mode

The A register is loaded with the number specified in the
instruction e.g. LDA #5

The A register is loaded with the number 5. The # symbol is
used to indicate the immediate mode.

Exercise:

                    10 LDA #5
                    20 STA &70

Return to the Edit mode, push the f2 key and input the above
program. Return to Monitor using f0 or the break key and
assemble it using the A command. Notice from the assembly
listing that the LDA #5 mnemonic has assembled into two bytes
of code. The first byte is &A9. This instructs the CPU to
load the A register with the byte immediately following. It
can be seen that this byte is the number &05 specified in the
instruction. This is the reason that this mode is referred to
as the immediate mode of addressing. Run the program. It
should load A with the number 5 and then store this number
into the store location &70.

Zero Page

The zero page is the first 256 bytes in the memory,
corresponding to the address range 0 to &FF and this is a very
valuable part of the memory on a 6502 microprocessor. Some
microprocessors have been designed so that they have many more
registers than the 6502 microprocessor used by the BBC
microcomputer. This can be an advantage as a register is a
particularly fast efficient method of handling data. This is
because the registers are contained inside the electronic CPU
chip and the relatively slow process of data transfer between
the CPU chip and the memory is not needed. In contrast the
6502 CPU has very few registers and so at first sight appears
to be a poor relation. This is not so, however, as the 6502

has been designed to operate very efficiently with the
zero-page of memory and in fact the whole of the zero-page can
be considered for many purposes as being equivalent to the
registers on other CPUs. It is interesting to note, therefore,
that the 6502 has in the zero page of memory the equivalent of
256 single byte (or 128 double byte) registers whereas say the
Z80 CPU has far fewer registers.

Many of the 6502 instructions have been designed to operate
very quickly with data from the zero- page of memory and the
term zero-page addressing mode is used to describe this fast
method of data access.

It is, in fact, the mode corresponding to the LDA &70
instruction already encountered. In this mode A is loaded
with the contents of the memory location specified. When the
location is in the zero-page of memory (address 0 to &FF) it
is said to be the zero-page addressing mode. The instruction
assembles to two bytes of code. The first is &A5 and this
instructs the CPU to load the A register with the contents of
the zero-page memory location specified in the next byte. In
this case this is the number &70. These zero-page addressing
instructions only take two bytes of code and this has two
advantages. First the instruction executes quickly as only
two bytes of instruction have to be read from the memory and
secondly the program length is reduced.

As we have already used this mode (without referring to it by
name) a separate exercise will not be given at this point.

Absolute Mode

If the address following the LDA is bigger than &FF it needs a
two byte number to specify it's value and it is then said to
be an absolute address rather than a zero-page address.

Exercise:

```
10 LDA &5000
20 STA &70
```

Enter and assemble the above program and notice that the LDA

&5000 now is equivalent to three bytes of code. The first
byte is the number &AD and this instructs the CPU to load the
A register with the contents of the address specified in the
following two bytes. The next byte is &00 corresponding to
the least significant byte of the address and the next is the
number &50 for the most significant byte of address.

This reversal of bytes in a 16 bit address is fairly common on
many microprocessors and may seem strange at first as when a
list of address contents are printed out the numbers do not
read correctly.

Set the contents of addresses &5000 and &70 to known but
different numbers and run the program to test its correct
operation.

Indexed Mode

The indexed addressing modes are very powerful methods of
specifying the source of data. The register X or Y is used
and A is loaded with the contents of the address formed by
adding X or Y to the address specified in the instruction.
Say for example that X contained the number 5, then LDA
&5000,X would load A with the contents of location &5005.

The indexed mode is available for certain instructions both on
full two byte addresses and also for zero-page addresses. The
full absolute indexed form takes three bytes of code whereas
the zero-page indexed form takes only two bytes.

Indirect Modes of Addressing

In computer terms the word indirect can best be translated
into ordinary terms by translating the word indirect into the
phrase "the contents of". Thus an indirect jump to say memory
location &5000 would not cause the computer to jump to the
address &5000 but would cause it to jump to the address
specified by the contents of &5000. Say that &5000 contained
&72 and &5001 contained &34, together containing the 16 bit
number &3472 then an indirect jump to &5000 would actually
cause the computer to jump to the address &3472.

The indirect mode is always indicated by the presence of parentheses (round brackets) in the mnemonic. Thus an ordinary jump to location &5000 is JMP &5000 whereas an indirect jump to the contents of &5000 is JMP (&5000).

Indirect Indexed Mode

This is a very powerful mode of operation which is frequently used. It allows the above indirect mode to be used in conjunction with the Y index register. A zero-page memory location is specified in the instruction and the CPU goes to this address and the one immediately above it and gets the 16 bit contents stored there. It then adds the Y register to this 16 bit number and then goes to the resulting address for the source of data. The description "indirect indexed" is given because of the order in which the operations are carried out. The indirect part is obeyed and then the index Y is applied to the indirect address obtained.

For example say that Y has the value 5, &70 contains &56 and &71 contains &23. The instruction LDA (&70),Y causes the CPU to go to &70 &71 and get the 16 bit number &2356. It then adds Y to it to get the value &235B and then loads A with the contents of &235B. To begin with this always seems a long way round of doing things but in effect it allows the zero-page memory locations to be used as indexed 16 bit pointers to address values. Further consideration is given in chapter 3.

Indexed Indirect Mode

The operations of indexing and indirection are carried out in the reverse order to the mode above. The indexing is carried out first and then the indirect look up of address is carried out. This instruction is written as follows LDA (nn,X) , where nn is a zero page address. The CPU first adds the X register to the number nn and then goes to the zero page memory specified by this result and gets the 16 bit address stored there. The A register is then loaded with the contents of this 16 bit address. For example say the stores &84 and &85 contain the numbers &00 and &50 and the X register

contained the number 4 the the instruction LDA   (&80,X) would
load A with the contents of address &5000.

This instruction is rather specialised and is not really used
much. Occasionally it can be used with X set to 0 and then a
simple indirect load of A takes place.

Implied Mode

Certain mnemonics contain or   IMPLY a source of data for the
data transfer and   the   source   of data does not follow the
mnemonic as above. An example is the TXA instruction which
causes the X register contents to be transferred to the A
register.

MOVING SMALL BLOCKS OF DATA IN THE MEMORY

The first simple program given was for moving a single byte of
data from one memory location to another. A common problem is
that of copying a sequence of many bytes from one section of
the memory to another. This problem is used here as an
introduction to the indexed addressing modes.

The basic method is to use the indexed forms of both the LDA
and STA instructions. The following two line section of
program illustrates this:

                    LDA &5000,X
                    STA &6000,X

Say X contained the value 5, then the first instruction loads
A with the contents of &5005 and the second stores A into
&6005. The advantage of the method is that there are special
instructions for incrementing and decrementing the value of X
and Y and so by altering the value of X in the above program
the same instructions may be made to operate on different
memory locations. The technique is to put the two
instructions in a program loop so that they are executed many
times with different values of X, rather like the FOR NEXT
loop in BASIC. The possible range of values of X is 0 to 255
as X is an 8 bit register so the technique may be used to move

blocks of memory up to 256 bytes long.

LOOPS AND LABELS

A program loop is a method of repeatedly executing the same
section of program many times. It needs the following:-

a) A loop counter to count the number of times that the loop
has been performed,

b) A test to see if the loop counter has reached the final
value and also a method of jumping back to the start of the
loop.

The start of the loop is usually identified with a LABEL. The
label is an identifying word inserted into the assembly
language so that a particular point in a program may be
referred to by a meaningful name rather than just the binary
address and the label serves as a target for a jump or branch
instruction. When inserted into the program the . prefix is
used to tell the assembler that the following text is to be
treated as a label. The end of the label may be denoted in
three different ways, by following it with a : space or by
pressing the RETURN key to start another line.

The three methods are shown below:-

1)   30 .LAB1
     40 LDA &5000,X
     50 STA &6000,X

2)   30 .LAB1:LDA &5000,X
     40 STA &6000,X

3)   30 .LAB1 LDA &5000,X
     40 STA &6000,X

In fact the : symbol is a general purpose separator for both
BASIC and assembly language and may be used to fit more than
one instruction on a line whether labels are used or not.
Thus yet another way of writing the above would be:-

```
30 .LAB1:LDA &5000,X:STA &6000,X
```

Thus any of the above methods may be used to make LAB1   refer
to the start of the loop.

Names for Labels

Certain names are not allowed as labels by the assembler. The
rule is that labels are not allowed to start with a number and
also must not begin with BASIC reserved words. The principle
BASIC words to beware of are the short ones such as   TO, END,
FOR and DEF. It is possible to avoid this problem altogether
by always using some convention such as, say using lower case
for labels or always beginning a label with some character
sequence which is known cannot clash with BASIC. The assembler
will report clashes that it finds with an error message.

As an example of a wrongly chosen name try to use the label
name TOWN in a program. This clashes with the BASIC TO and
thus produces an error message.

Loop Counter

The loop counter may take many forms, registers or memory
locations may be decremented to zero or incremented until some
end value is reached.   Although incrementing and decrementing
may both be used decrementing is often preferred because it is
easier to test for the final zero condition using the Z flag
than it is to test if a count is equal to some specified
number when counting up. For the present we shall use the Y
register and count down, using the DEY instruction which
decrements the value of Y by one, until the value zero is
reached. At the start of the program Y is loaded with the
number of times that the loop is to be obeyed and at the end
of the loop it is decremented and tested for being zero. If Y
is not zero then a jump (or branch) is made back to the start
of the loop. If Y is zero then execution of the loop is
terminated.

Conditional Branching

The conditional branch instructions test the flags and branch
depending on the state of the flag tested. For the above loop
the instruction BNE LAB1 may be used. This instruction will
branch to the label LAB1 if the result of some previous
operation was not equal to zero (Branch Not Equal to zero).
Just for comparison consider the opposite instruction BEQ
which would branch if the previous operation resulted in zero
(Branch if EQual to zero).

To complete the block move program we need to set the initial
values of X and Y before the start of the loop and increment X
and decrement Y just before the end of the loop.

The LDX and LDY instructions may be used to load X and Y with
values, for example LDX #0:LDY #10 will load X with the number
0 and Y with the number 10.

The instruction INX will increment (add one to) X and DEY will
decrement (subtract one from) Y. The program becomes:-

Exercise:

```
10 LDX #0
20 LDY #10
30 .LAB1
40 LDA &5000,X
50 STA &6000,X
60 INX
70 DEY
80 BNE LAB1
```

Enter the above program, assemble and run it, having first
used the M command to set the memory to some test data to
verify that the block move is carried out correctly.

It is important to note which instruction sets the Z flag
(that the BNE instruction tests) in the above example. Many
instructions can effect the flags and in the above example the
Z flag is effected by the LDA, INX and DEY instructions. The
BNE instruction operates on the condition of the Z flag as it
finds it , i.e. as it was left by the last instruction which

changed the Z flag. Thus in the above program it is
effectively testing if Y has been reduced to the value zero.
Note that the order of the INX and DEY instructions above is
therefore MOST IMPORTANT as if they were interchanged the BNE
would check if X were reduced to zero and not Y. This would
not be correct and the block move would not be carried out in
the way desired.

In general, therefore, when using the conditional branch
instructions to test the flags it is <u>VERY GOOD PROGRAMMING
PRACTICE</u> to try to keep the branch instruction immediately
following the instruction that sets the flag to avoid
intervening instructions having some undesired effect on the
flag.

Note similar instructions: DEX decrements X, INY increments
Y,INC increments memory, DEC decrements memory. e.g. INC
&5000 increments the contents of&5000 and DEC &5000 decrements
the contents of&5000. Unfortunately there are no instructions
for directly incrementing and decrementing the A register.

The above program amy be made more efficient by using the same
register both for the loop counter and also the index. Say
lines 20 and 70 are deleted then the same block transfer is
carried out starting with the high values of the index first.

MORE ADVANCED LOOP COUNTING

The method used above counted the Y register down to zero and
used the BNE instruction to test for Y zero. It is also
possible to count up using a register (INY to increment Y, INX
to increment X and INC to increment memory locations) but now
the register being used does not have a final value of zero
and so BNE may not be used. There are various comparison
instructions which may be used to test if a register or a
memory location is equal to a given number.

To test if Y is equal to a number the CPY instruction is used
and it can be used with immediate data or in various other
addressing modes. So for example CPY #8 will compare Y with
the number 8. If Y has the value 8 then the Z flag is set and
the BNE instruction (or BEQ instruction) may be used to test

for this condition. If Y is greater than or equal to 8 then C flag is set. The N flag is set to 1 if bit 7 of the result is 1. See Chapter 6 on positive and negative numbers. This is usually taken as meaning that Y is less than the value with which it is being compared.

Some examples illustrate the use of CPY:

Exercise:

```
10 LDY #0
20 .loop
30 INY
40 CPY #5
50 BNE loop
```

The loop is obeyed until Y has the value 5.

Test the program using the T command.

Exercise:

```
10 LDY #0
20 .loop
30 INY
40 CPY &5000
50 BNE loop
```

In this program the Y register is compared with the contents of &5000. Use the M command to set &5000 to some known value and run the program.

Exercise:

```
10 LDY #0
20 .loop
30 INY
40 CPY #8
50 BEQ exit
60 JMP loop
70 .exit
```

This example shows an alternative way of constructing a loop.

The BEQ instruction is used in this case to branch out of the loop when the end condition is detected. The JMP instruction is an absolute jump which always causes a jump to the label or address specified in the instruction.

The X register may be tested in the same way using the CPX instruction.

Exercise:

Repeat the above exercises using X instead of Y.

Memory locations may also be used as loop counters to count up or down. For counting down the DEC instruction is used and when the location has been decremented to zero the Z flag is set and may be tested in the usual way.

Exercise:

```
10 LDA #7
20 STA &5000
30 .loop
40 DEC &5000
50 BNE loop
```

Run the above program and check that &5000 has been decremented to zero at the end of the program.

Modify the program by including say an INX instruction inside the loop to check that it has been obeyed the correct number of times.

When counting up using a memory location INC is used and the comparison instruction used in this case is the CMP instruction. This compares A with a memory location with A containing the number to be tested against the contents of the memory location.

Exercise:

```
10 LDA #0
20 STA &5000
30 LDA #9
```

```
40 .loop
50 INC &5000
60 CMP &5000
70 BNE loop
```

Note that A is loaded with the test number before the loop and
that line 60 compares A with the contents of &5000.

If A is used inside the loop for some purpose, which is
usually the case, then it must be loaded with the test number
inside the loop just before the CMP instruction.

It is possible to use A itself for loop counting but this is
not usually done as there are no special instructions for
incrementing and decrementing A and the arithmetic addition
and subtraction instructions must be used instead. This is a
little more clumsy than the methods described above and in any
case the A register is usually needed for the operations
inside the loop.

Unconditional Jumps

The branch instructions branch depending on the condition of
the relevant flag. There are two JMP instructions that always
cause a jump to occur irrespective of the condition of the
flags. They are the 'JMP absolute' and the 'JMP indirect'
instructions. The 'JMP absolute' instruction is the simplest
and takes the form 'JMP address', where address is a two byte
address or a label standing for an address. When the
instruction is obeyed it causes the program to be obeyed from
the address specified i.e. a JUMP has been caused. The jump
may be to any point in the memory.

The indirect jump is rather different in operation. It takes
the form 'JMP (address)', where address is either an address
in the memory or a label standing for an address. When
encountered this instruction causes a jump, NOT TO the address
specified, but to the 16 bit value contained at the address.
For example if &5000 contains the number &12 and &5001
contains the number &34 then the instruction JMP (&5000) will

cause the next instruction at location &3412 to be obeyed (the
16 bit or 2 byte value at &5000 has the least significant
value in first and thus contains the number &3412).

Test at the Beginning of the Loop

The above programs all have the test of the loop counter at
the end of the loop. This is quite a normal method but it
does have two features which are sometimes not wanted.
Firstly, the loop is always obeyed at least once as the
program must pass through the loop in order to reach the
test. Secondly if the value of the loop counter is zero on
entry to the loop then it will be performed not zero times but
256 times. This is because the first decrement of the loop
counter will change its value from zero to the number 255
(&FF). The reason for this is connected with the way that the
computer handles negative numbers (&FF is actually a
representation of the number -1 but the detail of why is
complicated and covered in later chapters). The loop is then
executed a further 255 times making 256 in all. There are
several ways round these problems should the need arise. It
is possible to check for a zero loop counter before the loop
is entered and to cause a jump past the loop if this is the
case.

Exercise:

```
        10   LDX #0
        20   LDA &70
        30   BEQ exit
        40   .loop
        50   LDA &5000,X
        60   STA &6000,X
        70   INX
        80   DEC &70
        90   BNE loop
       100   .exit
```

This program moves a block of data up to 256 bytes long from
&5000 to &6000. The number of bytes moved is determined by the
number present in &70 before the program is run. If &70
contains zero then line 30 causes a branch past the loop to

the label exit.

Another way of solving the zero loop counter problem is to
rearrange the structure of the loop so that the decrement and
test of the loop counter is made at the start of the loop
rather than at the end. This is shown in the following
program.

Exercise:

```
              10   LDX #0
              20   INC &70
              30   .loop
              40   DEC &70
              50   BEQ exit
              60   LDA &5000,X
              70   STA &6000,X
              80   INX
              90   JMP loop
             100   .exit
```

The main thing to note with this program is the INC
instruction at line 20. This is needed as the loop counter is
decremented by 1 before the loop is actually obeyed. Without
it the loop would be obeyed 1 less times than it should.
Enter the program and test it using suitable data. It should
perform a block move of data from &5000 to &6000 with the
number of bytes moved specified by the contents of &70. Of
course this can be simplified by loading &70 with 1 more than
the number of transfers required and omitting the INC &70
instruction.

The examples of loop structure given are not the only ones
possible. It is possible to have many structures depending on
the application with the adjustment of the loop counter and
the test at various places inside the loop.

When analysing the operation of a loop structure it is helpful
to test the operation of the loop by writing down on paper the
values of the counter at various points in the loop. The
initial value of 1 should be tried in this way to see if the
loop is in fact obeyed once for this value and also the value
0 to see if this has the desired effect.

UNCOUNTED LOOPS   COMPARING MEMORY BLOCKS

It is also possible to have program loops which do not use a
loop counter.   The loop is repeated until some specific
condition occurs inside the loop.   For example a program could
be written to compare two sections of the memory.

Exercise:

```
10 LDX #&FF
20 .loop
30 INX
40 LDA &5000,X
50 CMP &6000,X
60 BEQ loop
```

At the start of the program X is set to the maximum possible 8
bit value so that when it is incremented for the first time it
becomes zero.

The loop is terminated if the contents of the two memory
locations being compared are not equal. Thus X contains the
position of the discrepancy in data in the two blocks.   Use
the M command to set up values in &5000 to say &5005 and the
same values in &6000 to &6005.   Then make &5006 and &6006
different and run the program.   The program should break with
the number 6 in X.

Range of Branches

All the branch instructions have a limited range that they can
branch over due to the fact that they only use two bytes to
specify the instruction (for reasons of speed of operation and
minimum program length).   This range is +127 byte and -128
bytes from the branch instruction itself.   The assembler
checks this point for us and if an error is detected it
reports the fact.

Most branches are in fact in this range but occasionally an
out of range branch will be needed.   The solution is to use a

combination of a branch and a JMP instruction. The JMP instruction is not limited in range and causes an absolute jump irrespective of any flag conditions to any point in the memory. Thus a conditional branch tests the flags and branches to the JMP instruction which then makes the "big jump" over the longer distance.

An alternative is to use a second branch instruction in place of the JMP instruction. This has the advantage that it is only two bytes in length but the disadvantage that the range of branch is limited.

FLOW DIAGRAMS (FLOWCHARTS)

Flow diagrams are a way of showing the structure of a program graphically on a chart so that it is easier to understand. Both assembly language and high level programs may be shown in flow diagram form and many readers of this book will have encountered the use of flow diagrams in connection with BASIC programs. The conventions are simple: normal program operations not involving decisions are drawn in rectangles and those involving a decision are drawn in diamonds.

The above program can thus be expressed as the flow diagram in figure 2.1.

SPEED OF PROGRAM OPERATION

In the introduction it was stated that machine code programs were much quicker in operation than BASIC. The speed of operation of the CPU is determined by an electronic clock which generates synchronising pulses at a fixed rate. In the BBC computer these pulses occur every 0.5 microsecond. This corresponds to a pulse repetition rate (or frequency) of 2 million pulses per second (or 2 MHz). The 0.5 microsecond time is known as the CYCLE TIME of the CPU and the speed of all the instructions is expressed in terms of the number of these cycles that are needed to complete it. Thus the LDA # instruction takes 2 cycles to complete and therefore occupies the attention of the CPU for 1 microsecond. The number of cycles that each instruction takes is given in the list of instructions given in the appendix.

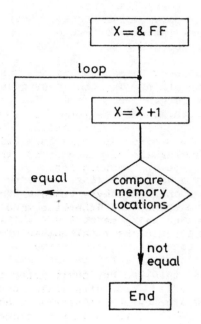

Figure 2.1

Some instructions take different numbers of cycles depending on the circumstances, for example the branch instructions. If no branch occurs these instructions take just 2 cycles but if a branch occurs 3 cycles are taken. Some of the indexed instructions also take an extra cycle if they address data which is in a different page to the instruction itself.

To work out the time that it takes a program to execute we consider each instruction and the number of times that it is executed and then perform a sum of all the cycle times involved taking full account of program loops.

For example the following program:

Instruction	Cycles
LDX #10	2
.LOOP	0
LDA &70	3
STA &71	3
DEX	2
BNE LOOP	2 OR 3

The LDX # takes 2 cycles and the loop is then obeyed for the first time and a branch made. Note that a label does not take any time up in the program as it is only exists in the text form of the program for the convenience of the programmer and does not assemble into any instruction.

Each time that the loop is obeyed and a branch made 3 + 3 + 2 + 3 = 11 cycles are taken and the last time that the loop is obeyed, with no branch being made, 3 + 3 + 2 + 2=10 cycles are taken. We thus calculate the total number of cycles to be 2 + 9*11 + 10 =111.

For long programs this is obviously going to be a difficult calculation if carried out with full precision so rough methods of estimation are frequently used where precise results are not required. We could for example assume that all the instructions which may vary in their number of cycles have a fixed number of cycles. A more rough and ready method might be to assume that all instructions have the same length say 3 or 4 cycles.

Effects of the Operating System on Timing

The above methods have a problem when used on the BBC computer. At the same time as running the user's program the 6502 CPU is also carrying out several tasks for the operating system. It is checking the keyboard, looking after a built in timer and also dealing with the hardware when necessary. This is achieved by what is called an INTERRUPT SYSTEM. At intervals, when necessary, the CPU suspends the running of the user's program and switches its attention to dealing with the event that caused the interruption. When the interrupt has

been serviced in this way the CPU resumes running the user's
program from where it left off.   This, of course, takes time
and the running of the user's program therefore takes longer
than anticipated using the above cycle time calculations.

If we are looking for ultimate speed and wish to dispense with
the facilities of the operating system we can switch off the
interrupts by issuing the SEI instruction but this is really
not recommended for general   purpose programming.   The
interrupt system can be switched back on with the CLI
instruction when needed.

The presence of the operating system interrupts means that the
regular operation of the CPU may not be used to provide timing
information to a program (a popular method of producing delays
is to produce program loops that just last the required length
of time).   Instead if a program needs to generate delays or
needs timing information then the timers built into the
computer hardware must be used.   The details of this are
covered later.

MORE ON Monitor

Disassembler

The X command in Monitor provides a means of converting binary
codes stored in the memory into the equivalent text mnemonic
form of the instructions.   In response to the X command
Monitor requests the address at which the conversion is to
commence and then the number of instructions to be converted.
It then disassembles the instructions using the paged mode of
display.   The SHIFT key is used to step onto the next screen
of information.

Some of the possible binary codes do not correspond to valid
instructions and it is therefore not possible to translate
them into mnemonics and they are printed just as the hex code
and also as the ASCII character corresponding to the code.
The codes cannot, of course, be obeyed by the CPU but are
usually part of a section of data in the memory.

You can try X by disassembling one of your own programs.   The

BASIC interpreter starts at address &8000 and may be disassembled if required.

The ESCAPE key may be used if you want to return to Monitor in the middle of disassembling.

List Command

The L command enables memory to be written to the screen as ASCII characters. Only printable characters are printed and invalid codes are printed as ~. The command is useful for picking out messages embedded in software and you could try to list the BASIC interpreter by responding to the request for a start address with &8000. The paged mode of presentation is again employed and the SHIFT key again used to bring up the next page. The ESCAPE key is used when sufficient memory has been listed.

When assembling programs Monitor chooses a safe place in the memory in which to put them. If you do not wish to take advantage of this feature, however, the start address of a program may be chosen using the S command which determines the start address of the assembler. There is not complete freedom of choice as to the address chosen, however, as Monitor itself and also the BASIC, and machine operating system all share the available memory. The S command does a simple check to ensure that Monitor is protected from overwriting although it is not possible to give the user complete protection from a poor choice of address.

Use the S command and enter &5000 in response to the request for an address. Then assemble a program and note that the program is assembled to the area starting at &5000.

Printing Programs

When in Edit mode most of the normal facilities of BASIC are available, with the exception of RENUMBER. The user's program resides in line numbers 10 to 10000 so that it may be printed as for any other program by switching on the printer and then typing CTRL B (or VDU 2) and then pressing key f1. The printer is switched off by CTRL C (or VDU 3).

Calculations

When writing programs in machine code we often like to carry
out a few calculations to say check the result of some binary
arithmetic. BASIC, of course, provides the necessary
facilities and they may be used in the Edit mode of Monitor
but a more convenient method is to use the C command of
Monitor. In response to the C command Monitor requests if a
hex or decimal result is required and then the calculation is
entered in the same format as for BASIC programs.   The
calculation may include any of the acceptable forms normally
used in BASIC and in addition any labels used in the user's
program are also recognised, following an assembly of the
program.

Exercise:

                    10 .label
                    20 LDA #1
                    30 STA qqq
                    40 JMP exit
                    50 .qqq:NOP
                    60 .exit

Enter the above program and assemble it. Then enter the C
command. We can now calculate various things with a
hexadecimal or decimal result as needed. For example specify
a decimal result and then enter exit - label to obtain the
length of the program. We can obtain the contents of the
storage location labelled qqq by entering ?qqq in decimal or
hexadecimal as required.

CONCLUSION

In this chapter we have introduced the various uses of Monitor
for developing assembly language programs and also some of the
simpler "building blocks" used in assembly language programs.

Rather than exhaustively describing all possible features of

the instructions a brief description has been used so that the
essential points have not been buried in a mass of detail.
The detailed information will be required from time to time,
however, and this is contained in the instruction set in
appendix A. This should be consulted as needed when
instructions are introduced in the book to see all the
possibilities concerning addressing modes, timings and flags.

To test your understanding of this chapter try to write a
program which copies a block of bytes from one part of the
memory to another and then checks the two copies to see that
they are the same.

3

Subroutines

The program loop is one method for repeatedly using the same set of instructions many times. This saves a lot of program space as otherwise instructions would have to be typed in many times. Another method is the use of the SUBROUTINE. Certain functions occur in many separate parts of a program, for example the instructions required to write characters on the screen of the computer. It makes sense to include such lines of instructions only once in a program and to have a technique for making them available whenever needed. Two extra instructions are used for this purpose, the JSR (Jump to SubRoutine) and the RTS (ReTurn from Subroutine) instructions. The JSR instruction is followed either by an address or a label to indicate the start of the subroutine. In actual use when the CPU obeys the JSR instruction it first remembers the address of the instruction following the JSR and then executes a jump to the start of the subroutine. It then obeys the instructions of the subroutine until it encounters the RTS instruction and then leaves the subroutine and jumps back to the instruction immediately following the JSR originally obeyed. For example Monitor contains a subroutine called PHEX which prints the contents of the A register onto the screen as a hex number. (If you are interested in how PHEX works try the disassembler X command and type PHEX when an address is requested. It uses 13 instructions and in turn calls a further subroutine.)

Exercise:

```
10 LDA #&12
20 JSR PHEX
```

Type in the above program and run it. The number 12 should be printed on the screen.

Exercise:

```
10 LDX #0
20 .loop
30 LDA &5000,X
40 INX
50 BEQ exit
60 JSR PHEX
70 JMP loop
80 .exit
```

The above program uses indexed addressing to print on the screen the contents of the memory between &5000 and &50FF using X as a loop counter as well as the index. Note that no spaces are printed in between the 2 digit hex values.

The BBC operating system also contains many useful subroutines that can be used. Two of the most often used subroutines are those which print a character on the screen and which read a character from the keyboard. Monitor recognises the names of these subroutines (unlike the BASIC assembler) and they may therefore be entered by name rather than referred to just by address.

CHARACTERS AND TEXT IN ASSEMBLY LANGUAGE

Characters and text are stored in the computer as binary codes, each character having its own unique code. The code used is an international standard called ASCII (American Standard Code for Information Interchange) and has been established so that computers and computer peripherals, such as printers and keyboards, use a standard system for communication. A list of ASCII codes is given in appendix C.

Strings

A string is just a list of characters stored in successive memory locations in the memory. There are various ways of indicating the end of the string but the most common on the BBC computer is to make the last character of the string a special code and the particular one chosen is the code &0D, which is the code for the RETURN key. Thus the string FRED would be stored as the codes &46, &52, &45, &44, &0D.

The M command in Monitor is able to input strings to the memory. The string is preceeded with the $ character and then all the following string plus a terminating &0D code are stored starting at the current address. For example to store the string "FRED" at location &5000 first press M and then type in the address &5000. Then $FRED is typed in as the contents.

OSWRCH

OSWRCH is a subroutine for writing a character to the screen. It is contained at address &FFEE in the memory and writes to the screen the character whose ASCII code is contained in the A register. On exit from OSWRCH the operating system leaves the values of A, X and Y unchanged from their values at the start of the subroutine. The flags, in general, are undefined (apart from D which is set to 0).

Exercise:

```
10 LDA #&41
20 JSR OSWRCH
```

The &41 is the code for the letter A so the above program should print a letter A on the screen.

Exercise:

```
10 LDX #0
20 .loop
```

```
30 LDA &5000,X
40 CMP #&0D
50 BEQ exit
60 JSR OSWRCH
70 INX
80 JMP loop
90 .exit
```

The above program uses a loop to write a sequence of characters (i.e. a string) stored in the memory starting at &5000 and terminated with a &0D, the ASCII code for the RETURN key (carriage return). Enter the above program and set up locations &5000 onwards to a string using the M command. Run the program and verify that it prints the specified string on the screen.

An alternative to using the M command is to input the string to &5000 using BASIC. The Edit command actually runs under BASIC so when in E all the BASIC facilities are available and thus the BASIC string input command may be used; e.g. $&5000="abcdefg" will set the locations &5000 onwards to the ASCII codes for the string abcedfg and terminate the string with the &0D code.

The Monitor L command will print memory as characters on the screen and so may be used to check that sections of the memory contain the desired strings. It prints ASCII characters less than &20 and greater than &7F as the ~ symbol. These codes do not represent characters and cannot be printed as they would be passed to the operating system to provide the functions analogous to the BASIC VDU commands. This is covered in detail in chapter 9. The ESCAPE or BREAK keys may be used to leave the L command.

Exercise:

Write a program to write on the screen the characters that have the codes &20 to &7F using the X register to store the code. (TXA will transfer it to A for printing.)

When this is working add a JSR PHEX in the appropriate place in the loop to print out the code after the character.

OSRDCH

This is the subroutine (address &FFE0) which reads a character
from the keyboard and places its code value into the A
register. Note that this routine does not print any value on
the screen, it only reads the keyboard and if you want
anything on the screen it has to be written there by your
program.

Exercise:

```
10 .loop
20 JSR OSRDCH
30 JSR OSWRCH
40 JMP loop
```

The above program is an example of this. It reads a character
from the keyboard and then prints it on the screen. Note that
as the program is an endless loop that you will need to press
the BREAK key to leave the program.

Exercise:

```
10 .loop
20 JSR OSRDCH
30 JSR OSWRCH
40 CMP #&0D
50 BNE loop
```

The above program is a modification which uses the RETURN key
as a terminator for the loop. It tests to see if the value
input from the keyboard is &0D, the ASCII code for the RETURN
key and if it is not the loop is repeated. If it is the
program is terminated.

The program could, of course, be modified to test for any
other key by substituting the required ASCII code for the &0D
in line 40. It is useful to note, however, that the assembler
also can use the BASIC ASC function to stand for ASCII values
e.g. in the above program line 40 could be replaced by:

```
40 CMP #ASC "."
```

The program now terminates when the . key is pressed.

There is a problem with the early version of the BASIC
assembler that ASC":" is not handled correctly. This has been
corrected in BASIC version 2.

It is simple to modify the above program such that it stores
the characters entered into the memory as a string.

This program also demonstrates that lower case letters may be
used for the mnemonics.

Exercise:

```
10   ldx #0
20   .loop
30   jsr OSRDCH
40   jsr OSWRCH
50   sta &5000,x
60   inx
70   cmp #&0D
80   bne loop
```

The use of upper or lower case mnemonics is not important to
the computer it is just a question of personal preference on
the part of the programmer.

Exercise:

This exercise involves a combination of the techniques covered
and thus forms quite a good test to see if you have mastered
the material.

Write a program which first reads in your name from the
keyboard as a string and then print it on the screen say ten
times using a loop.

As mentioned above, it is also useful to note that Monitor's
Edit command is in effect the normal BASIC operating system of
the BBC computer and that the normal BASIC facilities are
available, except for RENUMBER. Thus if you are curious about
the operation and structure of Monitor it may be listed in the

normal way using LIST, or backup copies may be made using SAVE
"Monitor". It is also possible to modify Monitor to your own
requirements as it seems that many people like to "customise"
programs to personal taste.

BASIC will recognise the names and values of any labels that
you have used (or Monitor uses) up until the point that you
start to edit programs and this can be an alternative to using
the Monitor commands for checking memory contents.

WRITING YOUR OWN SUBROUTINES

In general this is very similar to writing programs. The
subroutine is usually started with a label so that it can be
referred to by name and is left with the RTS instruction.

Exercise:

```
10 JSR test
20 JMP exit
30 .test
40 LDA #&41
50 JSR OSWRCH
60 LDA #&42
70 JSR OSWRCH
80 RTS
90 .exit
```

This program should print the letters AB on the screen. Note
that there is a jump around the subroutine itself to ensure
that it is only obeyed when actually called by the JSR
instruction. This is because if it were obeyed directly an
error would result when it tried to obey the RTS instruction
as there would be no JSR instruction to return to and results
would be unpredictable.

THE STACK

It can be seen in the example above that the subroutine test
calls other subroutines. This is known as nesting of
subroutines and is allowed up to a maximum of 128 levels. The

CPU is able to keep track of all the return addresses up to this number using a structure in the memory known as the stack.

The STACK is a special structure for holding data that the CPU controls in the memory. Data items can be stored in it, and recalled from it, but in an unusual way. Items are stored in order as they are sent to the stack, but when they are recalled it is not in the simple order in which they were stored. Instead when an item is recalled it is the LAST item that was sent to the stack and as items are recalled they are removed from the stack.

It can be compared to a pile of papers on a desk top. Sheets may be added to the top of the pile and the pile builds up as sheets are added. As sheets are removed from the top, the sheet removed is that currently at the top, i.e. the last one added to the pile and the structure is often known as a LAST IN FIRST OUT structure for this reason.

The area of RAM from &100 to &1FF (page 1 of memory) is used used for the stack.

As each JSR is encountered the return address, i.e. the address of the next instruction following the JSR instruction -1, is put onto the stack and as each RTS is encountered an address is taken from the stack incremented by 1 and the return performed.

A special purpose 8 bit CPU register called the STACK POINTER is used to automatically keep track of the current place in the stack. This is illustrated in Figure 3.1.

The stack pointer may be examined, if necessary, by transferring it to the X register using the TSX instruction and may be set by the TXS instruction which transfers the value in X to the stack pointer. These instructions are rarely used, however, as the CPU usually looks after the stack automatically.

When the computer is switched on the stack pointer is initialised to the value &FF. Each time that a subroutine is called the two byte address of the last byte of the JSR

instruction is stored on the stack and the value of the stack
pointer is decremented by two.   A jump is then made to the
subroutine and at the end of this subroutine the RTS
instruction takes this two byte value from the stack, adds 1
to it so that it is the correct return address, i.e.   the
point in the program after the JSR instruction.   The stack
pointer is incremented by two and the return is made to the
main program. An illustration is shown in Figure 3.2.

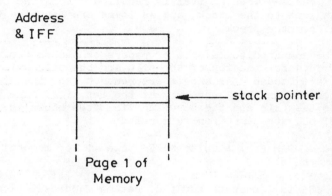

Figure 3.1

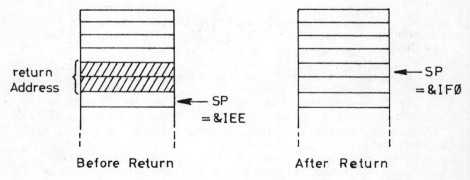

Figure 3.2

The stack also has an important use in assembly language
programming for the temporary storage of data. For example,
if say we want to temporarily store the value in A while A is
used for some purpose we can use the stack. The instruction
PHA (PusH A) copies the value in A onto the stack and then
decrements the stack pointer by one as shown in Figure 3.3.
The inverse operation (Figure 3.4) is the PLA instruction
(PulL A) which increments the stack pointer by one and then
copies the value pointed to into the A register.

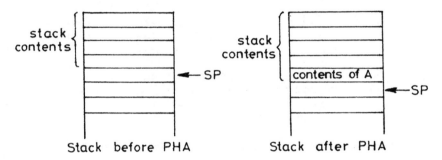

Figure 3.3

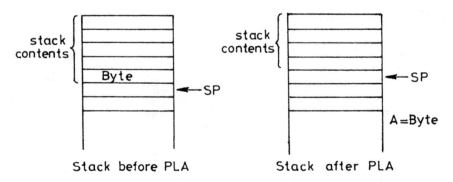

Figure 3.4

The stack thus appears to work upside down i.e. as values are
put on the stack the stack pointer is reduced and the stack is
built towards the low end of the memory. As values are taken
off the stack the stack pointer is increased and the stack is
shrunk towards the high end of page 1.

Some care is needed, however, to observe two important
points:-

The same stack is used for subroutines and data and when RTS
is obeyed it should find the appropriate return address and
not some stray data value inadvertently left on the stack.

If PHA or PLA is used in a loop then care should be taken to
ensure that there is no excessive build-up of values on the
stack.

It is very easy to have a mismatch in the number of PHA and
PLA instructions and thus leave values on the stack inside a
loop or subroutine and this is frequently a cause of error in
assembly language programming.

It is also important to know that Monitor makes extensive use
of the stack when single stepping or using breakpoints. If
you intend to use the stack other than for subroutines then
these Monitor facilities should not be used.

SAVING CPU STATUS

In general, when using a subroutine, the status of the CPU
will be changed by the subroutine. That is the numbers stored
in the registers and the condition of the flags will be
different at the start and finish of the subroutine. The
programmer must be aware of this and not rely on the CPU being
unchanged on exit from a subroutine. It is easy to make a
mistakes, however, and write subroutines which change register
values and then to use them in programs which rely on register
values not being changed.

It is possible to write subroutines which leave the status of
the CPU unchanged and it is good programming practice to use
this method, particularly for subroutines that will be used

many times in different applications. Certain types of
subroutine, which are called by the interrupt system, must be
written in this way as they are in effect called at random
instants while other programs are running and any interference
between the two has to be completely eliminated.

There are two methods of saving the status, one using fixed
memory locations and the other using the stack.

Saving Status Using Fixed Memory Locations

The method is basically to set aside a set of storage
locations in the memory and to use these on entry to a
subroutine to store all the flags and registers. Just before
the subroutine is left the contents of these locations are put
back into the CPU registers and flags. Say that stores called
SA, SX, SY and SP are used to hold the contents of the A, X, Y
and status registers then the following instructions at the
start of a subroutine will save the the CPU status:

```
            STA SA
            PHP: PLA: STA SP
            STY SY
            STX SX
```

The first instruction saves the A register into the store SA.
The next operation is to save the contents of the flags (P
register) on the stack and then to get it from the stack into
the A register and then save it into store SP. This is because
there is no instruction to directly store the status register
in the memory. Finally Y and X are saved into stores SY and
SX respectively.

Just before the RTS instruction the following instructions
will restore the values to the CPU from the stores:

```
            LDX SX
            LDY SY
            LDA SP: PHA
            LDA SA
            PLP
```

Most of these instructions are quite straightforward but

notice that the store SP contents are temporarily stored on
the stack and are only restored to the P register at the very
end. This is because the LDA SA instruction itself alters the
flags and might change the contents of the P register.

The following exercise demonstrates this. The subroutine
QUERY uses a program loop to print a number of ? characters on
the screen. The number of ?s printed is determined by the
contents of store &70. The subroutine, however, does not
change the status of the CPU.

Exercise:

```
          10    LDA #1: LDY #2: LDX #3
          20    JSR QUERY
          30    JMP FINISH
          40    .QUERY
          50    STA SA
          60    PHP: PLA: STA SP
          70    STY SY: STX SX
          80    LDX &70
          90    LDA #ASC"?"
         100    .LOOP
         110    JSR OSWRCH
         120    DEX: BNE LOOP
         130    LDX SX: LDY SY
         140    LDA SP: PHA
         150    LDA SA
         160    PLP: RTS
         170    .SA NOP
         180    .SX NOP
         190    .SY NOP
         200    .SP NOP
         210    .FINISH
```

In line 10 the CPU registers are set up to some known values
so that it can be verified that the subroutine does not change
them. The subroutine first saves the CPU status in lines 50
to 70 and then gets the desired numbers of question marks to
be printed from store &70. The X register is used as the loop
counter and the subroutine OSWRCH is used to carry out the
printing of the character in line 110.

Lines 130 to 160 restore the status of the CPU and return from
the subroutine. Lines 170 to 200 are interesting as they show
a simple method of reserving some storage locations. Each
label is followed by a single byte instruction which is never
obeyed as its only purpose is to occupy the single byte of
space until overwritten by the subroutine. Any single byte
instruction would do but the one chosen is NOP which is the
instruction which actually does nothing anyway.

Enter the program using the E command and assemble it using A.
When assembled use the M command to set store &70 to the
number of ?s to be printed and run the program. Note that at
the end of the program the contents of the registers have not
been changed by the subroutine.

Saving Status Using the Stack

This method is a little more elegant than the previous method
as it uses less instructions and no fixed memory needs to be
allocated. At the start of the subroutine the CPU status is
pushed on the stack a byte at a time and is left there until
the end of the subroutine, when it is recalled. Thus at the
start of the subroutine the following sequence of instructions
is used: PHP: PHA: TXA: PHA: TYA: PHA. At the end of the
subroutine the bytes are recalled in the reverse order to that
in which they were stored with the sequence: PLA: TAY: PLA:
TAX: PLA: PLP.

The method is shown in the following exercise.

Exercise:

```
         10   LDA #1: LDY #2: LDX #3
         20   JSR QUERY
         30   JMP FINISH
         40   .QUERY
         50   PHP:PHA
         60   TXA PHA
         70   TYA:PHA
         80   LDX &70
         90   LDA #ASC"?"
        100   .LOOP
```

```
110   JSR OSWRCH
120   DEX: BNE LOOP
130   PLA:TYA
140   PLA:TXA
150   PLA:PLP
160   RTS
170   .FINISH
```

COMMUNICATING WITH SUBROUTINES

There are three basic methods of data transfer between a
program and subroutines. The two most common methods have
already been encountered and these are the use of registers
and specified memory locations and these methods are
straightforward and recommended when starting assembly
language programming. The third method uses the computer
stack and is included here for completeness although it is
definitely not recommended for beginners. The method,
however, enjoys wide use amongst more experienced programmers
as it makes subroutines more general purpose.

The values to be sent to the subroutine are pushed onto the
stack and then the JSR executed. When the JSR is executed the
CPU automatically puts a further two bytes on the stack to
indicate the return address. The subroutine must then process
the data on the stack and then leave the stack such that when
the RTS is encountered at the end of the subroutine a correct
return is made. This process is VERY ERROR PRONE and
unfortunately, as the consequences usually result in a jump
into a random section of the memory, programs are frequently
corrupted. Unfortunately Monitor also makes extensive use of
the stack when using breakpoints or single stepping so that it
is not able to help in the usual way with programs which may
corrupt the stack. It does, however, have a built in
subroutine called STACK which prints the current value of the
stack pointer on the screen.

The following program shows how the stack may be used to send
a byte of data via the stack to a subroutine. The subroutine
prints the byte sent to it on the screen as an ASCII
character.

Exercise:

```
 10   LDA #ASC"A"
 20   PHA
 30   JSR PASC
 40   JMP FINISH
 50   .PASC
 60   TSX: INX: INX: INX
 70   LDA &100,X
 80   JSR OSWRCH
 90   TXS
100   DEX: LDA &100,X: PHA
110   DEX: LDA &100,X: PHA
120   RTS
130   .FINISH
```

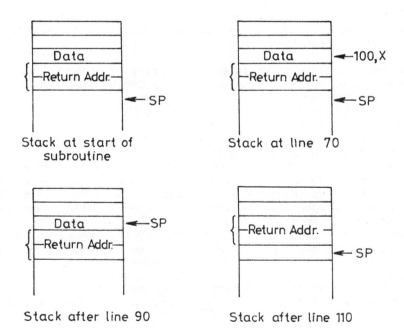

Stack at start of subroutine

Stack at line 70

Stack after line 90

Stack after line 110

Figure 3.5

Line 20 pushes the A register onto the stack and then a jump
to the subroutine is made.   The subroutine first gets the
value of the stack pointer into the X register in line 60 and
the X is incremented until it points to the data byte pushed
onto the stack in line 20. The byte is then loaded into the A
register using the LDA &100,X instruction and is printed in
line 80.

The next problem is to change the stack so that the data byte
is removed and the return address and stack pointer are set so
that when the RTS is encountered a correct return is made.
The stack pointer is set to the address occupied by the data
byte in line 90 and then the return address moved to this
position in lines 100 and 110.

The operation of the stack at various points in the program is
illustrated in Figure 3.5.

Enter, assemble and run the program.   The letter A should be
printed on the screen.

The above program is of interest because it shows how the
stack values can be accessed, not only by the built in PHA and
PLA instructions, but also by the normal instructions which
operate on memory.

Indirect Indexed Addressing Mode

Extra power may be given to the use of subroutines by the use
of the indirect indexed addressing mode. Consider the problem
of writing a subroutine to move a block of data from one part
of the memory to another. For the subroutine to be of general
application it should be able to move a block from any part of
the memory to any other. The absolute mode of addressing does
not provide this flexibility as the address is built into the
instruction and is therefore fixed. The indirect indexed mode
allows the address specifying the data to be itself contained
in the memory and so it can be varied on different subroutine
calls.

The real power of this mode of operation lies in the fact that

it effectively uses a pair of zero-page memory locations as a
pointer to the memory, with the added attraction of having the
Y register as in index to the pointer.

Instructions which use the mode take a pair of zero-page
locations and firstly get the sixteen bit contents. Then the
Y register is added to this sixteen bit number to get the
address of the memory location to be used in the instruction.
For example say that &70 contains the number &00 and &71
contains &50, then if Y contains the number &04 then the
indirect indexed load instruction : LDA (&70),Y will load the
A register with the contents of location &5004.

If we compare the instruction with the absolute indexed
instruction LDA &5000,Y which would also load A with the same
location (&5004) we can see the difference between the two
modes is that the absolute mode always refers to the address
&5000 but the indirect mode can be made to refer to other
addresses by changing the contents of the pair of zero-page
locations. In this sense the pair of zero-page locations acts
like a variable in a BASIC program.

Returning to the problem of moving a block of data say the
pair of bytes for the start address is in &70, &71 the end
address in &72, &74 and the number of bytes to be moved in the
X register then the following subroutine could be written.

```
            .MVE
            LDY #0
            .LOOP
            LDA (&70),Y
            STA (&72),Y
            INY
            DEX
            BNE LOOP
            RTS
```

Blocks of memory up to 256 byte in length may be moved by this
subroutine.

Printing a String

Another example is a subroutine to write a string of
characters to the screen. The writing of strings at a fixed
place in the memory has been covered earlier and now the
method can be developed to a more general purpose subroutine.

```
.PST
LDY #0
.PLOOP
LDA (&70),Y
CMP #&0D
BEQ PEND
INY
JMP PLOOP
.PEND
RTS
```

The locations &70 and &71 contain the start address of the
string. This subroutine will be found very useful in
conjunction with the VDU codes to drive the graphics built
into the operating system.

STRUCTURED ASSEMBLY LANGUAGE PROGRAMMING

We have now covered enough material to discuss the idea of
introducing structure into assembly language programming.

We begin by introducing the need for such an approach.
Consider a complex machine code program of say a few thousand
bytes in length and imagine the problems in trying to write
and develop it. It is difficult enough writing small programs
as so much detail has to be remembered and it is very very
difficult trying to follow all that is happening in long
programs.

One approach, when writing long programs, is to split the task
up into more manageable smaller sections and to write and
develop the smaller parts separately. This method is
frequently used by commercial software companies and different
programmers may be used to write the different sections. The
imposition of some method and structure then gives great

advantages as it simplies the task of joining together the
separate sections.

There are many methods and structures used in the various
applications of assembly language programming and this aspect
of program writing could indeed be the subject of a whole book
in its own right. It is profitable, however, to consider one
important   method involving subroutines as it is   quite
straightforward and well worth discussing before the reader
gets involved in writing long programs.

The task to be programmed is first broken down into a few
smaller sections. The break down being made such that the
interactions between the sections is minimised and these
sections are considered to be subroutines. The individual
sections are then considered and themselves broken down into
smaller sections which are again written as subroutines. The
process is repeated as many times as necessary until the task
has been effectively broken down into a large number of more
manageable subroutines. The advantage of this method comes as
at each level a task is clearly defined in terms of a
relatively small number of simpler tasks and the program
becomes easier to understand and modify.

Consider, for example, the writing of a word processor in
assembly language. There are many things involved but this
could be seen as comprising the following elements: editing
text in memory, storing text on disc and printing text. The
text editor could then be broken down into say: input of text,
display of text and modification of text. The input of text
could itself be broken down several subroutines.

It is difficult to make firm recommendations as to the ideal
length for a subroutine but it could be suggested that perhaps
the subroutines should consist of up to twenty instructions.

Once the functions have been broken down in this way it is
useful to make a list of the subroutines that need to be
written for each of the sections and then to look for
similarities so that common functions are not duplicated many
times but are included only once.

Although the program structure has been designed from the top

down the actual writing of the subroutines takes place from
the bottom up i.e. the simplest routine are written first and
thoroughly tested. The subroutines using these are next
written and so on until eventually the level of the main
program is reached. The main program then consists mainly of
decision making and the conditional calling of subroutines.

4

BASIC and Assembly Language

Up until this point the reader has been using the Monitor program to develop assembly language programs. Monitor serves to help the beginner with the details of inputting, running and debugging programs. There are times, however, when the space that Monitor occupies is too large or its use is too restricting to the programmer who wishes to use the full power of the computer to mix BASIC and assembly language programs.

When some confidence has been gained the support provided by Monitor can be dispensed with and use made of the powerful assembler built into the BASIC. The transition should be painless as Monitor itself uses the BASIC assembler when the A command is used and so most of the previous work is still relevant.

Before the assembler is described a discussion of some other useful features of BASIC will be described.

DISPLAYING AND MODIFYING MEMORY

BBC BASIC contains commands that allow memory locations to be examined and changed. The simplest of these is the ? operator. This operator is followed by the address of the memory location in question and then the combination is

69

treated by BASIC as a single byte integer variable. Thus
PRINT ?&3000 will display the contents of &3000 on the screen
and ?&3000=&41 will set the contents of &3000 equal to the
value &41. It is worth pointing out, in case the reader has
used other microcomputers, that BASIC on many of these
machines uses ? for the completely different purpose of being
shorthand for the PRINT statement i.e. equivalent to P. in
BBC BASIC.

There are two other such operators the ! and $ operators. The
! operator is similar in action to the ? operator but it deals
with memory locations as groups of four adjacent bytes.

For example !&3000=&789ADEF0 will set the contents of &3000 to
&F0, &3001 to &DE, &3002 to &9A and &3003 to &78.

BASIC integer variables are in fact stored in four adjacent
bytes and the combination of ! and an address behaves as if it
were a BASIC integer variable.

The $ operator is used to handle text strings in a similar
way. Thus $&2000="abcdef" will set location &2000 to the
ASCII code for the letter a, &2001 to the code for b and so on
until &2005 contains the code for the letter f. The ASCII
code for RETURN (&0D) is stored at the end of the string in
this case in location &2006. The strings may be used in other
ways by the BASIC e.g. PRINT $&2000 should print the string
starting at location &2000. In this case it will print
abcdef.

THE BASIC ASSEMBLER

The computer contains a very powerful fast assembler and also
systems for mixing BASIC and assembly language to obtain the
best out of both types of programming. The assembler is
operated from within BASIC using the special purpose
statements provided. The assembly language instructions take
exactly the same form as in Monitor with preceeding line
numbers. The assembly language program is preceeded by a [
instruction (printed in mode 7 as ◀) and terminated by the]
instruction (printed in mode 7 as ▶).

When the BASIC program is run the text form of the assembly
language is assembled into the binary codes. The codes are
stored into the memory and the place in memory that is used is
determined by the contents of the integer variable P% at the
start of the assembly.

Exercise:

```
          NEW
       10 P%=&2000
       20 [
       30 .prt
       40 LDA #&41
       50 JSR &FFEE
       60 RTS
       70 ]
```

The above program is in the form of a simple subroutine to
print a letter A on the screen. Note that P% is set to &2000
which will form the start address of the subroutine and that
the subroutine has been started with a label. This enables it
to be referred to by name. Enter and run the above program.

The program is assembled into the locations starting at &2000
onwards and as each instruction is assembled P% is increased
to the address at which the next instruction is to be
assembled. The name of PROGRAM COUNTER is thus sometimes
given to P% as it keeps a record of program addresses during
assembly. At the end of the assembly it contains the address
of the next free location following the assembled program.

Note that the machine code program is not obeyed at this time,
only the assembly is performed. The BASIC CALL statement may
be used to enter machine code subroutines. Thus the above
subroutine may be obeyed by typing CALL &2000 or CALL prt,
either in direct mode from the keyboard or from following
BASIC lines in the above program.

If your program is not arranged as a subroutine with a
terminating RTS statement then you must take responsibility
for what happens at the end of running the program. Automatic
return to BASIC is ONLY made by the RTS statement. If you
accidentally forget it then the program will just continue at

the end and obey whatever random code happens to be in the
memory. This frequently causes the system to crash and the
text of your program will probably be lost.

THEREFORE: DO NOT FORGET THE RTS AT THE END UNLESS YOU KNOW
THAT THE PROGRAM DOES NOT NEED TO RETURN TO BASIC.

Note that in Monitor the RTS was not used at the end of
programs. Instead Monitor terminated the program for the user
by inserting a special section of code at the end to print out
the registers.

BASIC also contains a special form of the DIM statement which
may be used to automatically allocate space for machine code
programs (or for other purposes). It reserves a space within
the BASIC program from which it is issued and sets a variable
equal to the start address of that space. This is very useful
as it takes the responsibility from the programmer of ensuring
that the assembled machine code does not overwrite the BASIC
program or part the memory used by the operating system.

Exercise:

```
              NEW
          10 DIM START% 100
          20 PRINT "START ADDRESS ";~ START%
          30 P%=START%
          40 [
          50 .prt
          60 LDA #&41
          70 JSR &FFEE
          80 RTS
          90 ]
```

LINE 10 reserves a space of 100 bytes within the BASIC and
sets the integer variable START% equal to the start address of
this space.

Enter and run the above program and notice that the program is
assembled to a different area of memory to that used
previously.

As this method of assembling code is so safe it is the method that is normally used for including sections of machine code within a BASIC program.

CALL although used simply above is actually an extremely powerful command. When encountered it copies the least significant bytes of the BASIC integer variables A%,X% and Y% into the CPU registers. A% is copied into the A register, X% into the X register and Y% into the Y register. The least significant bit of C% is also copied into the C flag. BASIC then performs a JSR instruction to the start of the program.

Exercise:

```
         NEW
10 DIM start% 100: P%=start%
20 [
30 .prt
40 JSR &FFEE
50 RTS
60 ]
```

Enter and run the above program. Set A% to an ASCII character code e.g. type A%=&42 and then jump to the subroutine by typing CALL prt. A% will be copied into the A register before the subroutine is called and thus the letter B should be printed on the screen.

Exercise:

```
         NEW
10 DIM start% 100: P%=start%
20 [
30 .prt
40 JSR &FFEE
50 RTS
60 ]
70 FOR A%=&20 TO &7F
80 CALL prt
90 NEXT
```

This program illustrates the assembly and calling of an assembly language program from the same BASIC program. The program is first assembled and then lines 70, 80 and 90 are used to print all the characters with codes &20 to &7F.

CALL also has the ability to pass further information from
BASIC to an assembly language program through the use of a
reserved section of the memory. This starts at location &600
and contains information on the types and addresses of extra
parameters that may be given to the CALL statement.

Another BASIC command named USR is also available for the
running of machine code subroutines but USR is different to
CALL in two ways. First, the complex parameter block method
of passing information is not available; and second, USR
returns a value to the BASIC program which may be printed or
put into a variable or expression in any of the usual BASIC
ways. The value returned is an integer and is generated from
the CPU registers at the end of the assembly language
program. The integer has the four byte value PYXA, where P is
the status byte (all the flags grouped together as a single
byte), Y,X, and A the bytes contained in the Y,X and A
registers.

Exercise:

```
            NEW
        10 DIM start% 100: P%=start%
        20 [ .prog
        30 LDA #1
        40 LDX #2
        50 LDY #3
        60 RTS
        70 ]
        80 PP%=USR( prog)
        90 PRINT ~PP%
```

Enter and run the above program. Notice that the value
returned by USR is put into the integer variable PP% and is
printed out in hex, thus showing that A contained 1, X
contained 2 and Y contained 3.

If required the individual parts of PP%, corresponding to the
CPU registers may be obtained using the BASIC AND statement.

e.g.   PP% AND &FF will select A

    (PP% AND &FF00)/&100 will select X

    (PP% AND &FF0000)/&10000 will select Y

    (PP% AND &FF000000)/&1000000 will select the
status register.

ESTIMATING PROGRAM LENGTH

When reserving space for assembly language programs we need to
know how many bytes of memory will be used to store the
assembled binary codes. The appendix A contains a list of the
instructions and the number of bytes that each one occupies
but it is clearly a tedious business to look up each
instruction and then add up the total number of bytes.   An
often used alternative is to notice that the maximum
instruction length is three and then to just multiple the
total number of instructions by three. Every instruction will
not be three bytes so that the resulting number of bytes will
be adequate to hold the program.

MEMORY MAP - ALTERNATIVE PLACES FOR MACHINE CODE

Undoubtedly the DIM statement provides the best general
purpose method of reserving space for a machine code program
but   there   are some other, less safe, methods that
exceptionally find use. If the DIM statement is not used to
locate assembly language within BASIC programs a detailed
knowledge of how the computer uses its memory is needed.
There are certain areas which are always used by the computer
and other areas which may or may not be used depending on the
model of computer (A or B) and on the options that are fitted
to the computer (disc, econet etc.). Finally the screen mode
alters the different areas of the memory used for storage of
the screen data.

Page 0 of memory is used by the operating system and BASIC but
some of these valuable locations have been set aside for the

user. The locations from &70 to &8F are in general the free
locations, with the exception that the ECONET command
*EXTENDPWF uses &8C to &8F. The free area is best used, not to
store programs, but in conjunction with the zero-page
instructions.

Page 1 of the memory is reserved for the stack.

Pages 2 to &C are used by the BASIC and operating systems.
The usage of pages &D onwards depends on which version of the
computer you have.

Page &D is available for storage of machine code programs, but
if a disc or ECONET filing system is in use then this area is
occupied by the operating system and will be corrupted as soon
as a filing system command is used.

The start of the BASIC program is given by the contents of the
BASIC variable PAGE which on a non-disc machine should be &E00
but on a machine with a disc interface is &1900. On a machine
with no disc but an ECONET system it is &1200. It will have
higher values on machines with more advanced options. If you
type PRINT ~PAGE the computer will print the value that is
used for your machine.

It is possible to reset PAGE to a higher value before a
program is input from the keyboard or filing system and to
locate the machine code program in the space thus created.

Exercise:

```
                    PRINT~PAGE
                    D%=PAGE
                    PAGE=PAGE+&100
                 10 P%=D%
                 20 [.prt
                 30 LDA #&41
                 40 JSR &FFEE
                 50 RTS
                 60 ]
```

Note that with this program the first three lines are in
immediate mode and must be entered before the program lines

are entered. These lines create a gap at the bottom of the
BASIC program of &100 (256 decimal) bytes.

It is important to note that PAGE can only be increased in
multiples of &100.

Enter the above exercise in the order given and RUN the BASIC
program. Type CALL prt to call the machine code program,
which should print the letter A on the screen.

Great care is needed when using this method as if the BREAK
key is pressed the value of PAGE is reset by the system to its
original value and you will get the message Bad program if you
type OLD to recover your program. You should then type in
immediate mode PAGE=PAGE+&100 and type OLD and press the
RETURN key to recover your program. An alternative is to
reprogram the BREAK key to reset the value of PAGE and to
recover the program. Thus say that the value &2000 is desired
for PAGE, this may be done by typing *KEY10 PAGE=&2000 |MOLD|M
and pressing the RETURN key.

Machine code programs may also be located in a free area of
memory between the BASIC program variables and a structure
known as the BASIC stack. BASIC uses the area starting at the
contents of a variable called LOMEM (which is normally the
same as TOP the end of the users BASIC program) to store
variables and the amount that it uses depends very much on the
BASIC program in question. The area between the end of the
variable storage area and the end of the BASIC stack is free
for use by machine code programs. The BASIC stack is a
software structure used by the BASIC interpreter to implement
GOSUBS, RETURNS and other BASIC functions. It starts,
normally, at the far end of RAM, just before the start of the
memory used for the screen. This point depends on the model
of computer and also on the screen mode. It is contained in
the BASIC variable HIMEM and so may be obtained by typing
PRINT ~ HIMEM.

The area between the BASIC variables and the BASIC stack may
be used for the storage of machine code programs but the
problem with using this area is that the size of the BASIC
stack and also the BASIC variable area must be known so that
the free space may be determined. These areas are program

dependent and so must be calculated for each program. It is
not too bad for simple programs where it is relatively
straightforward to put in some large safety margins for the
likely sizes of the stack and variable areas but for complex
programs or programs whose size of arrays or depth of
subroutine nesting may depend on data the method is best
avoided. You should also beware of using the MODE statement
in programs as the value of HIMEM is changed and this can lead
to errors.

It is better to change the value of HIMEM to some lower value
and use the space created between the BASIC stack and the
screen memory to store the machine code program.

Exercise:

```
        NEW
10 PRINT ~HIMEM
20 HIMEM=HIMEM-100
30 P%=HIMEM
40 [.prt
50 LDA #&41
60 JSR &FFEE
70 RTS
80 ]
```

The above program shows the method used to create a space of
100 bytes and a simple program being assembled into it.

LABELS

With the method of assembly given so far labels must be
entered with the . prefix before they are used as part of an
instruction. To show that this is the case try the following
program.

Exercise:

```
        NEW
10 DIM start% 100: P%=start%
20 [.STRT
30 JMP exit
```

```
40 .exit
50 RTS
60 ]
```

Enter and RUN the above program and see that the assembler
produces an error as it is not able to recognise the label
EXIT when it finds it in line 30 as it has not yet reached the
definition of the label in line 40.

TWO PASS ASSEMBLER

The solution is to use the assembler twice using a BASIC FOR
... NEXT loop. Each use of the assembler is called a pass.
The first time (or pass) the assembler is used to recognise
and work out the values of the labels and the second pass the
assembler is used to produce the correct machine code output.

The OPT statement is used as the first assembly language
instruction to control the assembler action during these two
passes through the assembly language. OPT is followed by a
number, or variable containing a number, which controls the
action of the assembler. Numbers 0 or 1 may be used for the
first pass of the assembler. 0 gives no listing and 1 gives a
list of assembler action during the first pass. Using 0 or 1
no errors are reported during the first pass. Normally 0 is
used for the first pass as a listing is usually not required.
In the second pass either 2 or 3 is usually used. OPT 2 gives
no listing whereas 3 will give a listing. The first pass is
usually run with OPT 0 and the second pass with OPT 3.

Exercise:

```
        NEW
10 DIM start% 20
20 FOR Q=0 TO 3 STEP 3
30 P%=start%
40 [OPT Q
50 JMP exit
60 .exit
70 RTS
80 ]
90 NEXT Q
```

AAL-D

Note that in line 30 P% is set up to the start address of the
assembly language for each pass of the assembler.   It is
important to remember to do this as otherwise the second pass
will not be located in the correct place.

Run the program and note that this time the program assembles
without errors.

Change line 20 to 20 FOR Q=1 TO 3 STEP 2 so that the form of a
listing in pass 1 can be observed. Note that the assembler
actually produces machine code output during pass 1 but that
unrecognised labels are set equal to a value which makes the
jump or branch instructions jump to themselves.

If line 20 is changed to 20 FOR Q=0 TO 2 STEP 2 then no
listing is output but any errors found are reported.   Once
confidence has been gained in assembly language programming
this is quite often used as it is the fastest form of two pass
assembly.

Of course if no forward labels are used then the fastest
assembly method is to use only one pass with OPT 2. If the OPT
statement is omitted then OPT 2 is assumed as the default
value.

BASIC VARIABLES AS SYMBOLS

The assembler is able to use BASIC variables as symbols. The
variables are given values in BASIC in the normal way in the
sections of program BEFORE the assembly language program and
the variables may then be used in assembly language
statements. The variables may be used to stand for either
addresses or data. If used for data the number contained in
the variable must be restricted to the single byte range 0 to
255 and if used for an address it must be restricted to the
double byte range of 0 to 65535. The assembler will report
errors if the range for data is exceeded but for addresses if
the range is exceeded no error is generated. It just takes
the lower two bytes of the value specified.

Exercise:

```
      NEW
10 OSWRCH=&FFEE
20 VALUE=&41
30 DIM start% 100: P%=start%
40 [.prog
50 LDA #VALUE
60 JSR OSWRCH
70 RTS
80 ]
```

Enter and RUN the above program and then CALL the subroutine by typing CALL prog in direct mode. The letter A should be printed on the screen. Note that the intelligent use of labels in this way can greatly increase the readability of a program.

Try making VALUE equal to a number greater than &FF to see the assembler error which results.

Exercise:

```
      NEW
10 FIRST=&3000
20 SECOND=&4000
30 DIM start% 100: P%=start%
40 [.prog
50 LDA FIRST
60 STA SECOND
70 RTS
80 ]
```

The above program illustrates the use of BASIC variables as 2 byte labels with the LDA and STA instructions. The program simply loads A with the contents of &3000 and then stores A into the store &4000.

Enter and RUN the program. Check the contents of &3000 and &4000 using the BASIC indirection operators i.e. P.? &3000 and P.? &4000.

BASIC EXPRESSIONS AS SYMBOLS

A very useful extension to the use of variables is a feature
of the assembler which allows a BASIC expression to be used to
calculate a data or address item. This gives great power and
really can help the readability of an assembly language
program.

Exercise:

```
          NEW
 10   FIRST=&3000
 20   SECOND=&4000
 30   DIM start% 100: P%=start%
 40   [.prog
 50   LDA FIRST
 60   STA SECOND
 70   LDA FIRST +1
 80   STA SECOND +1
 90   RTS
100   ]
```

This is based on the previous program but following the
transfer from &3000 to &4000 in lines 50 and 60 the byte in
&3001 is transferred to &4001 in lines 70 and 80.

RUN the program to assemble it and test with some sample data
placed in &3000 and &3001 using ?&3000= first data item and
?&3001= second data item.

IN AND OUT OF BASIC

We have seen how to start a program using a few lines of BASIC
to define some symbols but much more exciting things are
possible. BASIC and assembly language may be freely mixed as
many times as necessary. This sort of of technique is useful
for using BASIC to embed a block of data inside an assembly
language program.

The following program shows how this may be done and it again
shows the use of BASIC variables to communicate addresses to
the assembler.

Exercise:

```
        NEW
10   DIM START% 200
20   OSWRCH=&FFEE
30   FOR PASS = 0 TO 2 STEP 2
40   [OPT PASS
50   .PSTR
60   LDX #0
70   .LOOP
80   LDA MSG,X
90   CMP #&D
100  BEQ FIN
110  JSR OSWRCH
120  JMP LOOP
130  .FIN
140  RTS: ]
150  MSG=P%
160  $P%="HELLO "
170  P%=P%+7
180  [OPT PASS
190  .PROG
200  LDY #10
210  .PLOOP
220  JSR PSTR
230  DEY
240  BNE PLOOP
250  RTS
260  ]
270  NEXT
```

The subroutine PSTR prints a string and returns when it finds
the end of string code &D (the code for the RETURN key).   In
line 160 P% has the value of the next location following the
subroutine and the $P%="HELLO " puts the ASCII code of this
string plus a following &D code into the memory immediately
following the subroutine.   P% is then adjusted until it
contains the next address after the string and the &0D in line
170. Next the assembler is again used for a program which uses
the subroutine PSTR to print HELLO on the screen 10 times.

Note that the BASIC variable MSG is used to communicate the address of the start of the string to the assembler.

Enter CALL PROG to check that the program actually works.

BASIC II

Although many readers will not have issue II BASIC it is
interesting to look at some of the improvements to the
assembler that BASIC II contains. You can tell which version
of BASIC is fitted into your computer by typing the BASIC
statement REPORT immediately after switching on or after a
CTRL BREAK. If BASIC II is present the message "(C) 1982" is
printed rather than the "(C) 1981" for the original version of
BASIC.

There are two useful enhancements as far as the assembler is
concerned. The first allows code to be assembled into the
memory at a different place to that at which it is to be run.
This is done by using an extra integer variable O% to control
the place where the code is stored with P% containing the
address where the program is eventually to run. Bit 3 of the
number used by the OPT statement controls whether just P% or
both P% and O% are used. If bit 3 is 0 then the assembler
behaves in the normal way just using P% but if bit 3 is 1 then
both are used. In this case the code is assembled using P% to
determine the addresses for jumps and subroutines but the
binary code is actually stored in the memory starting at the
address specified by O%. In practice this means that instead
of OPT 0 to 3 we use OPT 4 to 7 instead to take advantage of
this feature.

This may not seem to be a great advantage but it actually is
useful as it allows code to be produced which will run from
tape or memory chips and make maximum use of the memory. This
type of operation is described more fully in chapter 8 where
the storage of machine code programs on tape is discussed.
For the sidewise ROM facility the start address of &8000 is
required but the program can be actually assembled into RAM at
a convenient address.

BASIC II also provides methods of inserting data bytes into
the machine code program. This is much more convenient than

the mixing of BASIC and assembly language shown above and is
given by the assembler operations EQUB, EQUW, EQUD, and EQUS.
The EQUB operation puts the number following it into the code
as a single byte, EQUW treats the number following it as a 16
bit value and puts into the code as a two byte value with the
least significant byte first. EQUD assumes that the number
following it is a 32 bit number (like a BASIC integer
variable) and puts four bytes into the code, again stored
least significant byte first in the usual way. The EQUS
operation puts a string into the code without the &D end of
string code used by the BASIC $ operator.

Exercise:

```
            NEW
       10   DIM START% 100
       20   FOR PASS = 0 TO 2 STEP 2
       30   P%=START%
       40   [OPT PASS
       50   .PROG
       60   NOP
       70   EQUB &A
       80   EQUW &9876
       90   EQUD &12345678
      100   EQUS "ABCDEFG"
      110   NOP
      120   ]
      130   NEXT
```

The above program may be assembled just to show that the data
is put into the program but it should not actually be CALLed.

MOVING LARGE BLOCKS OF DATA

The simple methods already given for moving blocks of data in
the memory are restricted to moving data blocks up to 256
bytes in length. This is adequate for many purposes but if a
larger block is to be moved other methods must be employed.
Perhaps the simplest method is to break the large block up
into blocks that are up to 256 bytes and then to use a
succession of small block moves. This can be a little clumsy,
however, and a better method is to take advantage of the

indirect indexed mode using a pair of zero page locations as a pointer.   In this case the index is set to zero and the pointer itself is incremented using double length arithmetic. The pointer can thus be incremented over the full range of the memory. Say that &70, &71 is used to specify the data source and &72, &73 the data destination then the following instructions move a single byte of data:

LDA (&70),Y : STA (&72),Y

These two 16 bit pointers may be incremented by the two byte increment given in chapter 6. A 16 bit loop counter will also be needed and this can be in say &74, &75.

The program following demonstrates the method and is written using the BASIC assembler using two passes. The loop counter is tested in lines 90 and 100 and if both bytes of it are zero a branch is made to the label FINISH. The transfer of a single byte from one location to the other takes place in line 120 and then in lines 130 to 190 both 16 bit pointers are incremented.   Then the loop counter is decremented in lines 190 and 200 and a jump back to the label loop is performed.

The lines of BASIC which follow are to set up the pointers and loop counter to values input from the keyboard.   Finally a CALL is made to perform the actual block move.

The program may be tested by setting up some memory to known values and then running the program to move the data.

Exercise:

```
        NEW
10   DIM S% 100
20   FOR PASS=0 TO 2 STEP 2
30   P%=S%
40   [ OPT PASS
50   .MV
60   CLD
70   LDY #0
80   .LOOP
90   LDA &74: BNE NZ
100  LDA &75: BEQ FINISH
```

```
110  .NZ
120  LDA (&70),Y: STA (&72),Y
130  INC &70: BNE S1
140  INC &71
150  .S1
160  INC &72: BNE S2
170  INC &73
180  .S2
190  SEC: LDA &74: SBC #1: STA &74
200  LDA &75: SBC #0: STA &75
210  JMP LOOP
220  .FINISH
230  RTS: ]
240  NEXT
250  INPUT "MOVE FROM" A$
260  ?&70=EVAL A$ MOD &100
270  ?&71=EVAL A$ DIV &100
280  INPUT "MOVE TO" A$
290  ?&72=EVAL A$ MOD &100
300  ?&73=EVAL A$ DIV &100
310  INPUT "NO OF BYTES" A$
320  ?&74=EVAL A$ MOD &100
330  ?&75=EVAL A$ DIV &100
340  CALL MV
```

5

Arithmetic

Arithmetic is one of the more involved areas of assembly language programming and has therefore been left until this later point in the book as there are quite a number of difficult and new concepts to be mastered. The computer has facilities for handling two different types of binary number system. One for numbers that are only ever considered to be positive (called unsigned binary integers). These are the simplest type of binary number already considered in chapter 1. The other number system is more involved and allows for numbers that can be considered to be positive or negative (known technically as twos complement binary numbers).

The situation is complex because the computer uses the same arithmetic circuits for both types of number and also decimal numbers and it is up to the programmer to interpret the results of arithmetic depending on the state of various flags before and after the arithmetic.

We begin by considering the simplest case, that is the addition of unsigned binary numbers which are of fixed length of one byte. The CPU has facilities for both binary and decimal arithmetic and it is necessary to specify the type of arithmetic required. This is done by setting the D flag to 0 using the CLD instruction which should be obeyed before any arithmetic is carried out.

All the following programs should be run with the aid of Monitor as the print out of flags that Monitor provides will prove helpful in understanding the operation of the arithmetic.

ADDING UNSIGNED NUMBERS

Unsigned numbers are added together using a combination of the A register of the microcomputer and a flag called the C (or carry) flag. The carry flag is a one bit register that is used to record if an arithmetic operation resulted in a carry i.e. a result too big to be contained in a single byte (greater than &FF).

First consider the numbers to be single byte numbers i.e. in the range 0 to &FF. The CPU adds together numbers in the A register using the ADC (AdD with Carry) instruction. This is available in many addressing modes and adds the data specified by the addressing mode PLUS THE NUMBER CONTAINED IN THE CARRY FLAG JUST BEFORE THE ADC INSTRUCTION to the number stored in the A register. The result is left in the A register. If the result is less than &FF the carry flag is set to 0 and A contains the correct result. If the result of the addition is too big to fit into a single byte, i.e. greater than &FF, then the carry flag is set to the value 1 and the A register contains the lower eight bits of the result.

This feature of always adding the carry flag as well as the specified data can be a nuisance. Although it makes the instruction more versatile, when we just want to simply add two numbers we HAVE TO REMEMBER TO RESET THE CARRY TO 0 BEFORE THE ADC INSTRUCTION.

The CLC (CLear Carry) instruction is used to set the carry flag to 0. There is also the opposite instruction available, should this be required, and it is SEC (SEt Carry), which sets the carry flag to a 1.

Thus if we just want to add some data to the A register we must use the CLC instruction just before the ADC.

Exercise:

```
10 LDA &5000
20 CLC: CLD
30 ADC #5
40 STA &5001
```

The above program adds 5 to the contents of storage location
&5000 and puts the result into &5001. Note that in line 20 the
CLD instruction is used to tell the CPU to use binary
arithmetic. Enter the program using the E command of Monitor.
Set the contents of &5000 to some number less than &FB (so
that no carry is generated) and assemble and run the program.
Check that the C flag is 0 after the program is run and that
the contents of &5001 are as expected.

Change the contents of &5000 to a number greater than &FB so
that a carry will be generated and notice that after running
the program that the C flag is set to 1.

The above program is an example of the immediate addressing
mode but other modes are possible.

Exercise:

```
10 LDA &70
20 CLC: CLD
30 ADC &71
40 STA &5000
```

This program adds together the contents of &70 to the contents
of &71 and puts the result into &5000.

The Details of Binary Addition

The computer performs the above additions using the binary
number system. We now study the details of binary addition.
The rules are very simple when compared with those of decimal
arithmetic. In decimal we have to remember a hundred results
for the addition of two decimal digits (0 + 0 = 0 carry 0, 0 +
1 = 1 carry 0, ... etc. up to 9 + 9 = 8 carry 1). In binary,
however, there are only two possible digits 0 and 1 and the

binary addition table for digits only has four possibilities.

```
0+0 = 0 carry 0
0+1 = 1 carry 0
1+0 = 1 carry 0
1+1 = 0 carry 1
```

A simple example illustrates the method:

```
        digit  position
        7 6 5 4 3 2 1 0

        0 0 0 0 0 0 1 1  ( = decimal 3)
       +0 0 0 0 1 0 0 1. ( = decimal 9)

carrys 0 0 0 0 0 1 1
       -----------------
result 0 0 0 0 1 1 0 0  ( = decimal 12)
       -----------------
```

We start with digit position 0 and determine that 1 + 1 is 0 carry 1. The 0 is written in the result and the carry in the carry position of the next digit. Moving to position 1 we then add 1 + 0 + the carry from position 0. This results in 0 carry 1 and the 0 digit is written into the result and the carry written in the next column to the left. We continue along the digit positions each time adding together the digits plus the carry from the previous position.

Adding a List of Numbers (total less than 256)

The indexed modes are also available and the following program shows how to add together a list of eight numbers stored in consecutive memory locations.

Exercise:

```
10   CLD: LDA #0
20   LDX #0
30   LDY #8
40   .loop
50   CLC
60   ADC &5000,X
70   INX
80   DEY
90   BNE loop
100  STA &70
```

The A register is used to hold the running total and is
initialised to zero in line 10. The X register is used to
perform the indexed addressing and Y is used as the loop
counter. The first time through the loop line 60 adds the
contents of &5000 and then &5001 etc until &5007. Note that
any carry generated by line 60 (if the result is bigger than
&FF) is neglected by this program as line 50 always resets the
carry flag to 0. The final result is stored in &70 and is also
displayed on the screen as the contents of A.

The program used the A register to hold the running total.
This means that A is not available for other uses. Instead a
memory location could be used to hold the running total.

Exercise:

```
10   CLD: LDA #0 : STA &70
20   LDX #0
30   LDY #8
40   .loop
50   LDA &70
60   CLC
70   ADC &5000,X
80   STA &70
90   INX
100  DEY
110  BNE loop
```

This program uses &70 to keep the running total. It is first
initialised to zero in line 10 and then lines 50 to 80 add the

contents of the next number to it inside the loop. The
process is illustrated in Figure 5.1.

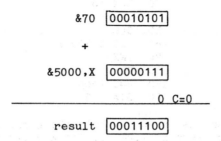

Figure 5.1

Double Length Result

The above program is only valid if the result is always less
than 256 (&100). If the result is too large after any of the
additions a carry will be generated and the problem is what to
do if this is the case. One approach is to regard the result,
not as an 8 bit number, but as a 16 bit or 2 byte number. If
any carry occurs after addition in the least significant byte
it is just added to the most significant byte of the two byte
result. Figure 5.2 illustrates the process.

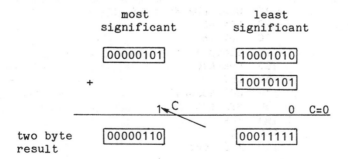

Figure 5.2

Thus the above program may be modified to allow for a 16 bit
total (up to 65535) by using say &71 as the most significant
byte of the two byte result.

Exercise:

```
10   CLD: LDA #0 :STA &70 :STA &71
20   LDX #0
30   LDY #8
40   .loop
50   LDA &70
60   CLC
70   ADC &5000,X
80   STA &70
90   LDA &71
100  ADC #0
110  STA &71
120  INX
130  DEY
140  BNE loop
```

In line 10 both bytes of the result are initialised to 0. Line
90 contains the start of the section which adds the carry flag
to the contents of &71. The contents of &71 are first loaded
into A and then the immediate number 0 PLUS THE CARRY FLAG are
added to it. Thus if carry was 1 after the ADC in line 70
then 1 will be added to the contents of &71.

Enter, assemble and run the program several times using
different sets of data to test if results greater than 255 are
correctly evaluated.

The method can be extended to results of any required number
of bytes. Say for a 3 byte result we could use &72 for the
third byte, initialise it to zero by changing line 10 to 10
LDA #0:STA &70:STA &71:STA &72 and then by inserting say a
line 115 LDA &72: ADC #0 :STA &72 to add the second byte carry
into the third byte.

Adding Two Byte Numbers

We have seen how a two byte result can be obtained by the

addition of single byte numbers. There are times when we need
to add such two byte numbers together. The method is
straightforward: we first add together the two least
significant bytes and then add the resulting carry plus the
two most significant bytes. Figure 5.3 shows the method for
adding the two byte number N1 (contained in &70 and &71) to
the two byte number N2 (contained in &72 and &73). The two
byte result is put into &74 and &75.

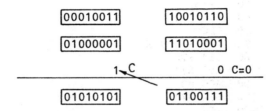

Figure 5.3

The program for this two byte addition is given below.

Exercise:

```
10   CLD: CLC
20   LDA &70
30   ADC &72
40   STA &74
50   LDA &71
60   ADC &73
70   STA &75
```

Note that if the result is bigger than two bytes then the
carry flag is set to 1 after the program is run.

Incrementing a Two Byte Number

A frequently needed task in assembly language programming is
the addition of 1 to a sixteen bit, or two byte value for
example the use of a two byte number used to represent an
address. Say the number is stored in &70 and &71. An
illustration is shown in Figure 5.4.

most   least
significant   significant

&71   &70

01000010   00010001

16 bit number = 0100001000010001

= &4211

Figure 5.4

One method of incrementing this 16 bit value is to use the
above addition methods to simply add 1 to the double byte
number. For example:

Exercise:

```
                        10   LDA &70
                        20   CLD: CLC
                        30   ADC #1
                        40   STA &70
                        50   LDA &71
                        60   ADC #0
                        70   STA &71
```

Enter and assemble the program and set &70 &71 to some known
values.   Run the program and check that the value has been
increased by 1.

A more efficient method is to use the INC instruction. This
increments a memory location by 1. Unfortunately INC does not
cause the carry flag to be set when the single byte range is
exceeded but it does, however, set the Z flag when the store
incremented goes from &FF to &00. The Z flag may thus be used
instead of the C flag to test whether or not to increment the
more significant byte.

Exercise:

```
10   INC &70
20   BNE SKIP
30   INC &71
40   .SKIP
```

This is much shorter than the method using addition.

A SIMPLE MULTIPLICATION PROGRAM

The 6502 microprocessor chip unfortunately does not have built
instructions for multiplication so that software must be
written to perform this function. Various methods are
possible and more detail is given in chapter 7. For the
present a simple (but slow) method will be given as an example
of the use of a combination of loops and addition.

It is possible to regard multiplication as repeated addition.
For example 7*5 could be interpreted as (5 + 5 + 5 + 5 + 5 + 5
+ 5) or of course (7 + 7 + 7 + 7 + 7). For small numbers the
method is reasonable but as the multiplication is performed
with large numbers many additions are needed and the method
becomes very slow compared to the methods discussed in chapter
7.

The following program and flow diagram Figure 5.5 shows the
method.

Exercise:

```
 10   CLD: LDA #0: STA &72: STA &73
 20   .loop
 30   CLC
 40   LDA &72
 50   ADC &71
 60   STA &72
 70   LDA &73
 80   ADC #0
 90   STA &73
100   DEC &70
110   BNE loop
```

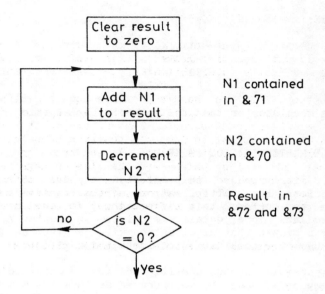

N1 contained
in &71

N2 contained
in &70

Result in
&72 and &73

Figure 5.5

A two byte result has been used as when two single byte
numbers are multiplied it is very easy to get a result which
is bigger than &FF, the maximum possible with a single byte
result. Line 10 sets the double byte result to zero. Lines
30 to 90 add the single byte number contained in &71 to the
double byte result contained in &72 &73.

Enter and assemble the program. Set &70 and &71 to the two
numbers to be multiplied and run the program.

There are two deficiencies with the program. The number
stored in &70 is reduced from its initial value to 0. This may
be overcome by taking a copy of the number in say X by 15 LDX
&70 and changing 100 to DEX. The second defect is that if &70
initially contains zero the loop is actually obeyed 256
times. A test for this condition could be incorporated at the
start of the program, e.g. the following lines could be added
12 LDA &70: BEQ exit and 120 .exit .

POSITIVE AND NEGATIVE NUMBERS

Before considering the action of the computer in performing arithmetic with negative numbers it is useful to review some decimal arithmetic rules that we often take for granted.

In everyday life we handle positive and negative numbers without thinking, automatically using arithmetic rules and conventions learned at school. Numbers are written in a form using a + or - sign to indicate positive or negative (or of course no prefix is equivalent to +) and the sign is followed by a set of digits which are the size or magnitude of the number. (Technically the numbers are sign plus magnitude decimal integers.) We do, however, treat negative numbers and results of arithmetic in a different way to positive numbers and results.

For example consider two simple arithmetic problems:

(a) 17 - 5 =
(b)   5 - 17 =

The results are of course 12 and -12 but we take for granted the mental processes involved in obtaining them. For 17 - 5 we perform a straightforward subtraction, 5 from 7 is 2 with no borrow and 0 from 1 is 1, to get the result 12.

For the second case of 5 - 17 we actually do not perform this calculation but instead say that the answer is - (17 - 5) or -12. Thus we have in effect performed a complex process. The 5 and 17 have first been compared to see which is the largest and only then has the subtraction been carried out to obtain a positive result. Finally the correct sign has been inserted in front of the result.

Let us see what happens if we forget the above method and try to directly subtract 17 from 5. We first take 7 from 5 (borrowing 1) to obtain 8 and then the borrow is subtracted from 0 (again borrowing 1) to obtain 9 and so on. The process never stops and the result is ....999998 with an infinite sequence of 9s before the 8 digit. Say that we restrict ourselves to a fixed number of places and stop after four digits of result then this result is 9998 (instead of -2).

Using our conventional ideas about arithmetic this result is
clearly wrong but in many ways it behaves as if it were
correct. Thus if we add the 9998 to a positive number say 6
and again restrict the result to four digits (neglecting any
carry into the fifth digit) then we get the result

$$
\begin{array}{r}
0006 \\
+9998 \\
\hline
=0004
\end{array}
$$

Adding the number 9998 has had the same effect as adding the
number -2.

It turns out that this alternative way of representing a
negative number is in fact a perfectly valid way of looking at
the problem. In this system, described as a TENS COMPLEMENT
SYSTEM, we use a fixed number of digits for all numbers. We
regard numbers as positive if the most significant digit is
less than 5 and negative if it is in the range 5 to 9. The
four digit decimal number thus can represent numbers in the
range -500 to +499.

We can get the negative of a number by taking it from zero.
For example the representation of the number -12 is found by
taking 12 from 0.

$$
\begin{array}{r}
0000 \\
-0012 \\
\hline
=9988
\end{array}
$$

Using this system we can add and subtract the positive and
negative numbers with freedom, using a fixed number of places
for the numbers and results and NEGLECTING ANY CARRY OR BORROW
FROM THE MOST SIGNIFICANT DIGIT. For example to reverse the
above problem we can evaluate -(-12).

$$0000$$
$$-9988$$

$$=0012$$

The correct result has been obtained.

It is the fact that the carry or borrow from the most
significant digit is ignored that makes this system of numbers
work and be different from the system which only allows
positive integers. Thus the programmer should take note: IF
USING COMPLEMENTS NEGLECT THE CARRY OR BORROW FROM THE MOST
SIGNIFICANT DIGIT - IF USING POSITIVE INTEGERS TAKE ACCOUNT OF
THE CARRY OR BORROW.

The complement system works correctly for addition and
subtraction operations but it breaks down completely if
multiplication or division is attempted. For multiplication
or division the numbers are converted into positive integers
and the sign of the result is adjusted following the result of
the operation with the positive integers.

This type of complement system has advantages when used in
computers. For example it removes the need to see which of
two numbers is the largest before performing a subtraction and
it also greatly simplifies the circuits of the arithmetic unit
as it is possible to use a single arithmetic unit both for the
ordinary unsigned numbers and the positive/negative numbers.

Tens complement numbers will be examined later in chapter 7
when decimal arithmetic on the BBC computer is studied but now
we proceed to a brief study of binary subtraction before
looking at the binary version of the complement system.

BINARY SUBTRACTION

As with binary addition the rules of binary subtraction are
very simple when compared with those of decimal arithmetic.
In decimal we have to remember many results for the
subtraction of two decimal digits (0 - 0 = 0 borrow 0, 0 - 1 =
9 borrow 1 ....5 - 3 = 2 borrow 0 ....etc. up to 9 - 9 = 0

borrow 0). In binary, however, there are only two possible digits 0 and 1 and the binary subtraction table for digits only has four possibilities.

$$0-0 = 0 \text{ borrow } 0$$
$$0-1 = 1 \text{ borrow } 1$$
$$1-0 = 1 \text{ borrow } 0$$
$$1-1 = 0 \text{ borrow } 0$$

A simple example illustrates the method:

```
              digit  position
              7 6 5 4 3 2 1 0

              0 0 0 0 1 0 0 1 ( = decimal 9)
             -0 0 0 0 0 0 1 1 ( = decimal 3)

    borrows   0 0 0 0 1 1 0
              ----------------
    result    0 0 0 0 0 1 1 0 ( = decimal 6)
              ----------------
```

Starting with digit position 0, 1 - 1 is 0 borrow 0. The 0 is written in the result and the borrow in the borrow position of the next digit. Moving to position 1 we then perform 0 - 1 - the borrow from position 0. This results in 1 borrow 1 and the 1 digit is written into the result and the borrow written in the borrow of the next column to the left. We continue along the digit positions each time subtracting the digits and the borrow from the previous stage.

Subtracting Unsigned Numbers in the CPU

It has been explained earlier that one of the advantages of the complement system is that the design of the hardware of the CPU is simplified. Internally subtractions are performed by adding the complement of the number to be subtracted. The CPU uses a fast method of converting a number to its complement, described later in this chapter, which relies on the carry flag being set to a 1 before the above addition of complement occurs. Although simplified hardware results a consequence of this is that on the 6502 CPU the carry flag acts as the inverse of the borrow described above.

The SBC instruction subtracts the data specified by the addressing mode and also the inverse of the carry flag, from the A register. The carry flag is set according to the result.

Until you get used to this feature of the 6502 the rule of thumb to remember is that if straightforward subtraction of two bytes is required then the carry flag is set to 1 (using SEC) before the subtraction is carried out.

Exercise:

```
10  CLD
20  LDA &70
30  SEC
40  SBC &71
50  STA &5000
```

This program subtracts the contents of &71 from the contents of &70 and stores the result in &5000.

If the number being subtracted is smaller then the result is positive and the C flag is 1 following the subtraction, (indicating no borrow). If the number being subtracted is larger then C is set to 0 (indicating a borrow).

The meaning of such a result is expanded in the description of 2's complement numbers.

Subtracting Two Byte Numbers

The addition of two byte numbers has already been covered and the method is easily extended to subtraction. The following program subtracts the double byte number in &72, &73 from that in &70, &71 and puts the result in &74, &75.

Exercise:

```
10  CLD
20  LDA &70
```

```
30  SEC: SBC &72
40  STA &74
50  LDA &71
60  SBC &73
70  STA &75
```

Note that in line 60 the borrow from the previous subtraction is used for the most two significant bytes.

Decrementing Two Byte Numbers

Two byte numbers are frequently used in many applications and we have already seen how to increment these numbers using an efficient method based on the use of INC. This suggests the use of the DEC instruction to perform the same operation for decrementing. Unfortunately DEC does not set any flag that can be used as an indication of whether or not to also decrement the most significant byte. The solution is to use the less efficient arithmetic instructions to subtract 1 from the double byte number.

Exercise:

```
10  CLD
20  SEC
30  LDA &73
40  SBC #1
50  STA &73
60  LDA &74
70  SBC #0
80  STA &74
```

This program is used to decrement the double byte number &73, &74 by 1. Note that at the end of the decrement the N flag may be used to detect if the decrement has resulted in a negative value and this is useful when using a two byte number as a loop counter. Try this by inserting 2 in &73, 0 in &74 and running he program three times.

Comparing Multiple Byte Numbers

Another task frequently needed when using arithmetic is the comparison of multiple byte numbers, say N1 and N2. There are three possibilities: the two numbers are equal, N1 is greater than N2 or N2 is greater than N1.

If the two numbers are subtracted (N1 - N2) then after the subtraction of the two most significant bytes the N flag is set according to the sign of the result. Thus N is set to 1 if N2 is greater than N1 and is 0 if N1 is greater or equal to N2. If the two numbers are equal then as the numbers are subtracted byte by byte each result will be zero and this occurrence has to be tested for as the subtraction is carried out.

Example:

```
10   CLD
20   LDA #0: STA &80
30   LDX #0: LDY #4
40   SEC
50   .LOOP
60   LDA &5000,X
70   SBC &6000,X
80   BEQ SKIP: INC &80
90   .SKIP: INX
100  DEY
110  BNE LOOP
```

This program compares the two numbers stored at &5000 and &6000 using a loop and indexed addressing. The bytes comprising the numbers are subtracted one at a time in lines 60 and 70. If the result of this is a byte which is non zero then &80 is incremented. Thus at the end of the program &80 will only contain zero if every result from subtracting individual bytes was zero and this can only be so if both the numbers being compared are equal.

TWO's COMPLEMENT BINARY NUMBERS

The radix or base of the binary system is two and a system of complements in binary is therefore known as the two's complement system. It operates in the same way as for the 10's complement system with a fixed number of bits for numbers and the most significant bit determining the sign of the number. The fixed number of bits used depends on the application but is usually a whole number of bytes. Single byte two's complement numbers are the simplest but two, three and four byte numbers (for BBC integer variables) are also used. For the moment consider single byte numbers. Bit 7 is the sign bit if it is 0 then the number is positive and if it is 1 then the number is negative. The most negative number is thus 10000000 which is equivalent to -128 and the most positive 01111111 which is equivalent to +127.

The two's complement form of a negative number is formed as above by subtracting the positive number from zero. Thus the number -4 decimal is equivalent to -(00000100) in a binary sign plus magnitude system and in two's complement form:

```
             digit  position
             7 6 5 4 3 2 1 0

             0 0 0 0 0 0 0 0 ( = 0 )
           - 0 0 0 0 0 1 0 0 ( = 4 )

           = 1 1 1 1 1 1 0 0
```

Thus the binary number 11111100 is equivalent to -4 in a two's complement system.

Another quick method of converting a number to its complement is to swap 0s and 1s in the number and then to add 1. Thus in the above example swapping 0s and 1s of the number 00000100 gives 11111011 and then adding 1 makes this 11111100 as before.

A commonly used number is -1. Using the above method this is converted by first taking the 8 bit number for +1 i.e. 00000001 and then swapping 0s and 1s to give 11111110. Then 1 is added to give 11111111 which is the two's complement form of -1. Expressed in hex this is of course the number &FF.

A useful way of looking at two's complement numbers is to

regard the most significant bit as representing the negative
of the power of two involved. Thus in an 8 bit system the
most significant bit represents the number - (two x two x two
x two x two x two x two x two) or -128 decimal. The rest of
the bits then have their normal values. Say we take the
number 11111111 then under this way of looking at things the
number may be converted to decimal as follows (1 x -128 + 1 x
64 + 1 x 32 + 1 x 16 + 1 x 8 + 1 x 4 + 1 x 2 + 1 x 1) or -1.

For readers interested in mathematics the system may be
likened to the method of performing arithmetic using logarithm
tables. In this method negative logarithms are formed by
having the most significant digit negative (denoted by a BAR
placed over it) and the rest of the number positive. In
effect a tens complement method of representing a negative
number.

Addition of Two's Complement Numbers

We have already seen how to add, in both single byte and
multiple byte fashion, unsigned binary integers and we now
proceed to the same thing using two's complement numbers. The
computer only has a single set of instructions which apply to
both ordinary unsigned numbers and also to the two's
complement numbers and the CPU does not know if it is dealing
with an unsigned number or a two's complement number. Instead
when performing arithmetic it treats the numbers as BOTH
UNSIGNED NUMBERS AND ALSO AS TWO'S COMPLEMENT NUMBERS and it
sets the flags for both number systems when an addition is
carried out. The programmer always knows which number system
he is using and must therefore use whichever flags are
appropriate to the task in hand.

The flags in question are the carry flag which we have already
encountered in the addition of multiple byte unsigned numbers
and a special flag for two's complement arithmetic, the
OVERFLOW flag. In unsigned arithmetic we completely ignore
the overflow flag. In two's complement addition, however, the
carry which occurs from the most significant bit is ignored
and as this carry is ignored the OVERFLOW flag is provided to
detect if a two's complement error has occurred during the
arithmetic.

Exercise:

```
10 CLD: LDA &70
20 CLC
30 ADC &71
40 STA &72
```

This Monitor program adds together the contents of &70 to &71
and puts the result into &72. It is equally valid if the
numbers stored in &70 and &71 are unsigned numbers or two's
complement numbers. If the numbers are unsigned we can test
the carry flag after the program to see if the result was
bigger than &FF. If the numbers are two's complement we test
the OVERFLOW (V) flag to see if things have gone wrong. Enter
and run the program. Load &70 and &71 with the numbers &05
and &FE. In two's complement &FE is equivalent to the number
-2 decimal so the result in two's complement should be 5 - 2 =
3. Run the program and examine the result. Notice that after
the program is run the V flag is 0 (i.e. everything OK) and
the carry flag is 1 (which we ignore in two's complement
arithmetic. If we were to look at the above program and data
in unsigned arithmetic then the number &FE is equivalent to
the decimal number 254 and the result of the addition would be
254 + 5 = 259, which in hex is the number &103, or &03 carry
1. Thus the same program can add data of either type and get
the right result depending on how we look at the flags after
the addition.

The number -2 was entered above as &FE but Monitor will also
accept input to the M command in the form of negative numbers
and thus the -2 could be entered as such into &71.

The Sign Flag - (N FLAG)

The sign, or N, flag is provided to indicate the sign of the
result of an arithmetic operation. It is essentially a copy
of bit 7 of the result and thus if the result is positive then
bit 7 and the N flag will be 0 and if negative then bit 7 and
N will be 1.

The flag is tested by two branch instructions BPL and BMI. The branch on positive BPL will cause a branch to be made to an address if a result is positive and branch on minus BMI branches on a negative result.

Subtraction of Two's Complement Numbers

As already described for the ADC instruction the CPU does not know which type of number it is dealing with and therefore sets the flags for both types of numbers. It is up to the programmer to work with the set of flags appropriate to the number being dealt with. Thus subtraction of two's complement numbers also uses the SBC instruction. As for addition any carry or borrow from the most significant byte of a subtraction is ignored. Overflow conditions are detected by the special purpose V flag.

Exercise:

```
10   CLD
20   LDA &70
30   SEC
40   SBC &71
50   STA &72
```

This Monitor program subtracts the contents of &71 from the contents of &70 and stores the result in &72. The program will subtract either ordinary unsigned numbers or twos' complement numbers and we use the appropriate flags. If the result exceeds the two's complement range then the V flag is set.

Overflow Conditions

The above methods of adding and subtracting break down under the circumstances when an arithmetic operation produces a result which is outside the allowable range.

The two's complement range possible in an 8 bit number is +127 to -128 and if the result is outside this range the V flag is set. For example try adding &7F (+127) to &7F using the program on page 108.

The correct result should be, of course, +254 but this is too big to fit in the single byte range. The actual result obtained is &FE, which is the two's complement representation of the number -2. The number 10000001 (&81) is the two's complement form of -127 and if the program is run with &70 and &71 both containing this number the correct result should be -254. This number is outside the allowable range and in fact the result obtained is &02 but the overflow flag is set to indicate the error.

The subtraction of numbers can also produce results which are out of range and the V flag is set for these cases too.

It is up to the programmer to monitor the condition of the V flag to check for overflow and to take action to deal with any errors which result.

6

Dealing with Bits

This chapter describes the techniques that are available for handling bytes as patterns of bits, rather than as binary numbers. The subject falls naturally into two areas, shifting data patterns and logical operations.

SHIFTING DATA PATTERNS

A function frequently required in assembly language is that of moving a binary number relative to the register or store that contains it. This is required for the software which divides and multiplies and also for other applications such as moving graphics on the screen and in sending serial data to computer peripherals.

The binary numbers stored in the accumulator and memory may be rotated or shifted relative to the location that contains them. For example if we consider the binary number 00001010 then the effect of a shift to the right is to give the number 00000101, and that of a shift to the left the number 00010100. The entire data pattern is moved one place to the left or right. When this is done a bit always "drops off the end" and a "hole" appears at the other end of the number. When a bit drops out of a number it is always placed in the carry flag so that it may be used subsequently. The hole that appears may be filled in two ways, either with a 0 as in the examples above, or with the contents of the carry flag before the operation took place.

The shift instructions ASL and LSR shift a number to the left or right respectively and a 0 is always inserted into the hole at the end. The rotate instructions ROL and ROR rotate the number to the left and right respectively and the hole is filled with the previous contents of the carry flag. With both sets of instructions the carry flag after the instruction is set to the value of the bit that drops out.

Multiplying and Dividing by Two

Note that if a binary number is shifted one place to the right it is equivalent to dividing its value by two and if it is shifted one place to the left it is equivalent to multiplying its value by two. The number 00001010 is the decimal number ten and the shifted version 00000101 is five whereas 00010100 is equivalent to the decimal number twenty.

Exercise:

```
10    LDA #&80
20    LSR A
30    LSR A
40    LSR A
50    LSR A
60    LSR A
70    LSR A
80    LSR A
90    LSR A
```

In line 10 the most significant bit of A is set to 1 and subsequent LSR A instructions move this bit down the A register with A going through the sequence (1000000) &80 (01000000) &40 (00100000) &20 (00010000) &10 (00001000) &08 (00000100) &04 (00000010) &02 (00000001) &01 (00000000) &00. Assemble the program and use the B command of Monitor to set a breakpoint on the first LSR A instruction and run the program. At the break A should have the value &80. Use the T command to single step through the program, A should successively have the values &80, &40, &20, &10, &08, &04, &02, &01, &00.

Note that on the last shift the bit which comes out of bit 0 goes into the carry flag.

The next exercise demonstrates that instead of shifting a 0 into bit 7 the rotate instruction shifts the contents of the carry flag.

Exercise:

```
 10   LDA #0
 20   SEC
 30   ROR A
 40   SEC
 50   ROR A
 60   SEC
 70   ROR A
 80   SEC
 90   ROR A
100   SEC
110   ROR A
120   SEC
130   ROR A
140   SEC
150   ROR A
160   SEC
170   ROR A
```

In this program the carry flag is set to 1 before each rotate instruction and thus a 1 is entered into bit 0 of A at each ROR A instruction. The number in A goes through the sequence (00000000) &00 (10000000) &80 (11000000) &C0 (11100000) &E0 (11110000) &F0 (11111000) &F8 (11111100) &FC (11111110) &FE (11111111) &FF.

Enter and run the program using the T command to see the sequence of shifts.

Multiple Length Shifts

Shifts and rotates of multiple byte numbers can also be
carried out by a combination of instructions using the carry
flag as the link between bytes. The bit that is shifted out
of the end of one byte is rotated into the hole of the next
byte. When shifting left the least significant byte is
shifted first, followed by the second then the third etc up to
the most significant. When shifting right we start with the
most significant byte first then the next most significant
etc., down to the least significant.

The method is illustrated by the following program which
divides a four byte integer by 8 using three successive
rotates to the right. The method is illustrated using the BBC
assembler instead of Monitor for a change.

Exercise:

```
          NEW
     10   DIM start% 50: P%=start%
     20   [.DV8
     30   LDX #3
     40   .loop
     50   LSR &3104
     60   ROR &3103
     70   ROR &3102
     80   ROR &3101
     90   DEX
    100   BNE loop
    110   RTS
    120   ]
```

Run the program and set the four bytes to some known value say
10000 using the ! operator i.e. !&3101=10000. Call the above
routine by entering CALL DV8 and print the contents of &3101
and the next three byte using P.!&3101 . The result should be
1250 i.e. 10000/8.

Fractional Result

Suppose we give the above program a number to divide which is

not an exact multiple of 8. Say we consider dividing the
decimal number 13 by 8. In binary the number 13 is 1101
(forgetting all the leading zeros) and when it is shifted to
the right three places to divide it by 8 we are left with the
number 1. The three bits 101 representing the remainder 5 drop
off the end of the binary number. We could collect the bits
that drop off in another store and regard the total result as
1.101, where the point in the result is a BINARY POINT. This
process is just the same as we would carry out in decimal if
we divide say 147 by 100. We shift the 147 right by two places
and collect the 4 and 7 digits that drop off to get the result
1.47. A more formal description of a fraction in a number
system is given in chapter 1. Thus we can see that the
complete binary result of 1.101 can be thought of as:

$$
\begin{aligned}
& 1 \\
+\ & 1 \times 1/\text{two} \\
+\ & 0 \times 1/(\text{two} \times \text{two}) \\
+\ & 1 \times 1/(\text{two} \times \text{two} \times \text{two})
\end{aligned}
$$

Which is the decimal number 1.625 .

We can also express the fractional results using the hex
number system in a similar way. Thus the above binary result
is written 0001.1010 (the zeros have been put in to make up
the binary groups to four digits) and this converts to the hex
number &1.A which is interpreted as:

$$
\begin{aligned}
& 1 \\
+\ & A \times 1/\text{sixteen}
\end{aligned}
$$

The following program is an extension of the above program and
collects the fraction part of the result in &3100.

```
      NEW
10    DIM start% 50: P%=start%
20    [.DV8F
30    LDX #4
40    LDA #0
50    STA &3100
60    .loop
70    LSR &3104
80    ROR &3103
```

```
             90   ROR &3102
            100   ROR &3101
            110   ROR &3100
            120   DEX
            130   BNE loop
            140   RTS
            150   ]
```

Set &3101 to some known value that is not a multiple of eight
perhaps !&3100=13 and run the program.   Call the subroutine
using CALL DV8F and check that the correct results have been
obtained. &3100 should contain the binary number 1010000
(&A0) and &3101 should contain 1.

Shift Register

Electronically the function of shifting is carried out in a
special type of register known as a shift register. We do not
need to know the details of this aspect of CPU design in order
to program in assembly language but the term shift register is
in common use for a circuit or piece of software which is used
to perform shifts on data patterns.

LOGICAL OPERATIONS

In a logic system two states are defined and these are often
described as the "true" and "false" states.   The system was
devised in ancient times for testing the validity of various
types of arguments (such as if proposition X is true when Y is
true and Z is false, or when Z is true and Y is false, is X
true under the conditions when Z and Y are both true?).   It
turns out that the system is not only good for confusing
ancient philosophers but is also ideal for the designing of
the   complex control and arithmetic hardware of   modern
computers.

The modern computer is built around the binary arithmetic
system and much of the operation of the computer is based on
the manipulation of binary   data using electronic logic
circuits.   Indeed the computer is itself largely composed of a
complex interconnection of logic circuits and it is therefore

natural that the CPU should contain instructions which perform
logic operations.

In assembly language a single bit is used to represent a logic
state with a 1 standing for the true state and a 0 standing
for the false state. (BASIC uses a slightly different
convention for its representation of logic states. It uses a
word which consists of all 1s, equivalent to the number -1,
for the TRUE state and a word consisting of all 0s for the
FALSE state.)

There are three basic functions upon which the entire system
of logic is based and returning to assembly language we
consider them in turn.

The NOT function says that a result, say R, is TRUE if some
propostion P is NOT TRUE. A table of the possibilities is
known as a TRUTH TABLE. For NOT then a short table may be
made.

P	R
0	1
1	0

The AND function gives a result R which is true if both of two
propostions P and Q are true and the truth table is therefore:

P	Q	R
0	0	0
0	1	0
1	0	0
1	1	1

Thus R is 1 only if P AND Q are both 1.

The logic OR function gives a result which is true if either
proposition P OR Q is true and the truth table is therefore:

P	Q	R
0	0	0
0	1	1
1	0	1
1	1	1

Thus R is 1 if P is 1 or Q is 1.

Another frequently used logical operation is the EXCLUSIVE OR function. This gives a result which is true if P is true OR Q is true but false if P and Q are BOTH true and the truth table is therefore:

P	Q	R
0	0	0
0	1	1
1	0	1
1	1	0

Another way of looking at EXCLUSIVE OR is that the result is true if P and Q are different and it therefore forms a sort of comparison on logical data. The EXCLUSIVE OR is an important function for binary computers as the arithmetic section of the CPU is usually based on EXCLUSIVE OR circuits. The detailed study of CPU design is not appropriate in this book, which concentrates on software, but it is instructive to note that if you refer back to chapter 5 it can be seen that part of the addition table for binary digits is the same as the table for the EXCLUSIVE OR table given above.

An everyday example of the EXCLUSIVE OR function is the operation of the two way electric light switch where a light at the top of the stairs is controlled by two switches, one at the top and one at the bottom. The light is off if both switches are on or both are off but the light comes on if both switches are in a different condition.

LOGICAL INSTRUCTIONS

The BBC microcomputer has four logical instructions which operate on the A register. The functions provided are AND, OR, EXCLUSIVE OR and BIT testing. Note that the NOT function is not provided explicitly and if required it must be obtained from the other instructions. The instructions always operate with A as one of the sources of data and the other specified by the addressing mode. Thus two bytes of input data are defined and eight parallel logic operations take place between

bits in the same digit positions in both bytes i.e. each bit
position is treated independently of the others.

AND

This instruction is available in a wide variety of addressing
modes and performs the logical AND between A and the data
specified. It is best illustrated by example:

```
                 digit  position
                 7 6 5 4 3 2 1 0

        A        1 1 0 1 0 1 1 1
        DATA     0 1 1 1 0 0 1 0
                 ----------------
        RESULT 0 1 0 1 0 0 1 0    Z=0 N=0
                 ----------------
```

The digit positions are taken individually and thus for digit
position 0 (1 AND 0) is 0, for digit position 1 (1 AND 1) is 1
and so on through each digit position until the complete
result has been obtained. The result is placed back into the
A register overwriting the original contents. If the result
is a zero byte then the Z flag is set. Bit 7 of the result is
copied into the N flag.

ORA

This is also available in a wide range of addressing modes.
The data in A is OR'ed with that specified by the addressing
mode and the result is placed in A. The flags are effected as
for the AND instruction e.g.

```
                 digit  position
                 7 6 5 4 3 2 1 0

        A        1 1 0 1 0 1 1 1
        DATA     0 1 1 1 0 0 1 0
                 ----------------
        RESULT 1 1 1 1 0 1 1 1    Z=0 N=1
                 ----------------
```

EOR

This instruction performs the EXCLUSIVE OR of the data in A
and that specified by the addressing mode again on a bit by
bit basis. An example follows:

```
                    digit  position
                    7 6 5 4 3 2 1 0

            A       1 1 0 1 0 1 1 1
            DATA    0 1 1 1 0 0 1 0
                    ----------------
            RESULT  1 0 1 0 0 1 0 1      Z=0 N=1
                    ----------------
```

BIT

This is an instruction which is used for comparing bytes in a
logical manner. The data in A is AND'ed with that specified
by the addressing mode but the result is only used to set the
flags and is discarded. A retains its value that it had
before the instruction.

```
                    digit  position
                    7 6 5 4 3 2 1 0

            A       1 1 0 1 0 1 1 1
            DATA    0 1 1 1 0 0 1 0
                    ----------------
            RESULT  0 1 0 1 0 0 1 0      Z=0 N=0 V=1
                    ----------------
```

If the result is zero the Z flag is set. Bit 7 of the memory
contents is copied into the N flag and bit 6 of the memory
into the V flag.

We now look at ways of using the above instructions to
accomplish various tasks.

SETTING BITS IN A

One way of changing the data in A is the use of the LDA
instruction. This, however, changes every one of the 8 bits
in A. There are occasions when we only want to change one of
the bits in A to set it to a 1 or 0 as required. It would be
possible to use the logical shift instructions to rotate the
bit required into the carry flag, perform the desired setting
operation on the carry flag and then rotate the bit back to
its correct position. For example say that we wish to reset
bit 3 in A to a 0. The following program shows this method and
should be tried using Monitor.

Exercise:

```
          10  .RST
          20  LDA #&FF
          30  ROR A
          40  ROR A
          50  ROR A
          60  ROR A
          70  CLC
          80  ROL A
          90  ROL A
         100  ROL A
         110  ROL A
```

Bit 3 is rotated into the carry flag, cleared and then rotated
back.

The problem with doing the job in this way is that it takes a
large number of instructions to carry out a relativly simple
task. A better way is to use the logical instructions.

For example if A is AND'ed with the binary number 11110111
then bit 3 will be set to zero. The pattern with which A is
AND'ed is called a MASK and the process is often referred to
as MASKING. Of course any of bits of A may be changed at the
same time with a single AND operation. The same operation
using the ORA function may be used to set a bit to 1. So to
set bit 3 to a 1, A is OR'ed with the binary number 00001000.

The two operations are often combined in successive

instructions so that say to reset bit 3 to 0 and also set bit
5 to 1 without changing the contents of the other bits we can
use the following program.

Exercise:

```
10 LDA &5000
20 AND #&F7
30 ORA #&20
40 STA &5001
```

The program copies the contents of &5000 into &5001 resetting
bit 3 and setting bit 5. Enter the program using Monitor and
assemble and run it after setting &5000 and &5001 to known
values (try &FF and also 0).

The NOT function

The NOT function is not explicitly given on the 6502 CPU.
Instead the EOR (EXCLUSIVE OR) may be used. If the contents
of A are EXCLUSIVE OR'ed with 11111111 then each bit of A will
be complemented (0s changed to 1s and vice-versa).

Exercise:

```
10 LDA &5000
20 EOR #&FF
30 STA &5001
```

The above Monitor program illustrates the method.

OBTAINING A 2's COMPLEMENT NUMBER

We have seen in chapter 5 that a number may be changed into
its two's complement form by interchanging 0s and 1s and then
adding 1. The NOT function does this interchanging of 0s and
1s and so we can easily obtain the 2's complement form of an
eight bit number.

Exercise:

```
10 LDA &5000
20 EOR #&FF
30 CLC: CLD
40 ADC #1
50 STA &5001
```

TESTING BITS IN A

We can test bits in A for being 0 or 1 using the AND function
to mask out the bits that are not being tested. Thus say that
the condition of bit 5 in A is needed then the instruction AND
#&20 will change A to a number which is all 0s apart from the
bit 5 position. If bit 5 is 0 then the Z flag will be set
whereas if it is a 1 then the Z flag will be not set.
Unfortunately the process changes the contents of A so that if
the data in A must be preserved then it must be saved in
memory or a register and recalled after the AND and test.

Exercise:

```
10 LDA &5000
20 AND #&20
```

The above program demonstrates the method.

TESTING BITS IN THE MEMORY

Bits in the memory can be tested as above after first
transferring the data to A. The BIT instruction may also be
used to test individual bits or combinations of bits in the
memory. Thus if BIT is used with A containing the data
00001000 then following the BIT instruction the Z flag will be
set if bit 3 of the memory address specified was a 0 and not
set if it was a 1. Note also that following the special action
of BIT that the N flag is set to the contents of bit 7 of the
memory and the V flag is set to bit 6 of the memory. The
following program tests the contents of location &5000. If bit
4 is 1 then the program leaves the Z flag reset to 0 whereas
if it is a 0 the the Z flag is set. The N flag is set to bit
7 and the V flag to bit 6 of the contents of &5000.

Exercise:

                        10 LDA #&10
                        20 BIT &5000

Try the program using Monitor with sample data in &5000 e.g.
&80 will set the N flag, &10 the Z flag and &40 the V flag.

PSEUDO-RANDOM NUMBER GENERATOR

A truly random number is a number which is taken from a set of
numbers which are totally unrelated to one another and all
have an equal chance of occurring in the set. This is very
difficult to achieve. In practice methods are used which
produce a set or sequence of numbers which, although not
random in the sense given above, are nevertheless, for
practical purposes, sufficiently unrelated so that they appear
random. Such sequences are called pseudo-random sequences and
usually take the form of a very long sequence of numbers which
look random in the short term but the sequence in fact repeats
after many numbers. It is like a very long endless loop of
tape in a tape recorder on which is stored a set of random
numbers. In the short term the numbers appear random but in
the long term the tape repeats the sequence of numbers and the
system is not truly random.

One technique of obtaining such a pseudo-random sequence is
the use of a so called M sequence. In this method a set of
memory locations is used to contain a long binary number.
This number is shifted one place to the left and the bit that
is shifted into the number at the least significant end is
obtained by forming the EXCLUSIVE OR of two of the other bits
in the word. There are many combinations of bits that will
work but for the moment we will take the bits in positions 4
and 22 for a 23 bit number, (bit 0 being the least significant
and bit 22 the most significant). Looking now at an
individual bit position in the binary word it is found that we

get a sequence which does not repeat until 2^{23} -1 shifts. To
obtain a random binary word of more than a single bit we
perform instead of one shift say 8 shifts and then take 8 bits

from the binary word as an 8 bit random number.

The following program shows the method in practice. The 23 bit number is contained in stores &70, &71, &72 and the name RNN is used to describe store &70. The exclusive OR of bits 4 and 22 is obtained in lines 90 to 170. First the bit in position 4 is examined in 90 and a branch made depending on whether it is a 0 or 1. Next the bit in position 22 is examined and if both bits are 0 the carry flag is made 0, (label ZC). If either is a 1 then the carry flag is set to 1 at label NZC. If both are 1, however, then the carry flag is made 0. Thus the carry flag is set to the exclusive OR of bits 4 and 22.

A multiple length shift to the left is then made n lines 190 to 210 and finally in the subroutine the X register is used to perform the above process 8 times. Thus after RAN has been called the location RNN contains a pseudo random byte.

In line 270 the 23 bit number is initialised to the number 1 and this is known as the seed of the sequence. Any number other than 0 may be used.

Some lines of BASIC are at the end of the program to plot 1000 random pixels on the screen.

```
            NEW
     10     DIM S% 100
     20     RNN=&70
     30     FOR PASS = 0 TO 2 STEP 2
     40     P%=S%
     50     [OPT PASS
     60     .RAN
     70     LDX #8
     80     .LOOP
     90     LDA RNN: AND #&10: BEQ RN1
    100     LDA RNN+2: AND #&40: BEQ NZC
    110     JMP ZC
    120     .RN1
    130     LDA RNN+2: AND #&40: BNE NZC
    140     .ZC
    150     CLC: JMP CONT
    160     .NZC
```

```
170     SEC
180     .CONT
190     ROL RNN
200     ROL RNN+1
210     ROL RNN+2
220     DEX: BNE LOOP
230     RTS
240     ]
250     NEXT
260     MODE 5
270     ?RNN=1: ?(RNN+1)=0: ?(RNN+2)=0
280     FOR K=1 TO 1000
290     CALL RAN: X= ?RNN * 4
300     CALL RAN: Y= ?RNN * 4
310     PLOT 69,X,Y
320     NEXT
```

7

More Advanced Arithmetic

This chapter concentrates on some of the more difficult aspects of arithmetic using machine code. In general most readers will not need to write their own routines for division and multiplication unless they are writing their own computer language as the high level language facilities provided by BASIC are so good. This chapter is provided for those who are interested in this more specialised area and might appeal to those interested in writing computer languages and developing programs involving decimal arithmetic. Many electronic measuring instruments have decimal outputs which are compatible with the type of decimal arithmetic used on the 6502 microprocessor (BCD) and the section on decimal arithmetic should be useful for working with these types of numbers.

DECIMAL ARITHMETIC

In chapter 5 we have studied binary addition and subtraction as this is the type of arithmetic most often used. The 6502 CPU, however, has powerful facilities for doing the same operations with DECIMAL numbers. Decimal numbers, of course, comprise decimal digits and a decimal digit can be any one of the ten symbols 0, 1, 2, 3, 4, 5, 6, 7, 8, 9. In a binary computer each decimal digit is represented by a group of four

binary bits and this system is known as BINARY CODED DECIMAL,
often abbreviated to BCD. Thus the binary number 0000 stands
for the decimal digit 0, 0001 for decimal 1, binary 0010 for
decimal 2 and so on until binary 1001 represents decimal 9. A
four bit binary number can have sixteen possible values, zero
to fifteen, and the BCD system only uses ten of these values.
The unused values 1010 to 1111 are not allowed and have no
meaning in BCD arithmetic.

The binary eight bit word can therefore store two of these BCD
digits and is thus able to hold numbers up to 99 decimal.
Remember that using binary the same eight bit word can store
numbers up to 255 decimal. The BCD system is obviously not as
efficient as binary at storing numbers as it takes more bits
to store the same number and for this reason most computers
work in binary.

Decimal addition and subtraction is carried out using the
instructions ADC and SBC in the same way as for binary
arithmetic but the computer is first set into the decimal mode
of operation by the SED (SEt Decimal mode) instruction.   This
sets the DECIMAL FLAG (D flag) to a 1 and makes all future
additions and subtractions occur using BCD arithmetic, until
the CLD (CLear Decimal mode) instruction is given to reset the
D flag to 0.

Exercise:

```
10 SED
20 LDA &70
30 CLC
40 ADC &71
50 STA &72
60 CLD
```

The above exercise (using Monitor) adds the BCD number stored
in &70 to that stored in &71 and places the result in &72.
Notice that the decimal mode is cleared in line 60 before the
program returns to Monitor. It is normal practice to do this
at the end of a decimal program and also before using many of
the computer's built in subroutines as these operate using
binary arithmetic.

Set the contents of &70 to the BCD number 56 i.e. the binary
number 01010110. Note that hex numbers and BCD numbers look
exactly the same, the only difference is that decimal digits
only go up to 9, and so we can use hex input and output
routines for the BCD numbers. The M command may therefore be
used on address &70 and the contents made equal to &56, which
of course is the same as BCD 56. Set &71 to BCD 27 and run the
above program. After the run &72 should contain the BCD
number 83 and the D command may be used to check this.

Exercise:

```
10 SED
20 LDA &70
30 SEC
40 SBC &71
50 STA &72
60 CLD
```

This exercise demonstrates decimal subtraction. The decimal
number stored in &71 is subtracted from that stored in &70 and
the decimal result is stored in &72. Set the contents of &70
to the BCD number 56 (entered as &56) and the contents of &71
to the BCD number 27 (entered as &27). Assemble and run the
program. The result stored in &72 should be, of course,
(56-27) = 29.

The decimal flag is cleared at the end of the program. The
decimal arithmetic is carried out using the 10's complement
system previously discussed. Using the above program set the
contents of &70 to BCD 27 and the contents of &71 to BCD 56.
The result of running the program should then be 27-56 = 71.
This is the 10's complement form of the number -(56-27) = -29.

BINARY TO DECIMAL CONVERSION

An example of the use of binary and decimal arithmetic is the
conversion of binary numbers to decimal. The basic method is
that of using a program loop together with a binary loop
counter. At the same time as the binary loop counter is
decremented a BCD number is incremented using decimal
arithmetic and at the end of the loop the binary number will

have been decremented to zero and the decimal number will have
been incremented to the decimal equivalent of the original
binary number.

Exercise:

```
             10  LDA #0
             20  STA &71
             30  .LOOP
             40  CLD:SEC
             50  LDA &70
             60  BEQ FINISH
             70  SBC#1
             80  STA &70
             90  SED:CLC
            100  LDA &71
            110  ADC #1
            120  STA &71
            130  JMP LOOP
            140  .FINISH
```

This program illustrates the method. Store &70 contains the
binary number to be converted to BCD. It is decremented, using
binary arithmetic with the D flag clear, in lines 40 to 80.
When it contains zero the program terminates.   On each pass
through the program loop, decimal arithmetic is used in lines
90 to 120 to add 1 to the BCD number stored in &71. Enter,
assemble and run the program using Monitor having first set
&70 to a binary number using the M command, say binary 1100
(entered as &0C). After the program has run then &71 should
contain the BCD number 12.

More sophisticated faster methods are available e.g. see
"Leventhall 6502 Assembly Language Subroutines p 163".

DECIMAL TO BINARY CONVERSION

A similar technique may be used to convert a BCD number to
binary.   Again a program loop is used but this time the
decimal number is used as the loop counter and a binary number
is incremented on each pass through the loop.

Exercise :

```
10   LDA #0
20   STA &70
30   .LOOP
40   SED:SEC
50   LDA &71
60   BEQ FINISH
70   SBC#1
80   STA &71
90   CLD:CLC
100  LDA &70
110  ADC#1
120  STA &70
130  JMP LOOP
140  .FINISH
150  CLD
```

This program converts the BCD number stored in &71 to binary
(in the store &70). Lines 40 to 80 use decimal arithmetic to
take 1 from the BCD contents of &71, branching to the end of
the program when zero is reached.   Enter   the   program using
Monitor and assemble it.   Set   the   contents   of &71 to the
decimal number 99 (entered as &99) and run the program. the
result left in &70 should be &63.

BINARY MULTIPLICATION

The multiplication of numbers is more difficult than addition
and so has been left until this later point in the book.   The
methods used require that the reader is familiar with multiple
byte addition, shifting data patterns and loops.

The   most   straightforward   introduction   is to consider the
binary version of long multiplication. For example consider
the binary multiplication 1010 x 0010, corresponding to the
decimal ten x two. As for decimal long multiplication the
multiplication is set out in Figure 7.1.

Lines 1 and 2 contain the two binary numbers to be multiplied
together. The 1010 in line 1 is successively multiplied by
the individual bits of the 0010 in line 2 and the result of

each of these partial multiplications is written down in lines
3 to 6, starting immediately underneath the bit of line 2
responsible for the multiplication.   One of the benefits of
binary arithmetic can now immediately be seen.   The binary
multiplication tables are extremely short (0 x 0 = 0 , 0 x 1 =
0, 1 x 0 = 0 and 1 x 1 = 1). Thus multiplying the 1010 by a 0
gives 0000 and multiplying it by a 1 gives 1010. Line 7 is the
result of adding the columns of figures in lines 3 to 6.

```
line 1                           1 0 1 0
line 2                           0 0 1 0
                                 -------
line 3                           0 0 0 0
line 4                         1 0 1 0
line 5                       0 0 0 0
line 6                     0 0 0 0
                           ---------------
line 7 result =            0 0 1 0 1 0 0
                           ---------------
```

Figure 7.1

Multiplication of Signed Numbers

If the two numbers to be multiplied together are two's
complement signed numbers then the above method does not
work. Any negative number must first be converted into its
positive equivalent and then the multiplication must be
carried out using positive numbers. After the multiplication
has been carried out the result is changed to two's complement
form.

Size of Result

The result of the above contains more bits than the original
two numbers to be multiplied and it can be seen that it can
potentially be 7 bits plus a carry or expressing the carry as
an extra bit the result can be up to 8 bits long from the
multiplication of two 4 bit binary numbers. The general rule

is that the result requires as many bits to express it as the
sum of the number of bits in the numbers to be multiplied.
Thus if three 6 bit numbers were to be multiplied together the
result could contain as many as 18 bits. More importantly the
result of multiplying two 8 bit numbers together gives a 16
bit or two byte result.

4 x 4 Binary Multiplication

The long multiplication method shown above can be easily
carried out by a combination of shifting and adding, using a
program loop. The two numbers, say N1 and N2, are contained
in storage locations and the 8 bit result is derived in a
storage location. We take one of the numbers, say N2, and
examine the least significant bit by shifting it to the right
into the carry flag.   If this bit is a 1 we add the number N1
to the result, if a 0, N1 is not added. The next operation is
to shift N1 1 place to the left ready to be added if the next
bit in N2 is a 1. The next bit in N2 is examined by again
shifting it into the carry flag.   The process is repeated
using a loop, each pass shifting N2 1 place to the right and
N1 1 place to the left with the shifted N1 being conditionally
added to the result.

The following program demonstrates the method.

Exercise:

```
        10    CLD:LDX #4
        20    LDA #0:STA &73
        30    .LOOP
        40    ROR &72
        50    BCC SKIP
        60    CLC
        70    LDA &73: ADC &70: STA &73
        80    .SKIP
        90    CLC
       100    ROL &70
       110    DEX
       120    BNE LOOP
```

This Monitor program uses &70 to store the number N1, &72 the

number N2 and &73 to store the result. The result is
initially set to 0 in line 20, (&71 has been left empty on
purpose to allow N1 to occupy 2 bytes for a later program).
Lines 40 and 50 shift a bit out of N2 into the carry flag and
test the bit shifted out. If the bit is a 1 then the contents
of &70 are added to the result whereas if the bit is a 0 the
addition is skipped. The number N1 is shifted left one place
on each pass through the loop. As there are 4 bits in N2 the
loop is passed through four times using X as the loop
counter.

Enter the program and assemble it. Put 4 bit numbers (0 to
&F) in &70 and &72 and either run or single step the program.
The result is left in &73 and the result may be checked using
the C command of Monitor. For example set &70 to 5 and &72 to
7. The result should be &23 (decimal 35).

Multiplication of 8 Bit Numbers

The multiplication of two 8 bit numbers generates a 16 bit
result and thus two bytes are needed for the result. Two
bytes are also needed for the number which is added to the
result as the shifts to the left which this number experiences
shift it out of the range of 8 bits. Thus say this number is
N1 then we allocate &70 and &71 for the number N1 and use the
multiple length shift left (CLC: ROL &70: ROL &71) to move
N1.

Exercise:

```
 10   CLD:LDX #8
 20   LDA #0: STA &71: STA &73: STA &74
 30   .LOOP
 40   ROR &72
 50   BCC SKIP
 60   CLC
 70   LDA &73: ADC &70: STA &73
 80   LDA &74: ADC &71: STA &74
 90   .SKIP
100   CLC: ROL &70: ROL &71
110   DEX
120   BNE LOOP
```

In line 20 the result and the most significant byte of N1 are
set to zero. The byte N2 is shifted into the carry flag in
line 40 as in the previous program. If a 1 is shifted into
the carry flag then the shifted number N1 (held in &70 and
&71) are added to the 2 byte result in lines 60, 70 and 80. N1
is shifted one place to the left in line 100.

Enter assemble and run the program using 8 bit numbers stored
in &70 and &72. The results can be checked using the C
command.

Multiple Byte Multiplication

The above ideas can be extended to allow for both N1 and N2 to
be multiple length numbers. The result will also then of
course be multiple byte, comprising a number of bytes equal to
the number of bytes in N1 plus the number of bytes in N2. N1
must also be padded out with zero bytes at the most
significant end so that it is the same length as the result.

Contracting the Result

Each time that a multiplication takes place the size of the
result is bigger than that of the numbers that have been
multiplied and there is obviously a potential problem as a
sequence of multiplications can result in products that occupy
many bytes. There are many possible applications involving
such multiplications but three sets of circumstances are
common.

1. All the result is wanted - in this case no contraction
    is required.

2. The original numbers were regarded as integers - in this
    case zero bits at the most significant end of the result
    may be discarded.   e.g.   00010000 * 00001010 =
    0000000010100000 which may be contracted to the single
    byte 10100000.

3. The original numbers were regarded by the programmer as
    being fractional i.e. a binary point was considered to
    be present at some place in the input numbers. In this
    case the programmer treats the numbers as if they were
    integers and then locates the binary point in the result
    after the multiplication. Bytes may then be discarded
    at the programmer's discretion.

For example consider 1.100000 * .10100000 :-

We first perform the multiplication 11000000 * 10100000 to
obtain 0011110000000000 and next we locate the binary point by
adding the number of places to the right of the point in both
input numbers, obtaining 14 places. The point in the result
thus also has 14 places to the right of it and the result is
therefore 00.11110000000000. In this case the zero bits at
either end of the result may be discarded.

TWO'S COMPLEMENT MULTIPLICATION

As mentioned above two's complement numbers cannot be
multiplied directly. They must first be converted into
positive numbers and then multiplied. The result is then
converted into a two's complement number at the end. For
simplicity we assume that the two numbers to be multiplied are
8 bit two's complement and that the result will be a two's
complement 16 bit number.

If the result is in the 8 bit two's complement range it can be
contracted to 8 bits by simply discarding the most significant
byte.

The next program listing is an example of the method. Storage
location &75 is used to deal with the sign of the result. It
is initially cleared to zero and then when each of the two
numbers to be multiplied are examined, store &75 is
incremented if the number is negative. Thus store &75 will be
0 if both numbers are positive (i.e. positive result) and will
be 1 if one of the numbers is negative (negative result).
Finally if both numbers are negative then store &75 will
contain the number 2 (binary 10) and this again means a
positive result. Thus it can be seen that if the least

significant bit of &75 is a 0 then the result is positive and
if it is a 1 then the result is negative.

The numbers to be multiplied are stored in locations &70 and
&72 and the result is derived in &73 and &74. In line 30 the
first number is checked to see if it is positive or negative
and if it is negative then it is converted into a positive
number by lines 50 and 60. The same process is carried out
with the second number in store &72 in lines 80,100 and 110.

When both numbers have been examined in this way and converted
to positive numbers a normal 8 x 8 multiply is performed to
give a 16 bit result which is obtained in &73 and &74.

Finally store &75 is examined to see if the result needs to be
converted to a negative number (if the least significant bit
of &75 is a 1 then the result is converted to a negative
number). Lines 260 to 290 convert the result to a two's
complement 16 bit number.

Try the following multiplications to see if you get the
results indicated.   Monitor allows the entry of negative
numbers when using the M command so the -5 and -7 numbers may
be entered in that format. They are automatically converted
to their two's complement form by Monitor.

$$5 \times 7 = \&0023 \quad (\text{decimal } +35)$$
$$5 \times -7 = \& \quad\quad\ (\text{decimal } -35)$$
$$-5 \times 7 = \& \quad\quad\ (\text{decimal } -35)$$
$$-5 \times -7 = \&0023 \quad (\text{decimal } +35)$$

Exercise:

```
10   CLD
20   LDA #0:STA &75: STA &71
30   LDA &70: BPL LAB1
40   INC &75
50   EOR #&FF
60   CLC: ADC #1: STA &70
70   .LAB1
80   LDA &72: BPL LAB2
90   INC &75
```

```
100   EOR #&FF
110   CLC: ADC #1: STA &72
120   .LAB2 LDA #0: STA &73:STA &74
130   LDX #8
140   .LOOP
150   ROR &72
160   BCC SKIP
170   CLC
180   LDA &73: ADC &70: STA &73
190   LDA &74: ADC &71: STA &74
200   .SKIP
210   CLC: ROL &70: ROL &71
220   DEX
230   BNE LOOP
240   ROR &75
250   BCC FINISH
260   LDA &73: EOR #&FF: STA &73
270   LDA &74: EOR #&FF: STA &74
280   LDA &73: CLC :ADC #1 :STA &73
290   LDA &74: ADC #0: STA &74
300   .FINISH
```

We can see that multiplication is quite a difficult process, particularly if two's complement numbers are used.

BINARY DIVISION

If anything division is more difficult than multiplication and this is easily seen by considering the binary version of long division. For example consider dividing ten by three, ten being in this case the NUMERATOR and three the DENOMINATOR. In binary this is 1010/11 and we set out the division as follows:

$$11 \overline{\smash{)}\,1010}$$

We take the 11 and test it against the most significant bits of the 1010. Starting on the extreme left hand end we have:

Does 11 go into 1 (i.e. is 11 bigger than 1):- NO write a 0 into the result and examine the next most significant bit of the 1010.

```
                              0
                           _____
                    11  |  1010
```

Does 11 go into 10:- NO write a 0 into the result and examine the next most significant bit of the 1010.

```
                             00
                           _____
                    11  |  1010
```

Does the 11 go into 101:- YES write a 1 into the result and subtract 11 from 101.

```
                            001
                          _____
                   11   |  1010
                           11
                           ---
                           10
```

We now bring down the 0 and see if 11 goes into 100

```
                            001
                          _____
                   11   |  1010
                           11
                           ---
                          100
```

YES write a 1 into the result and subtract 11 from 100

```
                           0011
                          _____
                   11   |  1010
                           11
                           ---
                          100
                           11
                           ---
                            1
```

We now have the result that 1010 divided by 11 is 11 remainder

1. If we wished a binary point could be inserted into the
result and the division continued to obtain the result as a
binary fraction.

There are several ways of expressing this process in a
program. Four separate numbers or elements can be identified
above. The numerator, denominator, result and remainder. The
remainder being the number left after the subtraction of the
denominator from the numbers brought down from the numerator.

One method is to consider the remainder and numerator together
as a double length number. A stage in the process is to first
shift the double length number one place to the left (to
"bring down a digit"). The denominator is then compared with
the most significant half of the number. If the denominator
is smaller it is subtracted from the most significant half of
the double length number and the new remainder from this
subtraction used to replace the most significant half of the
double length number. A 1 is then put into the result and the
above process repeated. If the denominator is bigger,
however, the double length number is left unchanged, a 0 is
put into the result and the above process repeated starting
with the shift left.

The following Monitor program illustrates the method for
dividing two 8 bit numbers to obtain an 8 bit result and
remainder. The program uses &71 for the numerator, &70 for
the remainder, &72 for the result and &73 for the
denominator.

Exercise:

```
10   LDA #0: STA &70
20   LDX #8: CLD
30   .LOOP
40   ASL &71: ROL &70
50   LDA &70: SEC: SBC &73
60   BCC SKIP
70   STA &70
80   .SKIP
90   ROL &72
100  DEX: BNE LOOP
```

In line 10 the remainder is initialised to zero. The double
length number comprising the remainder and the numerator is
shifted left one place in line 40 and the numerator is
subtracted from the most significant half of this number in
line 50. Note in this case the number is stored with the most
significant byte first unlike the normal case with addresses
where the least significant byte is stored first. If the
numerator is less than this most significant half the carry
flag will be 1 and the remainder is replaced by the result of
the subtraction. Line 90 shifts a 1 or 0 into the result as
required.

Enter the program and assemble it. Set the numerator,
location &71, and the denominator, location &73, to suitable
values and run or single step the program.

An interesting variation, which improves the efficiency of the
program is to let the result be formed in the same storage
location as the numerator. To do this line 90 is removed and
the ASL &71 in line 40 is replaced by ROL &71. The carry flag
comprising the bits of the result is then shifted into &71 as
the numerator is gradually shifted out on each pass through
the loop. An extra ROL &71 must then be added at line 110 in
order to insert the final shift.

The improvement in speed for this particular program is not
very great but if say 16 bit numbers are divided the
improvement becomes much more worthwhile.

FLOATING POINT NUMBERS

The binary numbers that we have studied so far are called
fixed point numbers. They have either been integers i.e. no
fractional part, or if fractional the number has been stored
with the binary point considered to be in a fixed place. This
class of numbers is by far the most common in assembly
language programming as it is the simplest, most efficient way
of representing a number. It is also widely used in much
commercial and business software for similar reasons but for
scientific applications another way of representing numbers is
often preferred, particularly when using high level
languages. This system, known as floating point, has certain

advantages. It is able to store both very small numbers and also very large numbers to a reasonably high degree of precision by storing the number in three separate parts. The first part contains the position of the binary point, in a special two's complement form. The second part is a sign bit which describes if the number is positive or negative and the final part is the actual number expressed in a particular fractional form. It is actually very similar to the E or exponent method of entering and printing numbers using BASIC, so that using E notation the decimal number 10000 can be written 1E4 and the number .001 can be written 1E-3. The main disadvantage with floating point representation is that the procedures for performing arithmetic are most complex and take much longer to run than the simpler fixed point alternative.

Although arithmetic using floating point numbers is beyond the scope of the present text the actual format of the floating point number will be described.

To start with consider a binary number 1011.01100 which may be written in exponential notation as

.101101100 * 2 ^ 4 and this process is known as STANDARDISATION or NORMALISATION. The first byte in the floating point number would contain the exponent, which is stored in two's complement form with the sign bit reversed. The number 0 would therefore be stored as &80. The exponent in this case is 4, to which this offset of &80 is added and it is thus stored as &84. The following 4 bytes contain the standardised fraction, in the example above this is 10110110 00000000 00000000 00000000. As in standardised form the most significant bit of the standardised fraction must always be a 1 the number 1 in this position is replaced by the sign bit which is 0 for positive and 1 for negative. The above example is positive so that the full 5 byte representation is 10000100 00110110 00000000 00000000 00000000 or &8436000000.

8

BASIC and the Operating System

The reader has already been introduced to the mixing of BASIC and assembly language in chapter 4. The subject is developed further in this chapter with descriptions of various features generally involving both languages and extended to alternative methods of using the machine operating system from assembly language.

SETTING UP REGISTERS

The registers in the CPU are only 8 bits in length and thus cannot hold 16 bit values. Often it is required that a 16 bit value is communicated to subroutine or section of program and if registers are used then two are needed. The software built into the machine frequently uses this method using the X and Y registers. The X register is generally used to hold the least significant byte and Y the most significant.

The BASIC functions MOD and DIV can be used as part of the assembler to split a 16 bit value into two halves. MOD is a function which performs a division using whole numbers and then delivers the remainder so that if a 16 bit value is operated on by MOD &100 (or MOD256 which is a bit quicker to type) the result will be the least significant half of the 16 bit value. If, say, L represents a 16 bit value then L MOD

&100 will be a value which is the least significant 8 bits of
L.

The function DIV similarly performs a 16 bit division using
whole numbers but instead of the remainder DIV produces the
actual result of the division, neglecting any remainder or
fractional part of the result. Thus L DIV &100 gives the most
significant part of L. An alternative, as above, which is
quicker to type is DIV256.

Exercise:

```
          10  LDX # LAB MOD &100
          20  LDY # LAB DIV &100
          30  .LAB
```

The above Monitor program illustrates the method. Enter the
program using Monitor and assemble it. Run the program and
check that X and Y are loaded with the least and most
significant halves of the label LAB.

CALL   PARAMETER BLOCKS

The simple use of the CALL command to call machine code
subroutines has already been described. CALL is an extremely
powerful command which can not only call machine code
subroutines but also pass BASIC variables to the machine code
using what is known as a parameter block. The use of CALL
outlined so far has been of the form "CALL address" where
"address" is a 16 bit value. Used in this way a JSR is
performed from BASIC to the address specified with the A, X
and Y registers being set on entry to the least significant
bytes of the BASIC integer variables A%, X% and Y%. The carry
flag is set to the least significant bit of the C% integer
variable.

Extra parameters can also be added to the CALL statement to
allow the addresses of BASIC variables to be communicated to
the machine code subroutine. For example CALL &4000, Z%, A$
will call the subroutine at address &4000 and pass the
addresses of the integer variable Z% and the string A$ to the
subroutine.   The information is passed through a PARAMETER

BLOCK which is located at address &600. The parameter block consists of a list of items. The first entry in the list is the number of extra parameters given to the CALL command. Then follows two bytes giving the address of the first parameter and then a single byte giving a description of the "type" of variable. Type 0 is a single byte, type 4 a four byte integer variable, type 5 a five byte floating point variable, type 128 a string and 129 a string variable.

The following exercise allows the structure of the parameter block to be investigated. The assembly language program just copies the first 20 bytes of the parameter block to address &3000 and sets up function key f0 to display this area starting at &3000. The parameter block is copied as when the RTS at the end of the program is executed control returns to BASIC and the parameter block can be changed from that present at the start of the subroutine.

Exercise:

```
        NEW
10   Z=100
20   A$="ABCD"
30   DIM S% 50
40   FOR PASS=0 TO 3 STEP 3
50   P%=S%
60   [OPT PASS: .PROG
70   LDX #20
90   LDY #0
100  .LOOP
110  LDA &600,Y: STA &3000,Y
120  INY
130  DEX: BNE LOOP
140  RTS: ]
150  NEXT
160  *KEY0 F.X=&3000 TO &3014:P.;~?X;" ";:N.|M
```

Lines 10 and 20 define two variables for use in testing the CALL statement. Run the above program to assemble the routine PROG then in direct mode type CALL PROG and press the return key. The parameter block may then be examined using function key f0. In this case the first byte should be 0 indicating that no extra parameters have been specified. Next try adding extra parameters.

e.g.   CALL PROG,?&1234

The first byte of the parameter block will now be 1 indicating
1 extra parameter. The next byte is the least significant
byte of the address of the parameter, namely &34 and the
following byte is the most significant byte, &12. The type of
a single byte variable such as this is 0 which is the next
byte.

The effect of extra parameters can be seen:

e.g.   CALL PROG,?&1234,A%,Z,$&5678,!&ABCD,A$

The parameter block now contains 6 parameters and is displayed
by pressing function key f0. In each case the address is
given followed by a byte giving the type of the variable.

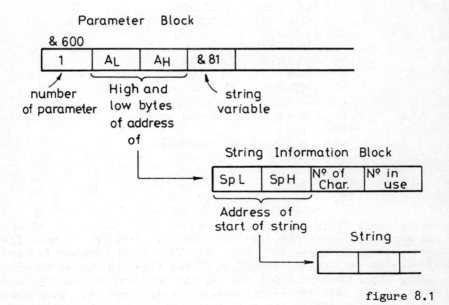

figure 8.1

The address given for the string variable is not the address
of the string contained in the variable but of the "String
Information Block". This is a block which contains first the
start address of the actual string followed by two bytes. The
first gives the the maximum number of bytes allocated for the
string and the second byte gives the current length of the
string. Figure 8.1 illustrates this.

This is demonstrated in the following exercise which
demonstrates the printing of a BASIC string variable.

Exercise:

```
           NEW
   10   SBLOCK=&70
   20   STRING=&72
   30   DIM S% 100
   40   FOR PASS=0 TO 3 STEP 3
   50   P%=S%
   60   [OPT PASS : .PROG
   70   LDA &601:STA SBLOCK
   80   LDA &602:STA SBLOCK+1
   90   LDY #0
  100   LDA (SBLOCK),Y : STA STRING
  110   INY:LDA (SBLOCK),Y: STA STRING+1
  120   INY: INY: LDA (SBLOCK),Y: STA &74
  130   LDY #0
  140   .LOOP
  150   LDA (STRING),Y
  160   JSR &FFEE
  170   INY: DEC &74: BNE LOOP
  180   RTS
  190   ]
  200   NEXT
  220   A$="test string"
```

This program takes the first address in the parameter block
and copies it into location &70 (called SBLOCK). This is
accomplished in lines 70 and 80. This 16 bit number is the
address of the string block and the first two bytes in the
string block are obtained in lines 100 and 110 using the
indirect indexed addressing mode.   These first two bytes are
the starting address of the string itself and are stored at

&72 and &73 (called STRING). The length of the string is
obtained in line 120 and stored in the address &74.

A program loop is then used to obtain each byte of the string
and write it on the screen using the OSWRCH subroutine address
&FFEE. Run the program to perform the assembly and then enter
CALL PROG,A$ to actually print the string.

Testing the Parameter Type

The purpose of the "type" information in the parameter control
block is to enable the machine code routines to take
alternative action if required, depending on the type of
variable presented to them. For example the above program
will always attempt to print a string even if it is presented
with a parameter of the wrong type.   To protect the routine a
check on the type of parameter can easily be introduced and an
error message generated if the wrong type of parameter is sent
to the routine.

Thus the addition of the following two lines to the above
program introduces the checking and prints a "?" on the screen
if an incorrect parameter type is given or no parameters are
specified.

```
 65   LDA &600:BEQ FAIL
 85   LDA &603: CMP #129: BNE FAIL
185   .FAIL: LDA #ASC "?": JSR &FFEE: RTS
```

The sequence JSR &FFEE: RTS can be replaced by the more
efficient JMP &FFEE. The return to BASIC being performed by
the RTS present at the end of subroutine &FFEE. This saves an
extra instruction and runs a little faster.

SAVING ASSEMBLY LANGUAGE PROGRAMS AND SECTIONS OF THE MEMORY

Assembly language programs may be saved in two different ways
on disc, tape or other filing system. The text (or source)
version of the program may be saved if using BASIC by the

normal BASIC SAVE command.   This method is good as the text
version may be edited and changed and is of course easily
readable.   The text mnemonics, however, must subsequently be
assembled before the program can be run.   If large programs
are being written the assembly process can take some time and
also as the text form occupies more memory than the assembled
machine code form and therefore the storing and retrieval of
programs takes considerably longer than if just the assembled
code is stored.

The alternative is to save the actual binary code of the
machine code program using the *SAVE command.

The command takes the form:

*SAVE "PROG" SSSS FFFF EEEE where PROG is the name of the file
which is to contain the data, SSSS is the start address of the
program or data to be saved written as a hex number. FFFF is
the end address plus 1 of the program again written in hex and
EEEE is the execution address of the program written in hex.
The following BASIC program illustrates this. The execution
address is the address that the program normally runs from and
if not given it defaults to the same address as that given as
the start of the section to be saved. It is used by the *RUN
command which will be covered later.

Exercise:

```
                    NEW
            10   P%=&3000
            20   [LDX #10
            30   .LOOP
            40   LDA #&41
            50   JSR &FFEE
            60   DEX
            70   BNE LOOP
            80   RTS
            90   ]
           100   *SAVE "TEST" 3000 3010 3000
```

The simple machine code program just writes the letter A on
the screen ten times.   Enter and RUN the program.   It
assembles the machine code program and when the program gets

to line 100 it saves the section of memory between &3000 and
&300F on the filing system currently in use in a file called
TEST. The quotes around the name of the file are optional.

The command *LOAD "TEST" may be used to recall the file called
TEST from the filing system and again the quotes around the
file name are optional. Switch off the computer (remember to
take your discs out if you have a disc machine) to guarantee
that the memory is clear and then switch it on again. Type
*LOAD "TEST" to recall the file from the system and when
loaded type CALL &3000 to run the program.

A useful command is *OPT 1,1 as this causes detailed
information on the starting, finishing and execution addresses
to be printed out when a file is loaded and this may be used
to check that the actual file on tape has the expected
addresses.

If required the file may be loaded at a different address from
that specified when the file was saved. A hex address is
given as a second parameter to the *LOAD command. Thus *LOAD
TEST 2000 will load the program TEST at address &2000 and not
at &3000. This particular program can be run from any address
and thus a subsequent CALL &2000 will cause the ten letter As
to be printed on the screen. Programs like this, which can be
positioned anywhere in the memory and still operate correctly,
are said to be RELOCATABLE. Most programs do not possess this
desirable feature, however, so that the ability to load a
program at a different address is not as useful as it appears
at first sight.

The instructions which make a program not relocatable are the
JMP and JSR instructions which jump to locations or routines
which are within the program as when the program is moved or
relocated the addresses in these instructions still point to
the place where the program was originally located. The
branch instructions, however, are perfectly relocatable as
they specify the address of the branching point relative to
the current program counter.

Instead of just loading a file in the above way it is also
possible to cause it to be first loaded and then run, starting
at the execution address. The command in this case is *RUN

"TEST" where the quotes around the file name are optional.
Try the effect of the command using the file TEST which you
have already created. Alternatively just *TEST may be
entered.

It is possible to add an offset to the JMP and JSR
instructions so that it is possible to assemble a program at
one place in memory but actually locate and run the code from
a different place. This is frequently necessary when writing
long machine code programs which, when actually run, have
large data areas or use graphics. The problem arises in these
cases because the screen and the text version of the program
both use large amounts of memory and there may not be enough
room for the text, machine code program and graphics screen to
be present in the memory at the same time.

Another case in which this sort of facility is useful is when
a program is being prepared for use by others and the text
version of the program is not being supplied to the user for
various reasons (text is easy to steal and modify but
assembled machine code is harder to tamper with).

BASIC version 2 provides facilities for assembling and running
programs from different areas of memory through the O% option
but it can also be done using the original version of BASIC.

The following exercise assembles a program, which may be run
from address &3000, into a section of the memory located
inside BASIC.

Exercise:

```
 10   DIM S% 20
 20   F%=&3000 - S%
 30   FOR PASS =0 TO 3 STEP 3
 40   P%=S%
 50   [OPT PASS
 60   JMP LAB+F%
 70   .LAB
 80   LDA #&41: JSR &FFEE
 90   RTS:]
100   NEXT
```

In line 10 the DIM statement is used to reserve 20 bytes of space for the machine code and S% records the start address of this space. The variable F% is used to hold a number that is the offset between the new origin required for the code and the present origin which is, of course, S%. F% is set up in line 20 and a normal two pass assembly of the program follows. The program has a jump to the label LAB at line 60 just in order to demonstrate the method. The offset F% is added to the address to be jumped to when the program is run so that when the program is relocated to the new origin of &3000 the jump will be to the correct place.

RUN the program and notice that it assembles to an area within the BASIC.

The program may be saved in a file using the *SAVE command using the start and finish addresses printed out when the program is assembled. For example if the first address of the program was &1F00 and the address of the RTS instruction was &1F0A and it was wanted to save the program in a file called PROG then the appropriate command would be *SAVE PROG 1F00 1F0A. To recall the file from the filing system the *LOAD PROG 3000 instruction would be needed and it could then be run by CALL &3000. Unfortunately the * commands will not accept BASIC variables so it is difficult to make this saving process automatic.

It is possible, however, to pass strings to the command line interpreter, the part of the operating system which deals with the * commands. A method is given later in the chapter, page 156 . Users of BASIC II have the advantage of a new command OSCLI allows a string to be derived from all the usual BASIC functions etc. to be passed to the command line interpreter.

SAVING PROGRAMS USING OSFILE

A better approach is to use the file handling subroutine OSFILE (address &FFDD) which is part of the operating system. Using OSFILE a program can be saved from one area of memory with information which will cause it to be loaded and run automatically from a different area of the memory.

OSFILE uses a section of memory as a control block to specify
the addresses used in saving and loading files and the address
of this block is communicated to the OSFILE subroutine using
the X and Y registers of the CPU. In addition the A register
is used to control the type of file operation desired. A zero
in A is used to specify that a write operation is taking
place.

The first two bytes of data in the control block specify the
address where the string describing the file name is stored.
Following this is a list of four byte addresses. Four byte
addresses have presumably been used by ACORN to allow for
future expansion to 16 bit microprocessors as two byte
addresses would have been sufficient for the 6502 CPU. For
saving files the first number is the address at which the file
will be loaded, the second is the address which will be used
to start running the file if *RUN is used. The third address
is the start address of the program or data to be saved and
the last number is the address immediately following the last
byte of program or data to be written.

The control block may be set up and OSFILE called either from
BASIC or assembly language. For the present purposes it is
more convenient to use BASIC as we are using BASIC anyway to
assemble the program and it also provides a demonstration of
the use of the indirection operators.

Exercise:

```
10    INPUT "START ADDRESS "A$
20    START%=EVAL A$
30    DIM S% 100
40    F%=START%-S%
50    FOR PASS=0 TO 3 STEP 3
60    P%=S%
70    [ OPT PASS
80    JMP LAB+F%
90    .LAB
100    LDA #&41
110    JSR &FFEE
120    RTS:]
130    NEXT
140    INPUT "FILE NAME" NAME$
```

```
150   $P%=NAME$: L=LEN NAMES$ +1
160   BLOCK%=P%+L
170   ? BLOCK%      =P% MOD &100
180   BLOCK%?1  = P% DIV &100
190   BLOCK%!2  = START%
200   BLOCK%!6  = START%
210   BLOCK%!10 = S%
220   BLOCK%!14 = P%
230   X%=P% MOD &100
240   Y%=P% DIV &100
250   A%=0
260   CALL &FFDD
```

The program in this example prints a letter A on the screen
when it is run. Line 10 reads in the start address of the
program as a character string which is then converted into a
number in line 20 using the EVAL function. This is a way of
inputting addresses in hex as otherwise the & prefix is not
recognised when inputting into a number direct. The integer
variable F% is again used for the offset to any JMP and JSR
instructions which are to be relocated and its value is
computed in line 40.

A normal two pass assembly follows with S% containing the
start address of the assembled code and following the assembly
P% contains the end address plus 1 i.e. the next free
location. The file name is then read in and stored as a
string immediately following the end of the program. The
OSFILE control block comes next, starting at address BLOCK%.
The first two bytes of the control block contain the address
of the string containing the file name. P% MOD &100 is used
to calculate the least significant byte and P% DIV &100 to
calculate the most significant byte. Line 190 sets the load
address of the file and line 200 the execution address of the
file, which is set in this case to the start of the file.
Lines 210 and 220 set the start and finish addresses of the
section of memory to be saved into the file. In this case S%
is the start of the assembled program and P% the end.

The start address of the control block is loaded into the X%
and Y% integer variables and 0 into A%. When OSFILE (&FFDD) is
CALLed these are loaded into the CPU X, Y and A registers and
the file is saved.

The file may subsequently be loaded using *LOAD without
specifying any address and it will load into the address
specified when the file was saved. The file may also be
executed or run using the *RUN command and it will be loaded
and run using the load and execution addresses saved with the
file.

Details of this and other uses of OSFILE are given on pages
454-5 of the USER MANUAL.

USING THE MACHINE OPERATING SYSTEM FROM MACHINE CODE

The BBC computer contains two distinct pieces of software.
The BASIC language and the MACHINE OPERATING SYSTEM (MOS). The
BASIC software is that needed to run the BASIC language
(including the ASSEMBLER) and the MACHINE OPERATING SYSTEM is
used to run all the hardware of the computer, the keyboard,
screen and printers and also the graphics and sound. The MOS
is, therefore, a very powerful piece of software and the
machine code programmer has full access to this power. You
have already been using the MOS by using the subroutines which
write to the screen (OSWRCH &FFEE), read the keyboard (OSRDCH
&FFE0) and deal with files (OSFILE &FFDD). The use of such
subroutines is perhaps the most common level of access to the
MOS and these are covered in the book as they are
encountered.

BASIC uses the MOS extensively and the user, in general, does
not need to be specifically aware of the MOS unless the more
specialised features of the machine are required. The *
commands are provided within BASIC to allow access to various
MOS features. All the commands that are preceeded by a * are
in fact not part of the BASIC language but are dealt with by a
separate piece of software in the operating system of the
computer. Following a * character at the beginning of a line
BASIC simply passes the rest of that line to the COMMAND LINE
INTERPRETER in the MOS. This is a subroutine called OSCLI,
address &FFF7, which interprets the line to provide the
required function in the MOS.

Assembly language programs can also use OSCLI to obtain the

commands normally available from BASIC. In general this
feature is not used as the access to the MOS through
subroutines is simpler and more efficient from machine code
but it may be required for more complex functions. Register X
is set to the least significant byte of the address of the
string to be interpreted and register Y to the most
significant. The string should be terminated in the normal
way with the ASCII RETURN code &D. The subroutine OSCLI is
then called using JSR &FFF7.

Exercise:

```
            NEW
      10    DIM C% 50
      20    FOR PASS=0 TO 3 STEP 3
      30    P%=C%
      40    [OPT PASS
      50    .PROG
      60    LDX # S MOD &100
      70    LDY # S DIV &100
      80    JSR &FFF7
      90    RTS
      100   .S
      110   ]
      120   NEXT
      130   $P%="KEY0 L.|M"
```

The X and Y registers are loaded with the address of the label
S which is at the end of the program. At the end of the
assembly the string "KEY0 L.|M" is stored into the memory
immediately following the program using the $ indirection
operator and thus S is effectively at the start of the
string.

Run the program to assemble the routine and then CALL it by
typing CALL PROG. Function key 0 should have been programmed
to give a listing of the program.

BASIC II users can change line 100 to

```
      100 .S EQUS "KEY 0 L.|M" :  EQUB &D
```

and delete line 130.

OSBYTE - THE *FX EQUIVALENT

Many assorted functions are provided in BASIC by the use of
the *FX command, followed by up to three parameters describing
the action required. One way of obtaining these functions
from assembly language is to use OSCLI, the command line
interpreter, as shown above. The functions are of such
importance, however, that a more direct method of access has
been provided through the subroutine OSBYTE (&FFF4).
Parameters are passed to OSBYTE via the CPU registers. The A
register contains the number that selects the *FX function
required, X contains the next parameter and Y the last. For
example *FX 139,1,0 would be expressed in assembly language as

```
LDA #139
LDX #1
LDY #0
JSR &FFF4
```

The range of OSBYTE functions is extensive although many are
not available in the early operating system 0.1. As most
readers will have some familiarity with the *FX functions
already by using BASIC the functions used in the book are
introduced as they are encountered rather than being grouped
together at this point.

OSWORD

Quite a number of operating system functions require more
storage for communication than the three CPU registers can
provide and in operating systems 1.0 and later the subroutine
OSWORD (&FFF1) is used. The A register then contains the
number specifying the particular function required but the X
and Y registers now contain the address of a parameter block
with X containing the least significant byte and Y the most
significant byte of the address.

Reading a Line of Characters

If A = 0 then OSWORD reads a line of text from the currently
selected input stream (the keyboard unless you have changed it
by *FX 2) and then stores it in the memory. The subroutine is
terminated if the RETURN key is pressed or an ESCAPE occurs.
On exit from the subroutine the Y register contains the number
of characters read in, including the RETURN if present. The
carry flag is 0 if the routine was terminated by the RETURN
key.

The parameter block pointed to by the X and Y registers is
structured as follows:

    1st byte :- least significant byte of address
    2nd byte :- most significant byte of address
    3rd byte :- maximum length of line
    4th byte :- minimum acceptable ASCII value
    5th byte :- maximum acceptable ASCII value

The address contained in the first two bytes is that where the
line that is read in will be placed. The DELETE key deletes
the last character entered and CTRL U deletes all line entered
so far. As the characters are entered they are echoed on the
keyboard. The following program shows the use of the method
to read a line into storage locations.

The parameter block is located at the end of the program
starting at the PBLOCK. The values are put into it in lines 90
to 160. The address contained in L% is first put into the
block in lines 120 and 130 followed by the maximum number of
characters to be read in in line 140. The minimum acceptable
ASCII character has been set to &1F and the maximum to &7F,
corresponding to the normal ASCII range of printable
characters in lines 150 and 160. Next A is set to 0 and X and
Y to the address of PBLOCK. The subroutine OSWORD is then
jumped to in line 200.

The program, when run, reads in a line and stores it at the
address contained in L% and thus, after it has run the line
read in may be examined by PRINT $L%. Try to read in more than
the 20 characters specified in line 140.

Further details of this OSWORD call are given in the USER
MANUAL page 459.

```
          NEW
10        DIM L% 21: DIM PBLOCK 5
20        DIM S% 100
30        OSWORD=&FFF1
40        PNT= &70
50        FOR PASS = 0 TO 2 STEP 2
60        P%=S%
70        [OPT PASS
80        .RDLIN
90        LDA #PBLOCK MOD &100: STA PNT
100       LDA #PBLOCK DIV &100: STA PNT+1
110       LDY #0
120       LDA #L% MOD &100: STA (PNT),Y: INY
130       LDA #L% DIV &100: STA (PNT),Y: INY
140       LDA #20: STA (PNT),Y: INY
150       LDA #&1F: STA (PNT),Y: INY
160       LDA #&7F: STA (PNT),Y
170       LDA #0
180       LDX #PBLOCK MOD &100
190       LDY #PBLOCK DIV &100
200       JSR OSWORD
210       RTS: ]
220       NEXT
230       CALL RDLIN
```

Reading and Setting the Time

The BBC computer contains two built in timers that may be used
using OSWORD. One is the timer, called the CLOCK, that is used
by the BASIC TIME function and the other is a separate timer
called the INTERVAL TIMER that can be used for a variety of
functions. Both timers consist of five byte binary values
that are incremented every hundredth of a second.

The clock is read using the subroutine OSWORD with A set to 1.
The X and Y registers contain the address where the five byte
binary result is to be stored.

To set the internal clock OSWORD is used with A set to 2. In
this case the clock is set to the five byte binary value

contained in the memory block pointed to by the X and Y registers.

The interval timer is similar in operation and may be read and set using A values of 3 and 4. A difference, however, is that the interval timer can also be used in conjunction with the interrupt system of the computer. When the timer is incremented and overflows an "event" is generated and a subroutine can be incorporated to take action when this occurs. For further details see chapter 10.

If You Have a Second Processor

When a second processor is fitted to the BBC computer programs will normally run on that processor. The original computer now becomes known as the Input/Output processor. As in the combined arrangement it handles the keyboard, screen, printer and discs. To access memory locations in the input output processor from a program running in the second processor the subroutine OSWORD is used with A set to 5 to read a byte and 6 to write a byte. The parameter block pointed to by the XY registers contains first a four byte address and then the data byte. Four byte addresses are used to allow for future expansion to 16 bit second processors.

SOUND

In general there is no advantage in using assembly language programming to control sounds. The high level facilities of BASIC are adequate and more convenient. If sound is required as part of a program which is all written in assembly language, however, then assembly language must be used. As the sound instructions are complex in operation it is recommended that before programming sounds in assembly language the BASIC SOUND and ENVELOPE statements should first be studied. The effects of the SOUND and ENVELOPE commands can then be directly translated into assembly language through the OSWORD subroutine with the A register set to 7 and 8 respectively.

For A = 7 the parameter block pointed to by XY contains 8

bytes and these are treated as four 16 bit numbers,
corresponding to the parameters used by the BASIC SOUND
statement. The first two bytes contain the channel number and
synchronisation information, the next two bytes the
amplitude. The pitch is contained in the next two bytes and
the final two bytes control the duration of the sound.

The ENVELOPE command is equivalent to using OSWORD with A = 8
and XY contains the address of a 14 byte parameter block with
each byte corresponding to a parameter of envelope.

As an example consider the equivalent of the two BASIC
statements:

```
            ENVELOPE 1,1,-26,-36,-45,255,255,255,
            127,0,0,-127,126,0
            SOUND 1,1,100,25
```

The following assembly language program performs the
equivalent of these two statements.

```
            NEW
      10    DIM SND 10
      20    DIM ENV 20
      30    DIM S% 50
      40    OSWORD =&FFF1
      50    FOR PASS = 0 TO 2 STEP 2
      60    P%=S%
      70    [OPT PASS
      80    .PROG
      90    LDX # ENV MOD &100
     100    LDY # ENV DIV &100
     110    LDA # 8
     120    JSR OSWORD
     130    LDX # SND MOD &100
     140    LDY # SND DIV &100
     150    LDA # 7
     160    JSR OSWORD
     170    RTS: ]
     180    NEXT
     190    ?SND  = 1 :   SND?1 = 0
     200    SND?2 = 1 :   SND?3 = 0
     210    SND?4 =100:   SND?5 = 0
```

```
220    SND?6 = 25:    SND?7 = 0
230    ?ENV  = 1 :    ENV?1 = 1
240    ENV?2 =-26:    ENV?3 =-36
250    ENV?4 =-45:    ENV?5 =255
260    ENV?6 =255:    ENV?7 =255
270    ENV?8 =127:    ENV?9 =0
280    ENV?10= 0 :    ENV?11=-127
290    ENV?12=126:    ENV?13=0
300    CALL PROG
```

Space is reserved for the two parameter blocks in lines 10 and
20. A simple assembly language program to first set up the
envelope and then to generate the sound follows. The data
bytes are put into the two parameter blocks in lines 190 to
290 and then the subroutine PROG is CALLed at the end of the
program to generate the sound.

An alternative to lines 190 to 290 is to use a BASIC FOR NEXT
loop to read in the values from a DATA statement e.g.

```
190    FOR Z = 0 TO 8
200    READ D: SND?Z=D
210    NEXT Z
220    FOR Z = 0 TO 14
230    READ D: ENV?Z=D
240    NEXT Z
250    DATA 1,0,1,0,100,0,25,0
260    DATA 1,1,-26,-36,-45,255,255,255
270    DATA 127,0,0,-127,126,0
280    CALL PROG
290
300
```

FILES IN ASSEMBLY LANGUAGE

The use of files for containing assembly language programs has
already been covered earlier in the chapter and this section
now concentrates on the use of files within assembly language
programs.

Files may be held on several different filing systems,
cassette tapes, discs, ECONET, ROM pack, and

Telesoftware/Prestel systems.   The type of system used is
selected by the appropriate * command e.g.   *TAPE, *DISC, *NET
etc.   These commands may be issued from assembler using OSCLI
as described earlier in the chapter.

OSFILE

Operations on complete files are carried out using the
subroutine OSFILE (&FFDD) using the A register to control   the
type of file operation required and also   a   parameter block.
It's use in saving machine code programs in files using BASIC
has already been described earlier in the chapter.

The parameter block contains five parameters, say P1 to P5.
The first, P1, is a two byte address which is the start
address of the string (terminated with a RETURN code &D) which
describes the file name.   The other parameters P2 to P5 are
four byte addresses which are set depending on the operation
being carried out.

Writing a File

OSFILE may be used with the A register set to 0 to write a
file.   The parameter block is set up with P4 set to the start
address of data to be written to the file and P5 set to the
address of the byte just past the last one to be written.   If
required an address can be stored with the file which
determines where it will be loaded when read back from the
file. This is specified by parameter P2. Also an execution
address may be stored with the file and this is specified in
P3.

As an example the following program uses the method   described
earlier for reading in a line of text up to 255 characters
long into an area of memory named BUFFER. The section of
memory is then saved into a file named TEXT. The parameter
block for OSFILE is contained in the memory starting at the
address FCB (file control block) and that for reading the line
in using OSWORD at the address PBLOCK as before.

Lines 110 to 220 read in the line of text using OSWORD and

then the section of program following the label SAFILE sets up
a parameter block (FCB) for OSFILE.

All the bytes in the FCB are first set to zero using a program
loop in lines 270 to 290. Many of the bytes in a typical FCB
are 0 so this saves setting them individually.   The first two
bytes of the parameter block are then set up to the address of
the file name string in lines 300 to 320.

The start address of the data to be written is L% and this is
put into the FCB in lines 330 to 350. The end address is E%
and this is put into the FCB in lines 360 to 380.

The X and Y registers are the set up to the start address of
the FCB in line 410 and the A register is set to zero.   The
subroutine OSFILE then writes the file.

The method works equally well for cassette files as well as
discs although, of course, discs are more convenient. If you
try the program with a disc system the resulting file can be
examined in hex form by *DUMP TEXT.

```
        NEW
10      DIM L% 256, PBLOCK 5, FCB 18, NAME 5
20      $NAME="TEXT"
30      PNT =&70: FCBPNT =&72
40      OSWORD=&FFF1: OSFILE=&FFDD
50      E%=L%+256
60      DIM S% 120
70      FOR PASS = 0 TO 2 STEP 2
80      P%=S%
90      [OPT PASS
100     .PROG
110     .RDLIN
120     LDA #PBLOCK MOD &100: STA PNT
130     LDA #PBLOCK DIV &100: STA PNT+1
140     LDY #0
150     LDA #L% MOD &100: STA (PNT),Y: INY
160     LDA #L% DIV &100: STA (PNT),Y: INY
170     LDA #255: STA (PNT),Y: INY
180     LDA #&1F: STA (PNT),Y: INY
190     LDA #&7F: STA (PNT),Y
200     LDA #0
```

```
210     LDX #PBLOCK MOD 256: LDY #PBLOCK DIV 256
220     JSR OSWORD
230     .SAFILE
240     LDA #FCB MOD &100: STA FCBPNT
250     LDA #FCB DIV &100: STA FCBPNT+1
260     LDA #0: LDX #18: LDY #0
270     .FLOOP
280     STA (FCBPNT),Y: INY
290     DEX: BNE FLOOP
300     LDY #0
310     LDA #NAME MOD &100: STA (FCBPNT),Y: INY
320     LDA #NAME DIV &100: STA (FCBPNT),Y
330     LDY #10
340     LDA #L% MOD &100: STA (FCBPNT),Y: INY
350     LDA #L% DIV &100: STA (FCBPNT),Y
360     LDY #14
370     LDY #E% MOD &100: STA (FCBPNT),Y: INY
380     LDY #E% DIV &100: STA (FCBPNT),Y
390     LDX #FCB MOD &100: LDY #FCB DIV &100
400     LDA #0: JSR OSFILE
410     RTS: ]
420     NEXT
430     CALL PROG
```

Reading a File

To read a file OSFILE is again used with a parameter block
containing five parameters (P1 to P5) as above but the A
register is set to &FF. The first parameter in the block is
again the two byte address of the string containing the file
name. The four parameters P2 to P5 following are four byte
addresses.

Each file contains as part of its catalogue or directory
information a load address. This is the address which was
contained in P2 when the file was written using OSFILE and the
file may be loaded at this address or alternatively forced to
load at another address. If the least significant byte of P3
is not 0 then the file loads at the address saved with the
file. If it is 0 the the file loads at the address given in
P2.

The following program reads the file created in the previous
program back into the memory and for convenience uses a BASIC
PRINT statement to display the data.

The file control block is first cleared to all 0s in lines 130
to 150. Then the address of the file name is put into the
first 2 bytes of the block in lines 170 and 180. The load
address of the file is then put into the block in 190 and 200.
The X and Y registers are then set to the address of the file
control block and A is set to &FF to indicate a read
operation. OSFILE is then called in line 230.

The whole program is the CALLed and the BASIC PRINT statement
used to print the area read back from the file.

```
            NEW
     10     DIM BUF 256, FCB 18,NAME 5,S% 100
     20     FCBPNT=&70
     30     OSFILE=&FFDD
     40     $NAME="TEXT"
     50     FOR PASS = 0 TO 2 STEP 2
     60     P%=S%
     70     [OPT PASS
     80     .RDFILE
     90     LDX #18
    100     LDA #FCB MOD &100: STA FCBPNT
    110     LDA #FCB DIV &100: STA FCBPNT+1
    120     LDA #0: LDY #0
    130     .RLOOP
    140     STA (FCBPNT),Y: INY
    150     DEX: BNE RLOOP
    160     LDY #0
    170     LDA #NAME MOD &100: STA (FCBPNT),Y: INY
    180     LDA #NAME DIV &100: STA (FCBPNT),Y: INY
    190     LDA #BUF  MOD &100: STA (FCBPNT),Y: INY
    200     LDA #BUF  DIV &100: STA (FCBPNT),Y
    210     LDA #&FF
    220     LDX #FCB MOD &100: LDY #FCB DIV &100
    230     JSR OSFILE
    240     RTS: ]
    250     NEXT
    260     CALL RDFILE
    270     PRINT $BUF
```

Files a Byte at a Time

OSFILE is used to read and write complete files but it is also possible to read and write files a byte at a time. This is similar to the BASIC file reading statements BGET# and BPUT#. The file is first opened and a channel number obtained from the filing system and then bytes can be read from the file or written to it. When all operation on the file have been finished it is closed.

The subroutine OSFIND is used for opening and closing files. The X and Y registers contain the address of a string giving the file name and A describes the type of file operation required, &80 for writing, &40 for reading and 0 for closing files.

When opening files the routine returns the channel number allocated to the file. The USER MANUAL says that the channel number is returned in the Y register but in fact this appears not to be correct as the number returned in Y is not subsequently recognised by the other routines on the author's machine, (A MODEL B with TORCH DISC PACK). Some experimentation revealed that the channel number appears to be returned in the A register.

Bytes are written to the file using the subroutine OSBPUT (&FFD4) which writes the byte in A to the file. The channel number should be contained in Y prior to this call. Reading is carried out by OSBGET (&FFD7) which gets a byte from the file and puts it in A. On exit from OSBGET the carry flag is set if an error occurs and this may be used to test for an end of file condition.

```
          NEW
10    DIM NAME 5, S% 50
20    $NAME="TEST"
30    BYTE=&70: OSFIND=&FFCE
40    OSBPUT=&FFD4
50    FOR PASS = 0 TO 2 STEP 2
60    P%=S%
70    [OPT PASS
```

```
        80   .WRFILE
        90   LDA #100: STA BYTE
       100   LDX #NAME MOD &100
       110   LDY #NAME DIV &100
       120   LDA #&80
       130   JSR OSFIND
       140   TAY
       150   .WLOOP
       160   LDA BYTE
       170   JSR OSBPUT
       180   DEC BYTE: BPL WLOOP
       190   LDA #0
       200   JSR OSFIND
       210   RTS: ]
       220   NEXT
       230   CALL WRFILE
```

This program writes a file containing 100 bytes consisting of the sequence 100, 99, 98 etc down to 0. The file, called TEST, is opened for writing in lines 90 to 130 and then a program loop is used in lines 150 to 180 to write the bytes to the file. Note that the channel number left by OSFIND is transferred to Y in line 140 ready for it's use by OSBPUT. Finally the file is closed in lines 190 and 200, the channel number required for the closing being still in the Y register. If you have a disc system then the resulting file may be dumped on the screen, in hex by *DUMP TEST.

For an example of file reading the following program reads back the above file into an area of memory called BUF.

```
             NEW
        10   DIM NAME 5, BUF 100, S% 50
        20   $NAME="TEST"
        30   OSBGET=&FFD7
        40   OSFIND=&FFCE
        50   FOR PASS = 0 TO 2 STEP 2
        60   P%=S%
        70   [OPT PASS
        80   .RDFILE
        90   LDX #NAME MOD &100
       100   LDY #NAME DIV &100
       110   LDA #&40
```

```
120    JSR OSFIND
130    TAY
140    LDX #0
150    .RLOOP
160    JSR OSBGET
170    STA BUF,X: INX
180    BCC RLOOP
190    LDA #0
200    JSR OSFIND
210    RTS: ]
220    NEXT
230    CALL RDFILE
```

The file is opened for reading in lines 90 to 120 and the
channel number put into Y in line 130. A loop is then used to
keep on reading bytes from the file and transfering them to
successive locations in the area BUF. When the end of file is
reached the carry flag is set following the OSBGET subroutine
and this is picked up by the branch in line 180. The file is
then closed.

The data read in can be checked by printing out the contents
of BUF as follows:

        FOR X=0 TO 99 : P.;~BUF?X; " ";NEXT

A useful thing to note when experimenting with files is that
if you forget to close a file then things may go wrong. You
may lose some data from the end of the file and subsequent
attempts to use the file will result in error messages.
Fortunately BASIC can help as it uses the same filing system
commands. If CLOSE#0 is issued then all files which are
currently open will be closed and all will be well.

Note that programs using OSBPUT, OSBGET and OSFIND will NOT
work with ECONET using the level 1 filesever software. The
level 2 fileserver will allow the use of these subroutines but
it requires a second processor to be fitted in order to work.

9

Graphics and Games

This chapter shows how the graphics facilities built into the operating system may be accessed from machine code. This includes all the powerful features normally obtained by using the BASIC PLOT and VDU commands. An advanced section on direct screen graphics is included for the circumstances when the operating system driven graphics are not fast or flexible enough. The advanced material in this particular section uses many of the more difficult techniques of assembly language and beginners should first master the preceeding chapters before progressing to direct screen graphics. Finally the chapter covers how the above ideas may be used to produce the animated graphics needed by computer games.

VDU CONTROL CODES

The functions of the operating system graphics normally obtained through the BASIC VDU command may also be obtained from assembly language. The facilities are extremely powerful and include the equivalent of PLOT, MOVE, DRAW, COLOUR, GCOL, MODE, CLS, CLG and VDU commands.

The subroutine OSWRCH (&FFEE) is used to give access to these facilities. We have already encountered this as it is the subroutine which writes the ASCII character in the A register

to the screen. The normal ASCII characters have codes in the
range &20 to &7A. The codes &00 to &1F are used to control the
graphics and are used by first sending the required code to
the operating system using OSWRCH and then sending in sequence
the required number of following bytes needed by the function
requested.

The use of OSWRCH in this way is the same as the use of the
VDU command in BASIC and readers familiar with VDU will be
able to transfer their knowledge directly into assembly
language.

A full list of the possible VDU commands is given in the USER
MANUAL (p.507)of the computer and will not be duplicated here
but some examples of the more commonly used functions will,
however, be given.

Clearing the Screen CLS and CLG

The VDU code for clearing the text area of the screen is &0C
and for clearing the graphics area &10. No following bytes are
needed so only a single subroutine call is needed and the
sequence LDA #&C: JSR OSWRCH for the equivalent of BASIC CLS
and LDA #&10: JSR OSWRCH for CLG.

Selecting a Graphics Mode

The graphics mode is selected by the code &16 and then the
next byte sent to the operating system sets the required
mode. Thus to set mode 5 LDA #&16: JSR OSWRCH: LDA #5: JSR
OSWRCH.

PLOT

All the functions provided by the BASIC PLOT statement are
available through the code &19. It requires a further five
bytes to be sent to the operating system. The first byte
defines the plotting action desired, exactly as in the BASIC
PLOT statement. The next two bytes give an X coordinate, the
least significant byte being sent first followed by the most

significant. Then follows a further two bytes for the Y
coordinate, again the least significant byte being sent
first. A line can be drawn by the BASIC PLOT 5,&123,&145 and
this is written in assembly language:

```
LDA #&19: JSR OSWRCH: LDA #&5: JSR OSWRCH:
LDA #&23: JSR OSWRCH: LDA #&01: JSR OSWRCH:
LDA #&45: JSR OSWRCH: LDA #&01: JSR OSWRCH
```

An example demonstrating a combination of the above follows.

Exercise:

```
        NEW
10      DIM P% 100
20      OSWRCH=&FFEE
30      [.line
40      LDA #&16: JSR OSWRCH
50      LDA #&05: JSR OSWRCH
60      LDA #&19: JSR OSWRCH
70      LDA #&05: JSR OSWRCH
80      LDA #&23: JSR OSWRCH
90      LDA #&01: JSR OSWRCH
100     LDA #&45: JSR OSWRCH
110     LDA #&01: JSR OSWRCH
120     RTS: ]
```

Lines 40 and 50 select screen mode 5 and then lines 60 and 70
select PLOT 5. The X coordinate follows in 80 and 90 and then
the Y coordinate.

Run the program and then CALL line to test the program.

Data Blocks

It can be seen from this example that many graphics
applications consist of the repetitive loading of A and the
jumping to the subroutine OSWRCH. It makes sense to automate
this process to some extent by containing the bytes to be sent
to OSWRCH in a data block and using a program loop to send
each byte in the block in sequence. The first item in the
data block can then be the number of items to be sent.

Exercise:

```
        NEW
   10   DIM S% 100
   20   PNT=&70: OSWRCH=&FFEE
   30   FOR PASS=0 TO 3 STEP 3
   40   P%=S%
   50   [OPT PASS
   60   .block
   70   LDY #0
   80   LDA (PNT),Y: TAX
   90   .LOOP
  100   INY
  110   LDA (PNT),Y
  120   JSR OSWRCH
  130   DEX: BNE LOOP
  140   RTS: ]
  150   NEXT
  160   INPUT "NUMBER OF BYTES" N
  170   DIM B% N+1
  180   ? PNT    =B% MOD &100
  190   PNT?1    =B% DIV &100
  200   ?B%=N
  210   FOR M=1 TO N
  220   INPUT A$: B%?M = EVAL A$
  240   NEXT
  250   CALL block
```

This program uses the assembly language subroutine called
block to send a block of data to the operating system
graphics. The block of data is read in using BASIC before the
assembly language routine is called. The space for the data
block is reserved using the DIM statement in line 170.

Colour

The colour of text is changed by the code &11 which should be
followed by number giving the colour of text required.   For
example when in mode 5 to get red text the sequence of
instructions LDA #&11: JSR OSWRCH: LDA #&01: JSR OSWRCH is
needed. As for the equivalent BASIC COLOUR statement   the

background colour may also be set by adding &80 to the value
of the colour code. For a yellow background in mode 5
therefore we use the following instructions:

LDA #&11: JSR OSWRCH: LDA #&82: JSR OSWRCH.

Graphics colours are determined by the code &12. This code is
equivalent to the BASIC GCOL statement and like GCOL it is
followed by two pieces of information. The first byte sets
the type of plotting action to be carried out. There are five
possibilities described in the User Manual although other non
documented values will work, however, giving various "striped"
effects. The five main possibilities are as follows.

0   Plot the colour specified by the next byte sent

1   OR the next byte sent with that already on the screen

2   AND the next byte sent with that already on the screen

3   EXCLUSIVE OR the byte sent next with that on the screen

4   Take the colour already on the screen and invert it.

The next byte sent is the colour to be plotted using the above
plotting action. The equivalent to say the BASIC GCOL 3,2 is
thus: LDA #&12: JSR OSWRCH: LDA #&03: JSR OSWRCH: LDA #&2: JSR
OSWRCH .

Speed of Operation

One of the main reasons for using assembly language
programming is the increase in speed of program operation
compared with using BASIC. It therefore comes as quite a
surprise to perform an actual test. The following BASIC
program draws 100 lines on the screen.

Exercise:

```
              NEW
        10    MODE 0: TIME=0
        20    FOR X%=0 TO 1000 STEP 10
```

```
                    30   MOVE 0,0
                    40   DRAW X%,1000
                    50   NEXT
                    60   PRINT TIME/ 100 "SECONDS"
```

Run the program and not the value of TIME printed.

The assembly language version of the same program can then be
tried.

Exercise:

```
                    NEW
             5   MODE 0
            10   DIM S% 100
            20   OSWRCH=&FFEE
            30   FOR PASS=0 TO 2 STEP 2
            40   P%=S%
            50   [OPT PASS
            60   .PLT
            70   LDA #&16: JSR OSWRCH
            80   LDA #0: JSR OSWRCH
            90   LDX #100
           100   LDA #0: STA &70: STA &71
           110   .LOOP
           120   LDA #&19: JSR OSWRCH
           130   LDA #4: JSR OSWRCH
           140   LDA #0:JSR OSWRCH: JSR OSWRCH
           150   JSR OSWRCH: JSR OSWRCH
           160   LDA #&19:JSR OSWRCH
           170   LDA #5: JSR OSWRCH
           180   LDA &70: JSR OSWRCH
           190   LDA &71: JSR OSWRCH
           200   LDA #&E0: JSR OSWRCH
           210   LDA #3: JSR OSWRCH
           220   LDA &70: CLC :ADC #10: STA &70
           230   BCC SKIP: INC &71
           240   .SKIP
           250   DEX: BNE LOOP
           260   RTS: ]
           270   NEXT
           280   TIME=0
           290   CALL PLT: PRINT TIME/100 "SECONDS"
```

Lines 70 and 80 set MODE 0. Zero-page locations &70 and &71 contain the X coordinate of the end of the line. The MOVE 0,0 equivalent is in lines 120 to 150 and the DRAW equivalent in lines 160 to 210.

The assembly language version is a bit quicker than the BASIC but not really so much quicker as to make it's use worthwhile. The reason for this surprising result is that the time taken by the assembly language instructions is relatively short It comprises approximately 3000 instructions most of which take 2 cycles to complete so the time taken is only 3 milliseconds. The whole program takes around 2.4 seconds to run so that it is obvious that the time is taken up not in the assembly language section of the program given above but in the operating system subroutine OSWRCH.

The same thing is true for the BASIC program. Most of the time is taken up not in BASIC but in the operating system routines. In effect we have speeded up a part of the plotting process which does not take very long anyway.

The example above was chosen deliberately to demonstrate the point. It is possible, particularly when dealing with individual pixels or points on the screen, to obtain useful increases in speed by using assembly language but really dramatic increases cannot be obtained in this way.

For really fast graphics we must dispense with the built-in graphics operating system and directly control the screen memory. We then lose the power of the operating system but gain significantly in speed.

DIRECT SCREEN GRAPHICS

The display screen is contained in the memory of the computer and we can change the contents of the screen by altering the memory contents. This process is extremely rapid as the STA instruction takes at most only a few microseconds to operate.

The memory is translated into the actual display by a combination of the video ULA chip and the 6845 DISPLAY

CONTROLLER chip. The ULA (Uncommitted Logic Array) is a
particular type of custom designed chip. The section of
memory used in a particular mode starts at the address given
by the BASIC variable HIMEM and goes up to the end of the RAM.
Mode 7 is the teletext mode and operates in a completely
different way to the other modes so the following discussion
applies only to modes 0 to 6.

Scrolling

When the screen system is initialised by switching on the
computer, pushing BREAK, a mode change or screen clearing
operations the screen is stored in the memory such that the
top left hand corner of the screen corresponds to the address
HIMEM. The rest of the screen is stored in successive
addresses. This continues to be the case until the screen is
full, i.e. BASIC or the operating system tries to write to a
region just off the bottom of the screen. When this occurs
the system carries out an operation known as SCROLLING. The
screen still occupies the same area in memory but the
correspondence between screen position and memory locations is
lost as the screen is "rotated" to fit on the extra
information. The following discussion applies to the screen
when it has not been scrolled in this way.

Screen Structure

The order in which the screen memory locations are addressed
takes a particular form because the screen is normally used to
display characters. Starting at HIMEM the memory is grouped
in sections of eight bytes, each of these sections describing
a rectangular area on the screen. The size of area depends on
the screen mode as shown in Figure 9.1. The individual bits in
a byte are used in different ways in the various modes. For a
two colour mode each bit describes the illumination of a
single point (or pixel) on the screen and the group of eight
bytes therefore controls a rectangular block of 64 pixels
(points). For four and sixteen colour modes the pattern of
bits also controls the colour of the points on the screen so
the group of eight bytes only controls 32 pixels for two
colour modes and 16 pixels for the 16 colour mode 2.

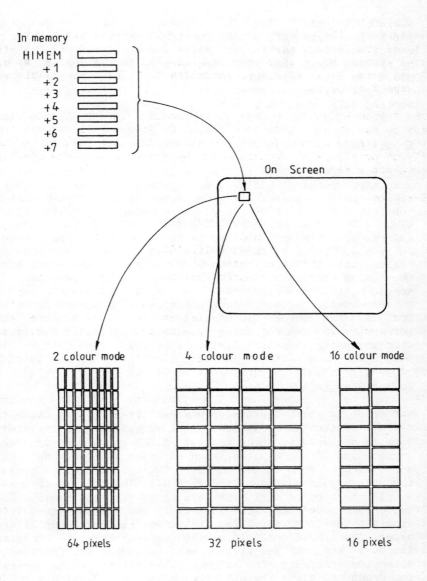

Figure 9.1

Going down the screen in the Y direction there are always 32
blocks but going across the screen in the X direction there
are either 40 or 80 blocks depending on the graphics mode.
Modes 4 and 5 use 40 blocks and modes 0, 1 and 2 use 80 blocks
in the X direction.

The following BASIC program shows the size of rectangle and
may be run in each graphics mode. On some telvision sets the
top left hand corner is off the screen and if this is so the
*TV255 or *TV 254 commands an be given to move the display
onto the screen.

Exercise:

```
          2   INPUT "MODE " M
          4   MODE M
          5   PRINT TAB(0,10)
         10   FOR K=0 TO 7
         20   ?(HIMEM+K)=&FF
         30   NEXT
```

Lines 2 and 4 read and change the mode and line 5 stops the
BASIC cursor and prompt from interfering with the displayed
rectangle which is plotted in the top left hand corner in
lines 10 to 30. Note that in mode 2 the block will be flashing
as the byte pattern is equivalent to COLOUR 15.

The two colour modes 0 and 4 are the most simple and so the
ideas of direct screen graphics will be introduced in terms of
these modes and then generalised to the multi colour modes
later.

Two Colour Graphics Mode

The top line of 8 pixels is set by the bits in the first byte
of the block, the next by the second byte and so on until the
bottom line of pixels is set by the eighth byte. The byte is
laid out on the screen as you would write it in binary with
the bit on the left controlling the pixel on the left. To see
first change mode and move the cursor out of the way by MODE
4: P. TAB(0,10) and then type ?HIMEM=&01 and ?HIMEM=&80

closely watching the top left hand corner.

Shapes are formed within the rectangle by writing the appropriate pattern of bits to the area of memory.

Exercise:

```
          NEW
  10  I."MODE ",M: MODE M
  20  P. TAB(0,10)
  30  DIM start% 50: p%=start%
  40  [OPT 0: .SHAPE
  50  LDA #&00: STA HIMEM
  60  LDA #&36: STA HIMEM+1
  70  LDA #&49: STA HIMEM+2
  80  LDA #&41: STA HIMEM+3
  90            STA HIMEM+4
 100  LDA #&22: STA HIMEM+5
 110  LDA #&14: STA HIMEM+6
 120  LDA #&08: STA HIMEM+7
 130  RTS: ]
 140  CALL SHAPE
```

First draw out the shape specified using a piece of graph paper with an 8 by 8 grid spacing and then run the program in each two colour mode (0 and 4).

Larger shapes can be created by a combination of shapes in these small rectangles. Successive groups of 8 bytes in the memory each describe a rectangle and the rectangles continue from the left of the screen to the right until the edge of the screen is reached. We then drop down a rectangle and then start again at the left.

The following program shows the layout of blocks on the screen. A program loop is used together with a subroutine called SHAPE to write blocks to the screen. Each time that a key on the keyboard is pressed another block is written until the RETURN key is pressed at which time the program ends.

The zero page location &70 is used as a pointer to the screen location and the bytes are written to the screen using the indirect indexed mode of addressing.

Exercise:

```
      NEW
 10   OSRDCH=&FFE0: PNT=&70
 20   DIM S% 100
 30   FOR PASS =0 TO 2 STEP 2
 40   P%=S%
 50   [OPT PASS
 60   .PROG
 70   CLD
 80   LDA #HIMEM MOD &100: STA PNT
 90   LDA #HIMEM DIV 6100: STA PNT+1
100   .LOOP
110   JSR SHAPE
120   LDA PNT: CLC: ADC#8:STA PNT
130   BCC SKIP: INC PNT+1: .SKIP
140   JSR OSRDCH: CMP #&0D: BEQ FINISH
150   JMP LOOP
160   .SHAPE
170   LDY #0
180   LDA #00:  STA (PNT),Y: INY
190   LDA #&36: STA (PNT),Y: INY
200   LDA #&49: STA (PNT),Y: INY
210   LDA #&41: STA (PNT),Y: INY
220             STA (PNT),Y: INY
230   LDA #&22: STA (PNT),Y: INY
240   LDA #&14: STA (PNT),Y: INY
250   LDA #&08: STA (PNT),Y
260   .FINISH
270   RTS: ]
280   NEXT
```

This approach, using the rectangular blocks, is fine and works
very quickly but it has restrictions. It is really similar to
using graphics via the redefination of characters as in the
BASIC VDU 23 command. The main problems occur when the object
to be plotted has to start at any given point on the screen
rather than at the convenient points on the edges of
rectangles.

Plotting a Byte Anywhere on the Screen

We approach the problem of writing objects to the screen in a
structured way by first by considering how to plot a single
byte at any given point on the screen. A byte in this context
contains 8 bits and, in the different modes these are
translated into 8, 4 or 2 pixels on the screen depending on
the graphics mode used.

Screen Coordinates

In order to define a starting point for the plotting some
system of coordinates is needed and the natural system is to
define the origin to be in the top left of the screen. The X
coordinate then goes from left to right, 0 to the screen width
expressed in pixels. The number of pixels across the screen
depends on the mode and is 160 for modes 2 and 5, 320 for
modes 1 and 4 and 640 for mode 0. In the Y direction top left
is 0 and bottom left is 255 in all modes. This is illustrated
in Figure 9.2.

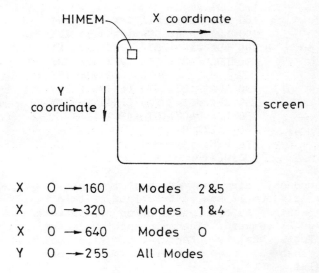

Figure 9.2

It can be seen that a single byte is sufficient to hold the
value of the Y coordinate but that two bytes may be needed for
the X coordinate depending on the mode in use.

When plotting at a given starting point, the byte to be
plotted will not in general lie exactly on top of a screen
byte but will overlap two of them. In order to plot the byte
we must first calculate the address of the screen bytes which
overlap and then shift the byte to be plotted into the correct
position in relation to them. The simplest mode is mode 4 and
we shall first consider the way to calculate the address of
the first byte in mode 4.

MODE 4 GRAPHICS

In mode 4 there are 40 rectangular blocks of 8 bytes across
the screen in the X direction. Taking the Y coordinate first
we note that for Y = 0 to 7 the Y value is just added to the
start address of the screen. For Y = 8 to 15 the number to be
added to the screen address is in the range 320 (8 x 40) to
327 and for Y = 16 to 23 we have to add 640 to 647. The
process can be expressed in terms of the BASIC DIV and MOD
functions and the Y addition is then given by:

$$YADD= Y \ MOD \ 8 + (Y \ DIV \ 8) * 8 * 40$$

In assembly language the function MOD 8 is simply accomplished
by ANDing with &7. The complex looking DIV 8 * 8 is also easy
to perform. The function DIV 8 is division by 8 with the
fraction discarded. In binary this is equivalent to three
shifts to the right with the bits that drop into the carry
flag being ignored. Then *8 is simply equivalent to three
shifts to the left, with 0s being shifted into the least
significant end of the number. All we have done in effect is
to make the three least significant bits of the number equal
to 000 with all the higher bits the same as in the original
number. In assembly language this is simply accomplished by
ANDing with &F8.

There remains the multiplication by 40. It would be possible
to use the general purpose multiplication methods but it is
faster to use a simple programming trick. To fast multiply a

number by 10 a common method is to shift it left twice to
multiply it by 4, then add the original to make it times 5. A
shift left then makes the multiplication times 10. To multiply
by 40 a further two shifts left are required. The following
lines of program labelled YCALC take the Y coordinate stored
in YC and calculate YADD.

```
1000    .YCALC
1010    LDA YC: AND #&F8:STA YADD
1020    LDA #0: STA YADD+1
1030    ASL YADD: ROL YADD+1
1040    ASL YADD: ROL YADD+1
1050    LDA YC: AND #&F8
1060    CLC: ADC YADD: STA YADD
1070    BCC Y1: INC YADD+1
1080    .Y1
1090    ASL YADD: ROL YADD+1
1100    ASL YADD: ROL YADD+1
1110    ASL YADD: ROL YADD+1
1120    LDA YC: AND #7: CLC
1130    ADC YADD: STA YADD
1140    BCC Y2: INC YADD+1
1150    .Y2
```

Note that this will not work yet as it stands as it is not a
complete program. The extra lines needed to complete the
program will be developed in the course of the text. When
incorporating these additions care should be exercised if they
are entered using AUTO as the line numbers do not always
follow a regular sequence.

In lines 1010 and 1020 YADD is made equal to (YC MOD 8) * 8.
This is multiplied by 4 in lines 1030, 1040. The addition to
make it times 5 is carried out in lines 1050 to 1080 and then
in lines 1090 to 1110 three further shifts to the left make
the total multiplication up to times 40. In lines 1120 to 1150
the addition of YC MOD 8 is carried out.

Consider next the X coordinate and the calculation of the
screen address. For X = 0 to 7 the address is contained in
the first byte and no addition needs to be made to the start
address of the screen. For X = 8 to 15 then 8 must be added
to the start address. For higher X the addition can again be

expressed in terms of the BASIC DIV function as

$$XADD= (X \text{ DIV } 8) * 8$$

The other thing that needs to be considered is the shifting of
the byte to be put on the screen relative to the screen
bytes. Say that X = 5 then the byte would have to be shifted
five places to the right before it is put onto the screen.
For higher values of X this can be expressed as

$$XSHIFT= X \text{ MOD } 8$$

The two calculations can be carried out in assembly language
as follows.

```
1500    .XCALC
1510    LDA XC: AND #7: STA XSHIFT
1520    LDA XC: AND #&F8: STA XADD
1530    LDA XC+1: STA XADD+1
```

Where XC and XC+1 contain the double byte X coordinate.

The next thing is to calculate the actual address of the first
screen byte by adding YADD and XADD to the start address of
the screen and storing the result in ADDR.

```
1550    LDA #HIMEM MOD &100
1560    CLC: ADC YADD: STA ADDR
1570    LDA #HIMEM DIV &100: ADC YADD+1
1580    STA ADDR+1
1590    LDA ADDR: CLC
1600    ADC XADD: STA ADDR
1610    LDA ADDR+1: ADC XADD+1
1620    STA ADDR+1
```

The byte to be put on the screen must be shifted relative to
two screen locations as shown in Figure 9.3. If the byte to be
put on the screen is in a location called BYTE then the
following lines will shift it relative to that location and
the next (BYTE+1) and then put both the bytes onto the screen
by logic ORing them with the existing contents of the screen.
This has the effect of adding the contents of BYTE to the
display, and the display then consists of the old display plus

the contents of byte. Alternatively the screen contents could
instead be completely overwritten by just using STA in lines
1730 and 1760.

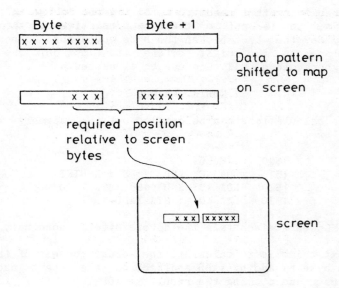

Figure 9.3

Sometimes we need to remember to contents of the screen before
the byte was written. Here some lines have been added to save
the contents of the screen such that after this section of
program then locations BYTE and BYTE+1 contain the previous
screen contents.

```
1650     LDA #0: STA BYTE+1
1660     LDA XSHIFT: BEQ WR1
1670     .XLOOP
1680     LSR BYTE: ROR BYTE+1
1690     DEC XSHIFT
1700     BNE XLOOP
1710     .WR1
1720     LDY #0: LDA (ADDR),Y: PHA
1730     ORA BYTE: STA (ADDR),Y
1740     PLA: STA BYTE: LDY #8
```

```
1750    LDA (ADDR),Y: PHA
1760    ORA BYTE+1: STA (ADDR),Y
1770    PLA: STA BYTE+1
```

The above line numbers are compatible and the following lines
can be added to make the whole process into a subroutine
called PUT.

```
  10    MODE 4
 900    XC=&70: YC=&72: ADDR=&74
 910    YADD=&76: XADD= &78:
 920    BYTE= &7A: XSHIFT= &7C
 930    DIM S% 600
 940    FOR PASS=0 TO 2 STEP 2
 950    P%=S%
 960    [OPT PASS
 970    .PUT
 980    CLD
1800    RTS
1810    .TEST
1820    LDA#0: STA XC: STA XC+1
1830    STA YC: LDX #200
1840    .TLP
1850    LDA #&80: STA BYTE
1860    JSR PUT
1870    INC XC: INC YC
1880    DEX: BNE TLP
1890    RTS
1900    ]
1910    NEXT
1920    CALL TEST
```

The subroutine TEST tests the subroutine by drawing a line on
the screen. In line 1850 BYTE is set to &80 to write just a
single pixel and it is written to the screen in 1860. The XC
and YC coordinates are incremented on each pass through the
loop.

Using PUT in this way to write a single pixel to the screen is
rather like using the BASIC PLOT 69 command.

WRITING OBJECTS TO THE SCREEN

An object can be any size but let us consider first a
character sized object comprising 8 bytes. The bytes are
stored in successive locations and transferred to the screen
using the subroutine PUT.

Delete lines 1810 to 1920 in the above program using DEL.
1810,1920 and then the following may be added.

```
 945    OBJ=&7E: OBJIND=&80
1900    .PUT8
1910    LDA #0:STA OBJIND
1920    LDX #8
1930    .OBLP
1940    LDY OBJIND
1950    LDA (OBJ),Y: STA BYTE
1960    JSR PUT
1970    INC OBJIND: INC YC
1980    DEX: BNE OBLP
1990    RTS
2000    .TEST
2010    LDA #shape MOD &100: STA OBJ
2020    LDA #shape DIV &100: STA OBJ+1
2030    LDA #100: STA XC: LDA #0: STA XC+1
2040    LDA #100: STA YC
2050    JSR PUT8
2060    RTS
5000    .shape
5010    ]
5020    NEXT
5030    FOR Z=P% TO P%+7
5040    READ A$
5050    ?Z= EVAL A$
5060    NEXT
5070    DATA 0,&36,&49,&41,&41,&22,&14,&8
5080    CALL TEST
```

The bytes defining the shape of the object are put into the
memory in lines 5030 to 5070. The label "shape" at the end of
the assembly identifies the start of this area. The
subroutine TEST sets up the X and Y coordinates to 100,100 and
initialises OBJ to point to the shape being plotted.

The subroutine PUT8 takes the shape a byte at a time and plots it on the screen using PUT. On each successive PUT the Y coordinate is incremented by 1 ready for the next byte to be sent. As the Y register is used in PUT the store OBJIND is used to hold the index used for stepping through the bytes defining the object.

Figure 9.4 shows the relationship between bytes and the shape on the screen. Each 0 bit corresponds to a black pixel and each 1 bit a white pixel.

&0	0 0 0 0 0 0 0 0	&0
&3	0 0 1 1 0 1 1 0	&6
&4	0 1 0 0 1 0 0 1	&9
&4	0 1 0 0 0 0 0 1	&1
&4	0 1 0 0 0 0 0 1	&1
&1	0 0 1 0 0 0 1 0	&2
&1	0 0 0 1 0 1 0 0	&4
&0	0 0 0 0 1 0 0 0	&8

Figure 9.4

WRITING LARGER OBJECTS

Larger objects are just built up of bytes in the same way as the simple character sized object above. We could adopt various conventions for storing the bytes depending on the application. One approach is to simply extend the single character method to a larger rectangle on the screen. The subroutine PUTOBJ transfers a rectangular object whose size is contained in locations YL and XL. YL contains the number of pixels in the Y direction and XL the number of bytes in the X direction. The number of pixels per byte is 8 in mode 4 and this is set using XP to allow the subroutine to be easily generalised to other modes.

OBJIND holds the index which is used to step through the list of bytes which define the shape to be plotted and YCT is used to count the the number of bytes transferred in the Y direction. The lines 2270 to 2300 reset XC to the value that it had on entry to the subroutine.

```
946    XL=&81: YL=&82: YCT=&83
947    XP=8
2110   .PUTOBJ
2120   LDA XL: PHA
2130   LDA #0:STA OBJIND
2140   .PU1
2150   LDA YL: STA YCT
2160   .PU2
2170   LDY OBJIND
2180   LDA (OBJ),Y: STA BYTE
2190   JSR PUT
2200   INC OBJIND: INC YC
2210   DEC YCT: BNE PU2
2220   LDA XC: CLC: ADC #XP: STA XC
2230   BCC PU3: INC XC+1
2240   .PU3: LDA YC: SEC: SBC YL: STA YC
2250   DEC XL: BNE PU1
2260   PLA: STA XL
2270   .PU4
2280   LDA XC: SEC: SBC #XP: STA XC: BCS PU5
2290   DEC XC+1: .PU5
2300   DEC XL: BNE PU4
2310   RTS
```

The following lines can be added to test the subroutine.

```
2050   LDA #2: STA XL: LDA #16: STA YL
2055   JSR PUTOBJ
5030   FOR Z=P% TO P%+31
5070   DATA &3C,&42,&41,&40,&40,&21,&12,&A,&12   } LHS.
5071   DATA &21,&40,&40,&41,&42,&3C,&0
5072   DATA &1E,&21,&41,&81,&1,&C2,&24,&28,&24   } RHS
5073   DATA &C2,&1,&81,&41,&21,&1E,&0
```

The data bytes defining the shape start at the point X=0 Y=0.
The next byte is X=0 Y=1, the X=0 Y=2 and so on until the
first column is full. Then follows X=1 Y=0 and so on until
each column is complete.

Figure 9.5 shows the relationship between the codes and the
shape, the 0s in the shape have been omitted so that the shape

is easier to see.

```
              !  . . . . . .  !  !  . . . . . . !
         N hex                              hex  N
         1 &3C   1 1 1 1             1 1 1 1   &1E 17
         2 &42  1           1      1        1  &21 18
         3 &41  1             1   1         1  &41 19
         4 &40  1              1            1  &81 20
         5 &40  1                           1  &01 21
         6 &21   1          1 1 1          1   &C2 22
         7 &12     1     1       1     1       &24 23
         8 &0A       1   1       1   1         &28 24
         9 &12     1     1       1     1       &24 25
        10 &21   1        1 1 1           1   &C2 26
        11 &40  1                         1   &01 27
        12 &40  1              1          1   &81 28
        13 &41  1             1   1       1   &41 29
        14 &42  1           1       1     1   &21 30
        15 &3C   1 1 1 1             1 1 1 1   &1E 31
        16 &00                               &00 32
```

Figure 9.5

N is the order that the bytes are put onto the screen using the subroutine PUT. Another object, of the same size, that you might like to try is given by the following bytes: &00, &00, &00, &00, &00, &1F, &2C, &4C, &8C, &4C, &2C, &1F, &00, &00, &00, &00, &00, &10, &28, &44, &44, &28, &91, &46, &3E, &46, &90, &28, &44, &44, &28, &10.

ERASING AN OBJECT

To remove an object from the screen the pixels which have been put on the screen must be removed. If the object was originally written on to a blank section of screen the this may simply be done by overwriting the object with zeros. In general, however, the object may have been written onto a non-blank part of the screen and when the object is removed we would usually like the original contents to be restored. This means that when an object is written to the screen we have to store the area of screen that is overwritten and then, to

delete the object, the area of screen is restored from the
stored data.

The subroutine PUT, which has already been encountered, was
written with this process in mind. PUT is used to put a byte
of 8 pixels on the screen and on exit from PUT it leaves
information on the area of screen overwritten. The two stores
BYTE and BYTE+1 contain the two bytes of screen that were
overwritten and the stores ADDR and ADDR+1 contain the address
of the first screen byte. Each time that PUT is used to write
an object as a sequence of bytes this information could be
stored in a list and when the object is to be erased the
information is restored to the screen.

The following lines can therefore be added to the object
writing subroutine PUTOBJ to save the area overwritten into
another area beginning at address labelled ST.

```
2111    LDX #0
2191    LDA ADDR: STA ST,X: INX
2192    LDA ADDR+1: STA ST,X: INX
2193    LDA BYTE: STA ST,X: INX
2194    LDA BYTE+1: STA ST,X: INX
```

Space can be reserved for ST by adding a suitable DIM
statement.

```
935     DIM ST 128
```

As each byte in the object results in four bytes of storage
being needed the above DIM statement reserves enough storage
for an object 32 bytes long.

All that is needed now is a subroutine to restore the
information to the screen to erase the object.

```
948     STP=&84
2400    .REST
2410    LDX STP
2420    .RSTLP
2430    LDY #0
2440    LDA ST,X: STA ADDR: INX
2450    LDA ST,X: STA ADDR+1: INX
```

```
2460    LDA ST,X: STA (ADDR),Y: INX
2470    LDA ST,X: LDY #8
2480    STA (ADDR),Y
2490    TXA: SEC: SBC #7: TAX
2500    BPL RSTLP
2510    RTS
```

The data is restored to the screen in the reverse order to that in which it was stored. The location STP contains the position of the last address in the list of data. For an object M bytes long STP would contain (4 x M) -4. This address is obtained in lines 2440 and 2450 and then the screen bytes are obtained and stored back on the screen in lines 2460 to 2480. The index is then adjusted so that it points to the next address in the list.

With the previous program in the memory enter the above program lines and run the program. The flower shape should be drawn on the screen. To remove it type ?STP=124: CALL REST.

EXCLUSIVE OR-ing OBJECTS ON AND OFF THE SCREEN

An alternative method can be used if the background onto which the object is to be written is always blank. If in the subroutine PUT the OR statements which write bytes to the screen are replaced with EOR (exclusive OR statements) then the first time that the object is written it goes onto the screen as before (because exclusive ORing with zero is the same as ORing with zero). If, however, now the object is rewritten to the same place it is exclusive ORed with itself and this results in zero - the object disappears.

The following lines show the modifications needed if the reader wishes to experiment with the method.

```
1730    EOR BYTE: STA (ADDR),Y
1760    EOR BYTE+1: STA (ADDR),Y
```

The method is not as fast as the previous one as all the screen addresses must be recalculated to erase the object but it does not require the use of the extra memory.

Unusual effects occur if the screen is not blank. Wherever
the object is written, the screen is reversed but when the
object is rewritten to erase it the screen resumes its
previous condition.

ANIMATION- MOVING OBJECTS ON THE SCREEN

We have seen how to write objects of various sizes and also
how to erase them. The creation of movement on the screen is,
of course, an optical illusion. The object is not continually
moved but is written to a place on the screen, then left there
stationary for a short length of time.   It is then erased and
written at a new position close to where it was before. If
the timing and distance moved are suitable the illusion of
movement is created but if not then flickering images or jerky
movement results. The flickering effects are demonstrated in
the following program. Firstly an object is written to the
screen and then immediately erased and moved to a new position
one place to the right. A single byte X coordinate is used so
the object goes across the screen to X=255 and then starts
again on the left at X=0.

The shape is shown in Figure 9.6

```
                  ! . . . . . ! ! . . . . . . !
        &00                                              &00
        &80       1                                      &00
        &C0       1 1                                    &00
        &E0       1 1 1                                  &00
        &F0       1 1 1 1                   1 1 1        &1C
        &FF       1 1 1 1 1 1 1 1 1 1 1       1          &F4
        &C0       1 1               1 1 1 1 1 1 1 1      &FE
        &FF       1 1 1 1 1 1 1 1 1 1 1 1 1 1 1 1        &FF
```

Figure 9.6

First delete lines 2000 to 2060 and 5071 to 5073 of the
previous program to remove unwanted bits specific to the
earlier examples and then add the following lines.

```
     5000    .fly
     5010    LDA #PLANE MOD &100: STA OBJ
```

```
5020    LDA #PLANE DIV &100: STA OBJ+1
5030    LDA #0: STA XC: STA XC+1:LDA #100: STA YC
5040    .SPLP
5050    LDA #2: STA XL: LDA #8: STA YL
5060    LDA #60: STA STP
5070    JSR PUTOBJ
5080    JSR REST
5090    CLC: LDA XC: ADC #1: STA XC
5100    JMP SPLP
6000    .PLANE
6010    ]
6015    NEXT
6020    FOR Z=P% TO P%+15
6030    READ A$
6040    ?Z=EVAL A$
6050    NEXT
6060    DATA &0,&80,&CO,&EO,&FO,&FF,&CO,&FF
6070    DATA &0,&0,&0,&0,&1C,&F4,&FE,&FF
6080    CALL fly
```

The BREAK key is used to leave the program and resume using
BASIC. Use the OLD command to retain the program for the
following work in the chapter.

The object moves across the screen but the flickering is very
bad. There are two main reasons for this, the object is
removed as soon as it is written and therefore the whole
object does not remain still before the eyes for long enough
to become established, and secondly there is the effect of
interference between the built in normal TV scanning system
and the program. The television screen is not itself a static
thing as it is continually being written by a moving spot at a
rate of fifty screens a second. Most readers will have
probably noticed the effects of this in normal TV viewing;
spoked waggon wheels, when turning, appear to go backwards
after they have reached a certain speed and if a TV camera
takes a picture of a TV screen to which it is not
synchronised, then black bands move up or down the screen.

Synchronising the Animation

The operating systems 1.0 and later allow the user to

synchronise the writing of information to the screen so that
the interference can be avoided.

There are two methods that can be used. One is rather complex
using the interrupt system to generate an interrupt
synchronised with the picture refresh rate. The other is a
simpler method that is a subroutine which waits until the
start of the next screen to be displayed. Here we concentrate
on the simpler method which uses the operating system
subroutine OSBYTE (&FFF4) with the A register set to the value
19 (&13). This is equivalent to the BASIC command *FX 19 and
causes a delay until the start of the next screen (or frame)
of the picture. It thus provides both the functions of delay
and synchronisation needed for smooth motion and we can add
the following subroutine to the program.

```
2600    .SYNC
2610    LDA #19
2620    JSR &FFF4
2630    RTS
```

If now this subroutine is called before the object is removed
from the screen smooth motion results.

```
5075    JSR SYNC
```

Moving Quickly

The above object is only moving one pixel per frame scan and
as there are 50 scans per second we are getting a movement of
50 pixels per second. To get faster movement instead of just
adding one to the value of XC in between each frame a larger
number is added. Thus line 5090 is modified to say:

```
5090    CLC: LDA XC: ADC #8:STA XC
```

Experiment with adding different values to XC to see the
effect. If too large a number is added the effect of motion
is lost as the object just seems to jump instantaneously from
one place to the next.

The Y coordinate can also be changed to move the object up and down the picture.

Using equal X and Y movements results in diagonal movement and
this can be used to demonstrate one of the problems of using
this simple method of synchronising the animation.

```
5090    CLC: LDA XC: ADC #1: STA XC
5095    CLC: LDA YC: ADC #1: STA YC
```

Now, part of the object disappears in the top left hand corner
of the screen. The synchronisation starts in the top left
hand corner and the problem is caused by the time taken by the
program that we have written. The longer that it takes the
program to run the larger the area of screen effected. Once
the object stops, however, all is well and its display is
continuous.

The message is simple. When designing moving graphics, try to
keep away from the top left hand corner and in particular try
to keep the action near to the bottom of the screen if you
want to use this simple method of synchronisation.

Controlling Movement From the Keyboard

Many applications need the movement on the screen to be
controlled from the keyboard. Unfortunately the usual
keyboard reading routine OSRDCH poses certain timing
difficulties as it waits for a key to be pressed. If the key
is held down an auto repeat is used and the characters are
held in a queue in the input buffer. This complicated type of
action is not usually required when controlling objects and we
in general just want to know if a key is held down at a
particular instant or not. There is a subroutine built into
the operating system which simply tests the keyboard to see if
a particular key is pressed at the time the subroutine is
called.

The subroutine in question corresponds to the BASIC command
INKEY using a negative number. OSBYTE (&FFF4) is used with
the A register set to &81 and the X register set to the
negative number given for the character in the User Manual
description of INKEY, page 275. The Y register is set to &FF.

On exit both X and Y contain 0 if the character specified was
not pressed and &FF if it was pressed. The following
subroutine TESTKEY uses the method to test if a particular key
is pressed. On exit from TESTKEY the A register contains &FF
if the key was pressed but 0 if it was not pressed.

```
2650    .TESTKEY
2660    LDY #&FF
2670    LDA #&81
2680    JSR &FFF4
2690    TXA: RTS
```

The X register is loaded with the negative number which
specifies the key to be tested. For example if the "U" key is
to be tested we look up from the User Manual entry on INKEY
that the negative number is -54 and this can be put into the X
register using the instruction LDX #(-54 AND &FF). The AND &FF
is needed as -54 is represented in BASIC by 4 bytes &FFFFFFCA
and this is too big to fit into X. The AND &FF reduces this to
the single byte &CA which will fit into X.

The following lines can be added to the program to move the
object around the screen using the U, D, L and R keys for up,
down, left and right.

```
5085    LDX #(-54 AND &FF): JSR TESTKEY
5086    BEQ NTU: SEC: LDA YC: SBC #2: STA YC
5087    JMP SPLP
5088    .NTU: LDX #(-51 AND &FF): JSR TESTKEY
5089    BEQ NTD: CLC: LDA YC: ADC #2:STA YC
5090    JMP SPLP
5091    .NTD: LDX #(-87 AND &FF): JSR TESTKEY
5092    BEQ NTL: SEC: LDA XC: SBC #2:STA XC
5093    BCS SPLP:DEC XC+1: JMP SPLP
5094    .NTL: LDX #(-52 AND &FF): JSR TESTKEY
5095    BEQ SPLP: CLC: LDA XC: ADC #2: STA XC
5096    BCC SPLP: INC XC+1: JMP SPLP
```

These lines test the keyboard for the U, D, L and R keys. If
one of these keys is detected the corresponding coordinate is
altered so that the object is moved by 2 pixels in the
required direction. The speed of movement is easily changed
by altering the number that is added to, or subtracted from,

the coordinates from 2 to another number.

Try moving the object to all parts of the screen to see the extent of the area subject to the object disappearing whilst in motion.

The program developed so far is given on the tape under the name of "PLANE4".

Detecting Collisions

When writing games or other software involving animated graphics we often need to know when objects collide or if one object is moved on top of another object. One method is to examine the X and Y coordinates of all objects on the screen and to detect collisions between specific objects by comparing the coordinates. This method is straightforward but if a large number of objects are to be tested quite a lot of comparisons need to be done.

Another method is to examine what is actually on the screen before objects are written to it. If the screen already contains some pixels which are "on" in the place where the object is to be written then it must be colliding with some previously written object. The subroutine PUT leaves the previous screen contents in the two locations BYTE and BYTE+1. These two locations overlap the byte ORed to the screen so to test the actual eight pixels used by PUT some further information is needed. The solution is to generate a mask with which the contents of BYTE and BYTE+1 can be tested. The following lines can be added to PUT to leave a suitable mask in the two locations MASK and MASK+1.

```
1655    LDA #&FF: STA MASK
1656    LDA #0: STA MASK+1
1685    LSR MASK: ROR MASK+1
```

Following PUT then BYTE and BYTE+1 can be tested using MASK and MASK+1.

```
LDA BYTE: AND MASK: BNE COLL
LDA BYTE+1: AND MASK+1: BNE COLL
```

Where COLL is the label of the section of program that deals
with collisions.

MODE 0 GRAPHICS

Mode 0 is very similar to mode 4. The difference is that there
are twice as many pixels across the screen in the X direction
and the subroutine PUT must be modified. Instead of
multiplying by 40 the multiplication factor is 80 and we can
add some extra shifts to accomplish this.

> 1115   ASL YADD: ROL YADD+1

ADD this line to PLANE4 and change line 10 to:

> 10   MODE 0

COLOUR DIRECT SCREEN GRAPHICS

We have already seen how in the two colour modes a single byte
of the screen describes 8 pixels which are either on or off.
For a colour mode the byte of screen also has to contain the
colour information and so less pixels can be fitted into a
byte.

For four colour modes each byte controls four pixels laid out
on the screen P3, P2, P1, P0. P0 is controlled by bits 0 and 4
in the byte, P1 by bits 1 and 5, P2 by bits 2 and 6 and
finally P3 by bits 3 and 8 in the byte. The two bit binary
number for each pixel is the colour on the screen : 0 BLACK, 1
RED, 2 YELLOW, 3 WHITE using the standard colour allocations.

Mode 2 is the sixteen colour mode and thus four bits per pixel
are needed. Each byte of the screen thus only describes two
pixels P0 and P1 laid out on the screen P1, P0. P0 is
controlled by the binary number comprising bits 6,4,2,0 (bit 0
least significant) and P1 by the number comprising bits
7,5,3,1 (bit 1 least significant). The four bit binary number
specifies the colour of the pixel.

The methods and subroutines developed so far can also be used, with some modification, for the coloured modes. Objects are composed of bytes and can be written and moved using the same system of X,Y coordinates.

MODE 5 GRAPHICS

As a demonstration, the design and movement of a coloured arrow in mode 5 will be discussed. The arrow is shown below in Figure 9.7

```
10000000   &80      y   w          10001000   &88
01000000   &40       y   w         01000100   &44
00100000   &20        y   w        00100010   &22
00001111   &0F      rrrrrrrr        00001111   &0F
00001111   &0F      rrrrrrrr        00001111   &0F
00100000   &20        y   w        00100010   &22
01000000   &40       y   w         01000100   &44
10000000   &80      y   w          10001000   &88
```

Figure 9.7

Where y is a yellow pixel, w a white pixel and r a red pixel.

The main difference between mode 5 and mode 4 is that in mode 5 each byte only contains four pixels instead of 8 and thus some account needs to be made of this when shifting bytes into the correct position before ORing them onto the screen. For example consider the byte 00010001, which is a white pixel on the right hand end of a rectangular block. If this is shifted one place to the right the effect desired is that of moving the white pixel into the next byte into the left-most position, i.e. the code 10001000 is wanted. Figure 9.8 illustrates the process and it is apparent that a straight forward double length shift right does not accomplish this, so a more complex shift must be devised.

The type of operation needed is to first shift the byte one place to the right. We then note the bit that is shifted into bit position 3 and replace it with 0. The bit that comes out of the end into the carry flag is also noted. Next the byte

to the right is shifted one place right and the bit, in the
previous byte, that was shifted into bit 3 is put into bit 7
of this byte. The contents of the carry flag are put into bit
position 3 to complete the shift. The other bit positions are
correctly dealt with by shifting to the right.

| 00010001 | | 00000000 |

One shift right is required to give:

| 00000000 | | 10001000 |

Figure 9.8

```
2700    .SHIFT5
2710    ROR BYTE+1: LDA #&77: AND BYTE+1
2720    STA BYTE+1
2730    LDA BYTE: AND #&11
2740    ASL A:ASL A: ASL A
2750    ORA BYTE+1: STA BYTE+1
2760    LDA BYTE: LSR A
2770    AND #&77: STA BYTE
2780    RTS
```

BYTE+1 is shifted to the right in 2710 and bit positions 3 and
7 are set to 0. In lines 2730 and 2740 the bits in positions 0
and 4 in BYTE are selected out and shifted up into positions 3
and 7. They are then ORed into BYTE+1 in line 2750. Finally
BYTE itself is shifted right and bits 3 and 7 set to 0.

The subroutine PUT also needs some modification to allow for
only 4 pixels per byte. The calculation of the screen address
now should be :

$$XADD = (X \ DIV \ 4) * 8$$

and we modify PUT as follows.

```
1510   LDA XC: AND #3: STA XSHIFT
1520   LDA XC: AND #&FC: STA XADD
1535   CLC: ASL XADD: ROL XADD+1

1680   JSR SHIFT5
```

The new subroutine for shifting is incorporated in line 1680.

The mode is set in line 10 and the number of pixels per byte in line 947.

```
10     MODE 5
947    XP=4
1115
```

The blank line 1115 removes any statements that may have been added to test mode 0.

Note that the flashing cursor may be removed by adding the BASIC statement VDU 23;8202;0;0;0; as described in the User Manual p.77 and this could be added in say line 20 above.

Finally the DATA statements are changed to the new object:

```
6060   DATA &80,&40,&20,&0F,&0F,&20,&40,&80
6070   DATA &88,&44,&22,&0F,&0F,&22,&44,&88
```

The resulting program is contained on the tape and is called "ARROW5".

MODE 1 GRAPHICS

This is similar to mode 5 as it is a four colour mode but the difference is that there are 80 rectangles across the screen instead of 40. The change is accommodated by incorporating an extra line:

```
1115   ASL YADD: ROL YADD+1
```

MODE 2 GRAPHICS

In mode 2 there are only two pixels per byte and there are 80
bytes across the screen and there are thus 160 pixels in the X
direction.   The 4 bits controlling the pixel   are stored   in
alternate bits in the byte and the process of shifting a pixel
to the right must be modified.

```
2800    .SHIFT2
2810    ROR BYTE+1: LDA #&55: AND BYTE+1
2820    STA BYTE+1
2830    LDA #&55: AND BYTE: ASL A
2840    ORA BYTE+1: STA BYTE+1
2850    LDA BYTE: AND #&AA
2860    LSR A: STA BYTE
2870    RTS
```

Byte+1 is shifted 1 place to the right in 2810 and alternate
bits are set to 0. Alternate bits in BYTE are selected in 2830
and shifted into place and put into BYTE+1 in 2840. Finally
byte is itself shifted right and the leftmost pixel set to
zero in 2850, 2860.

The subroutine PUT must also be changed to accommodate the
change to 2 pixels per byte and the XADD is now computed :

$$XADD = (X \ DIV \ 2) * 8$$

The program lines needed to accomplish this are:

```
1510    LDA XC: AND #1: STA XSHIFT
1520    LDA XC: AND #&FE: STA XADD
1535    ASL XADD: ROL XADD+1
1536    ASL XADD: ROL XADD+1
1680    JSR SHIFT2
```

Other modifications needed are:

```
10      MODE 2
947     XP=2
1115    ASL YADD: ROL YADD+1
```

The design of an object will now be discussed.

The object chosen is a space invaders type "thing" and this is
laid out first in terms of pixels in Figure 9.9.

               ! is the start of a byte.

                  column   !0!1!2!3
        row
         0   G
         1   GYG
         2   GYG
         3   BGYGB
         4   BBGYGBB
         5   B GYG B
         6   B r B
         7   rcr

                                              Figure 9.9

G is a green pixel, Y a yellow pixel, B a blue pixel, r a
red/cyan flashing pixel, c a cyan/red pixel.

To work out the data bytes corresponding to this we take the
pixels in pairs. Starting at top left (row 0 column 0) the
first pixel and the one on its right are blank giving a data
byte of &00. Moving down one position the next pair (row 1
column 0) are also blank, again giving &00. Moving down again
we also get &00. The next position (row 3) is not blank,
however, as there is a blank in the left position followed by
a blue pixel to its right. The code for a blue pixel is 0100
binary and this code occupies alternate bits in the byte, the
other bits being 0000 for the blank pixel to its left. The
resulting code is thus 00010000 binary or &10. A good way of
forming this code is to first write down the binary code for
the pixel on the right with gaps in between the bits, thus we
get 0 1 0 0. Then starting at the left write down the binary
code for the left hand pixel and fill in the gaps to get the
result. The next two pixels (row 4) are both blue so we get
the binary code 00110000 (&30) followed by row 5, a blue pixel
and blank, 00100000 (&20). The same pattern follows in row 6:
&20. In row 7 there are two blanks &00.

The first eight data bytes are thus &00, &00, &00, &10, &30, &20, &20, &00.

We next move to the top of column 1 and moving down column 1 taking pixels in pairs we obtain &04, &0D, &0D, &0D, &0D, &0D, &41, &D6.

Going down column 2 we obtain &00, &08, &08, &18, &18, &08, &00, &82. and the last column (3) gives &00, &00, &00, &00, &20, &20, &20, &00.

The statements to read these bytes into the program are:

```
6020    FOR Z= P% TO P% +31
6060    DATA &00,&00,&00,&10,&30,&20,&20,&00
6065    DATA &04,&0D,&0D,&0D,&0D,&0D,&41,&D6
6070    DATA &00,&08,&08,&18,&18,&08,&00,&82
6075    DATA &00,&00,&00,&00,&20,&20,&20,&00
```

Line 5050 needs to be changed to :

```
5050    LDA #4: STA XL: LDA #8: STA YL
```

to set the X and Y lengths of this object and also location STP which is used by the restoring subroutine needs to be changed for this object to the value 124 (32 * 8 -4) and this is done in line 5060.

```
5060    LDA #124: STA STP
```

The revised program is given on the tape under the name "THING2".

10

Interfacing and Interrupts

An interface in computer terms refers to a part of the
computer which connects to external devices or signals and the
BBC microcomputer contains several such interfaces for
communicating with the outside world. It can respond to
digital signals from other computers or digital circuits and
also read the analog voltage signals generated by such
external appliances as joysticks.

Digital interfaces are of two types SERIAL, in which a single
wire is used and the digital byte to be communicated is sent
as a sequence of pulses, and PARALLEL, in which a byte is sent
on 8 wires all at the same instant in time. In each case the
digital signal is represented by two voltages, a low voltage
(approximately 0 volts) for logic 0 and a high voltage
(approximately 5 volts) for logic 1. Standard systems for both
types of communication exist and the BBC computer supports two
of them, the RS423 serial data link and the CENTRONICS printer
port. It also provides a separate USER PORT for the use as an
additional parallel or serial interface.

A digital voltage only has two values, high and low, but in
general a voltage signal can have any value. In computer and
electronic terms a non-digital value such as this is called an
analog value. The computer can use these analog voltages
using the built-in analog TO DIGITAL CONVERTOR. This reads an

analog voltage and converts it into a digital number. It
cannot, however, without additional circuitry, generate analog
voltages to send to other equipment.

BUFFERS

The computer's handling of interfaces takes place as a
sequence of events in time and in very simple computer systems
the user has the responsibility of looking after the timing
and synchronisation of the data flow. The BBC microcomputer
is more advanced, however, and uses instead a system of
BUFFERS to insulate the user to some extent from the timing
problems. To communicate using a BUFFER bytes are read from,
or written to, the BUFFER instead of to the actual interface
involved. The operating system then looks after the transfer
so that say, when writing a byte, the users program does not
have to wait until one character has been written before it
sends the next and also so that, when reading a byte, the
device sending the data does not have to wait for the user's
program to be ready . By this means the user's program is
essentially isolated from the timing and synchronisation
problems. Of course if desired the user can communicate
directly with for example the serial interface but this is
only necessary in specialised applications

The subroutine OSBYTE is used for buffer operations using the
Y register to contain the data byte. To write to a buffer the
A register is set to &8A and to read from a buffer A is set to
&91. The X register is set to a number specifying the buffer
required according to the following list.

X	BUFFER
0	keyboard
1	RS423 input
2	RS423 output
3	printer
4	sound channel 0
5	sound channel 1
6	sound channel 2
7	sound channel 3
8	speech synthesiser

The buffers are effectively queues of bytes awaiting attention
and the operating system can inform the user concerning
whether a particular queue is full or empty using EVENTs as
described later in this chapter.

The queues can be emptied or FLUSHED using OSBYTE with A set
to 21 (&15) and X set to specify the buffer required as
above.

Alternatively all the buffers can be flushed at once using
OSBYTE 15 (&F) with X set to 0.

THE RS423 SERIAL DATA LINK

As explained already a serial interface handles communication
as a sequence of pulses on a single wire. Although not always
needed two other wires are often used: the handshaking lines
REQUEST TO SEND and CLEAR TO SEND. These are provided so that
the flow of information can be synchronised and transmission
can be suspended if the computer is busy doing a more
important task.

The speed of transmitting and receiving pulses is known as the
BAUD rate (1 bit per second is 1 BAUD) and is set by using the
subroutine OSBYTE. There are eight standard speeds provided on
the BBC computer and these are 75, 150, 300, 1200, 2400, 4800,
9600, and 19200 baud. The X register is used to select the
required speed, the above speeds corresponding to X=1 to X=8.
The A register is set to 7 to select the receive baud rate and
is set to 8 to select the transmit baud rate.

To write a byte to the serial output it is placed into the
serial output buffer using OSBYTE with A=&8A and X=2, the Y
register containing the character, and the operating system
looks after the actual transmission. Reading a byte from the
serial link consists of taking a byte from the buffer (if
there is one there) and this is done using OSBYTE with the A
register set to &91 and X set to 1. The byte is returned in
the Y register and the carry flag is set to 1 if the buffer
was empty.

Before the RS423 receiver is used it must first be enabled by

OSBYTE with A set to 2 and X set to 1.

The following program is an illustration of the above. It shows how the BBC computer may be used to act as a terminal Video Display Unit (VDU) to another computer. Such terminals have a keyboard and a screen and characters typed on the keyboard are sent down the serial link to the remote computer. Characters sent from the remote computer via the serial link are displayed on the screen of the VDU.

```
           NEW
     10    OSBYTE=&FFF4
     20    OSWRCH=&FFEE
     30    DIM S% 60
     40    FOR PASS = 0 TO 2 STEP 2
     50    [OPT PASS
     60    .TERM
     70    LDA #7: LDX #3: JSR OSBYTE
     80    LDA #8: LDX #3: JSR OSBYTE
     90    LDA #2: LDX #1: JSR OSBYTE
    100    .RDKEY
    110    LDA #&91: LDX #0: JSR OSBYTE
    120    BCS RDLINK
    130    .TMIT
    140    LDA #&8A: LDX #2: JSR OSBYTE
    150    .RDLINK
    160    LDA #&91: LDX #1: JSR OSBYTE
    170    BCS RDKEY
    180    .WSCREEN
    190    TYA: JSR OSWRCH
    200    JMP RDKEY
    210    ]
    220    NEXT
    230    CALL TERM
```

The baud rate is set to 300 baud in lines 70 and 80 and the RS423 receiver is enabled in line 90. Line 110 reads the keyboard buffer and if no character was present line 140, which transmits a character is skipped. The RS423 receive buffer is next checked in lines 160 and 170. If a character is present it is written to the screen in 190 and if not a branch is made back to read the keyboard.

Two BBC machines can be linked together in this way with the above program running on each. Denoting the two machines as A and B the following RS423 connections will enable messages typed on one machine to be displayed on the other.

```
        COMPUTER A              COMPUTER B

        data in --------------data out
        data out -------------data in
           RTS -----------------CTS
           CTS -----------------RTS
        0 Volts --------------0 Volts
```

Note that the RETURN key only causes the cursor to return to the start of the current line. To move to the next line the LINEFEED control character CTRL J must be typed. If the JSR OSWRCH in line 190 is replaced by JSR &FFE3 (OSASCI) then the linefeed control characters will be inserted automatically.

ANALOG TO DIGITAL CONVERTOR

This converts an analog input voltage to a digital number. There are four input channels that are available for use and these are designated 1, 2, 3 and 4 corresponding to the BASIC ADVAL channels. The conversion of the voltage on a channel is not instantaneous and in fact takes approximately 10 msec. Normally the computer scans each channel in turn performing conversions automatically and thus each channel is converted every 40 msec.

This state of things can be changed, however, by the programmer. The number of channels used can be reduced so that the scanning is made more rapid and also the start of the conversion on a particular channel can be synchronised to a program operation.

The assembly language programmer uses OSBYTE to carry out these control functions and also to read the analog to digital converter.

OSBYTE with A set to 16 (&10) is used to set the number of
channels to be used. The X register is used to specify the
number of channels X=0 disables all channels, X=1 enables
channel 1, X=2 enables channels 1 and 2, X=3 enables channels
1,2 and 3 and X=4 enables all 4 channels.

OSBYTE 17 (&11) with X set to the channel number will force a
conversion to start on a particular channel. Osbyte 128 (&80)
can be used to see if a conversion is complete and also to
read the value of a complete conversion.

If X is set to 0 on entry to OSBYTE 128 then on exit Y
contains the number of the channel which was last converted.
If X is set to the channel number on entry then the last value
converted on that channel is returned in X and Y as a 16 bit
number (X least significant and Y the most significant). The
conversion is actually only performed to 10 bit accuracy by
the hardware but it is converted to a 16 bit number by the
operating system.

THE PRINTER PORT

This is normally used, of course, for driving parallel
printers and bytes can be written to such printers by writing
them to the printer output buffer using OSBYTE as described
above. It can also be used as an 8 bit digital output port
without the buffer if a parallel printer is not being used.
It appears to the computer as a memory location to which a
byte may be written. The address of the printer port is &FE61
and A may thus be written using STA &FE61. If use of a second
processor is anticipated, however, this method will not work
and instead and OSBYTE call is needed. In this case A is set
to &97 and X to &61,and the character to be written being
placed in Y.

THE USER PORT

The user port is an 8 bit port which may be arranged to be an
input port or an output port or indeed a mixture of the two.
Like the printer port it also appears to the computer as a
memory location, in this case &FE60. Also associated with it

is location &FE62 which controls if the port is input or output. Each bit position in &FE62 corresponds to a bit position in the user port and if a bit in &FE62 is a 1 then the corresponding bit in the user port is an output but if it is a 0 then the bit is an input. Thus to set all the bits of the port as inputs the instructions: LDA #0: STA &FE62 and to set it to all outputs: LDA #&FF: STA &FE62. If the programs have to work using a second processor these are written LDA #&97: LDX #&62: LDY #0: JSR OSBYTE for an input port and LDA #&97: LDX #&62: LDY #&FF: JSR OSBYTE for an output port.

Reading the port consists of reading the memory &FE60 for example LDA &FE60. This will not work if run on a second processor, however, and under these circumstances then the OSBYTE subroutine with A set to &96 and X set to &60 must be used, the value being returned in the Y register. Thus reading the port becomes : LDA #&96: LDX #&60: JSR OSBYTE.

Similarly to write to the port using a second processor we have LDA #&97: LDX #&60: JSR OSBYTE which will write the byte contained in the Y register.

AN EXPERIMENT BOARD

In order to make any significant progress in understanding digital interfacing using the computer some hardware is necessary. Figure 10.1 gives the circuit diagram of a simple electronic experiment board, developed at the University of Salford, and this may be constructed by readers with a little electronics experience. It contains three types of output device connected to the printer port: light emitting diodes so that a visual display of all 8 bits is obtained, a power transistor on bit 0 so that higher power devices such as relays and motors may be driven and also a DIGITAL TO analog converter so that a voltage output of the digital number is obtained. It also contains 8 switches connected to the user port so that digital input to the computer can be obtained.

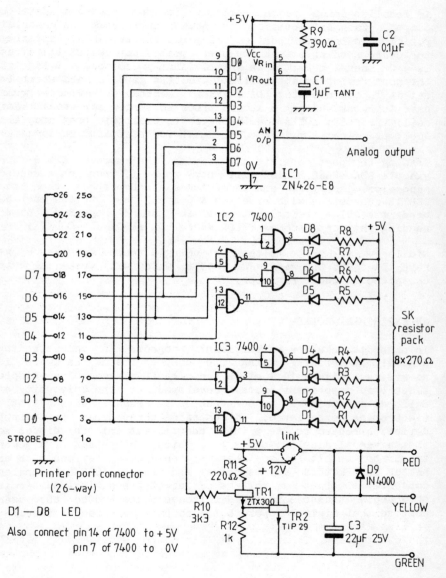

Figure 10.1a

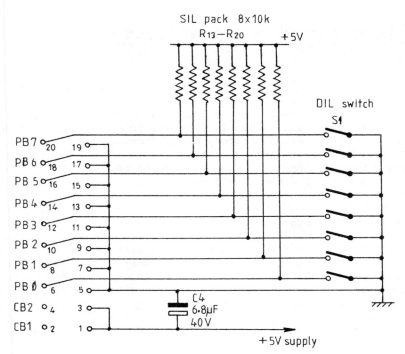

SIL pack 8×10k
$R_{13} - R_{20}$ +5V

DIL switch
S1

PB7 o 20   19 o
PB 6 o 18   17 o
PB 5 o 16   15 o
PB 4 o 14   13 o
PB 3 o 12   11 o
PB 2 o 10   9 o
PB 1 o 8   7 o
PB 0 o 6   5 o
CB2 o 4   3 o
CB1 o 2   1 o

C4
6.8μF
40V

+5V supply

User port connector
(20-way)

Figure 10.1b

The digital to analog converter has a voltage output which is
proportional to the digital number presented to it's input.
It has a maximum output of 2.55 volts which corresponds to the
byte 255 (decimal) and the constant relating output to input
is therefore 0.01 volts per bit.

The design of the circuit board is presented as an example and
readers with some electronic experience will no doubt be able
to modify the design to their own requirements e.g. to extend
the number of power outputs or use different types of inputs
or say a better digital to analog converter.

Three simple programs which use the circuit board will be
given as examples. First the reading of the switches and
using them to control the LEDs, then displaying binary
counting and finally waveform generation using the digital to
analog converter. The first two programs given are in the
form suitable for use with Monitor which should be loaded into
the computer. The programs are entered using the E command
and assembled and run in the usual way.

Switches and Leds

The printer port does not need to be initialised as this is
done by the operating system but the user port needs to be set
up as all inputs. The following program initialises the user
port in lines 10 and 20, reads it in in line 30 and then
transfers the number to the LEDs connected to the printer port
in line 40.

```
                  10    LDA #00
                  20    STA &FE62
                  30    LDA &FE60
                  40    STA &FE61
```

Each time that the program is run using the R command of
Monitor the switches are read and transferred to the LEDs.

Binary Counting

The following binary program counts up in the X register and
after each increment of X the result is transferred to the
LEDs for display. In between each increment the program reads
a character from the keyboard. The character read is not used
as the only purpose of this operation is to slow the program
down for otherwise the changes on the LEDs would be too quick
to be seen. The space bar on the keyboard can be conveniently
used to step through the count which terminates when the
complete binary 8 bit sequence has been performed.

```
10   LDX #0
20   .LOOP
30   STX &FE61
40   JSR &FFE0
50   INX
60   BNE LOOP
```

Waveform Generation

Monitor is not used for this program which relies on an
mixture of BASIC and assembly language to exploit the best
features of each. A data block consisting of 256 bytes is
first set up using BASIC for its power in performing
arithmetic. An assembly language subroutine is then used to
quickly transfer this block repetively to the printer port
where the DAC converts it into a voltage waveform.

```
     NEW
10   DIM BLOCK 256
20   DIM S% 50
30   FOR X = 0 TO 255
40   BLOCK?X = 128 + 127 * SIN (X*PI*2/255)
50   NEXT
60   FOR PASS = 0 TO 2 STEP 2
70   P%=S%
80   [OPT PASS
90   .TFER
100  LDX #0
110  .LOOP
120  LDA BLOCK,X
```

```
130    STA &FE61
140    INX
150    JMP LOOP
160    ]
170    NEXT
180    *KEY 10 OLD |M
190    CALL TFER
```

The lines 30 to 50 set up a sine function in the store area labelled BLOCK. This is scaled and offset so that 1 complete cycle fits into the data block and the amplitude goes between 0 and 255.

Of course these lines may be modified to place any desired function in the data block so that we can generate waveforms of an arbitrary shape.

The assembly language TFER contains an infinite loop that continually repeats, taking bytes from BLOCK in sequence and transfering them to the printer output port. The BREAK key must therefore be used to leave the program.

If you have access to an oscilloscope you can view the resulting waveform which ideally should be a sine shape. It is not, however, completely sinusoidal in shape. Obviously it contains small steps due to the limited way in which the 8 bit output port can represent quantities but also if you look carefully, an occasional larger step or disturbance can be viewed on the waveform. This is due to the interrupt system of the computer as every so often an interrupt is generated and this causes the running of the user's program to be suspended while the operating system looks after some task. In the program above this effectively means that instead of the waveform moving on to the next value at the appropriate time it is held constant giving the effect of a disturbance in the otherwise regular output sequence.

The solution to the problem is to switch off the interrupt servicing, by the use of the SEI instruction which sets the I (interrupt disable flag) to a 1 and inhibits the maskable interrupts. This can be entered in the above program by say 95 SEI. When the BREAK key is pressed to leave the infinite loop the flag will be reset and the interrupts will be re-enabled.

The use of 256 data items to control the waveform gives quite
a smooth approximation to the sine curve but reduces the
maximum frequency that can be obtained. A complete loop
through all the values takes approximately 2 milliseconds and
this is a frequency of only 500 Hertz (cycles per second). If
fewer data items are used for one repetition of the waveform
then the steps in the waveform are more coarse but the speed
is improved.

VECTORS

The operating system uses many subroutines in carrying out its
operations and we have already seen a selection of these e.g.
OSWRCH, OSFILE etc. When a program wants to call, say, OSWRCH
the instruction JSR &FFEE is used.   The code at this address
&FFEE causes a JMP (&20E) instruction to be carried out. The
locations &20E and &20F are jointly known as a VECTOR and
contain the 16 bit address of the code back in the operating
system that will write a character to the screen. This is a
very roundabout method of getting access to the subroutine.
We have first performed a JSR &FFEE (&FFEE is in the ROM),
which has then carried out JMP (&20E) (&20E is of course in
the RAM) and this has caused a jump back into the ROM.

The whole point of the exercise is that the call is indirected
through a pair of RAM locations.   The user can if needed
change these locations to change the effect of the standard
operating system subroutine. A list of operating system
routines and associated vectors is given on p.512 of the USER
GUIDE.

To intercept an operating system routine in this way the user
replaces the contents of the vector by the address of the
routine which is to be obeyed instead of the standard one. At
the end of the user's routine several different actions are
possible. If the new routine is to completely replace the one
from operating system the RTS instruction may be given (RTI if
an interrupt routine see later). Alternatively if the user's
routine is to be carried out as well as the original operating
system routine then a jump must be made to the address

originally contained in the vector. This of course implies
saving the original contents of the vector so that the jump to
the operating system routine can be made.

Vectors are also widely used by the interrupt system and when
interrupts occur the calls to the subroutines which service
the subroutine are made through vectors.

INTERRUPTS

The CPU of the computer is a very busy device as it has to
look after many things at the same time. These include
controlling the discs, printer, reading the keyboard and other
tasks. All of this at the same time as running the user's
BASIC or assembly language programs. The CPU cannot actually
do more than one thing at once, however, and it has to share
itself between all the above, spending some time doing each.
There are many ways of making this sort of thing happen,
particularly on large computers, but here we shall concentrate
on the method used on the BBC microcomputer.

As most of the above activities only require attention from
time to time the computer runs the users program as its main
activity but stops running it when one of the other tasks
requires attention and resumes running it when the task has
received the necessary service from the CPU. This type of
organisation is known as an INTERRUPT system as the tasks
requiring occasional attention interrupt the running of the
main program. As each interrupt occurs the users program is
stopped and the flags and program counter address are saved on
the stack. The computer then runs a subroutine called an
interrupt service routine for the interrupting task. At the
finish of this a return to the main program is made using the
information saved on the stack.

Non Maskable Interrupts

There are three kinds of interrupts on the BBC microcomputer
only two of which are available to the user. The type of
interrupt which cannot be used is the NON MASKABLE INTERRUPT
as it is reserved for certain important system functions.

This type of interrupt is caused by an electronic input to the
CPU input NMI and a logic signal on this always causes an
interrupt to occur. There is no way that the users program
can stop this occurring hence the name NON MASKABLE and these
interrupts are always used for tasks that must receive
immediate attention e.g. the disc or ECONET controllers.

Maskable Interrupts

The second type of interrupt is also caused by electronic
inputs to the CPU but has the feature that the interrupts may
be switched on or off under control of the users program using
the I flag. The third type of interrupt is the software break
caused by the BRK instruction. This simulates the second type
of interrupt described above, the difference being that the B
flag is set to 1 when this type of interrupt occurs.

Many maskable interrupts may be connected to the CPU and the
interrupt software must be able to determine which one caused
a particular interrupt and then to take the appropriate
action. On the BBC computer the operating system fortunately
helps a little in this task as it checks first to see if one
of its own devices caused the interrupt and if this is the
case it deals with it, via the vector &204. Some of these
interrupts provide information which is needed by the user and
the EVENT system can then be used. However, if the operating
system does not recognise the source of the interrupt it
provides the user with a method of incorporating specialised
software to service the interrupt, via the vector &206.

EVENTS

Certain conditions that occur during the standard interrupt
handling by the operating system may be of interest to the
user and provision is made for this.   There are ten such
conditions, known as EVENTS and numbered 0 to 9, and the
operating system allows the user to incorporate subroutines
which are called when the event occurs. If the user wishes
this to occur the event is enabled using OSBYTE with A set to
14 (&E) and X set to the event number that is to be enabled.
The user places the address of subroutine that is to be called

in the vector &220, &221 and when the event occurs the
operating system then calls the user's subroutine. Events are
disabled OSBYTE with A set to 13 with the X register set to
the number of the event to be disabled.

The user's subroutine is entered with the A register set to
the number of the event responsible for the call. The X and Y
register contents on entry depend on the particular event.
The operating system takes all the responsibility for looking
after the interrupts so the subroutine should not enable
interrupts and should finish, just as any other subroutine,
with the RTS instruction.

The events will now be outlined in turn and a simple example
showing the use of events is given for event number 2, the
keyboard interrupt.

The buffers are handled by events 0 and 1. Event 0 occurs when
a buffer has become empty and event 1 when a buffer has become
full. On entry to the user's subroutine the X register
contains a number which describes the buffer in question using
the numbers given on page 208 .

Event number 2 occurs each time that a key is pressed on the
keyboard. A simple example of the use of this might be to
count the number of key presses that are made, storing the
result in say &70 and &71.

```
                   NEW
        10    CNT=&70: EVECTOLD=&80
        20    OSBYTE=&FFF4
        30    EVECT=&220
        40    DIM S% 100
        50    FOR PASS = 0 TO 2 STEP 2
        60    P%=S%
        70    [OPT PASS
        80    .ROUT PHP
        90    INC CNT : BNE SKIP
       100    INC CNT+1
       110    .SKIP
       120    PLP: RTS
       130    .PROG
       140    LDA EVECT: STA EVECTOLD
```

```
150    LDA EVECT+1: STA EVECTOLD+1
160    LDA #ROUT MOD &100: STA EVECT
170    LDA #ROUT DIV &100: STA EVECT+1
180    LDA #14: LDX #2: JSR OSBYTE
190    LDA #0: STA CNT: STA CNT+1
200    STA CNT+2: STA CNT+3
210    RTS
220    .normal
230    LDA #13: LDX #2: JSR OSBYTE
240    LDA EVECTOLD: STA EVECT
250    LDA EVECTOLD+1: STA EVECT+1
260    RTS: ]
270    NEXT
280    CALL PROG
```

The subroutine for keeping the count is in lines 80 to 120 and just increments the contents of the double byte counter. Notice that it preserves the CPU status register by pushing it on the stack and recalling it. The address of ROUT is placed into the contents of &220 in lines 160 and 170 and then event number 2 is enabled using OSBYTE with A set to 14 in line 180. The count, and also the next two bytes, are initialised to 0 in 190 in lines 170 and 200. This is so that the ! operator can be conveniently used from BASIC to print the contents of the count.

Once this program has run all future use of keys will be counted, even while running BASIC. To examine this type P.!&70 and then press the RETURN key. This sequence itself contains 7 key presses and so will add 7 to the number contained.

When the facility is not required CALL normal will disable the event and restore the vector &220 to its initial value. Alternatively pressing the BREAK key will reset the entire event system to normal.

Event 3 is used with the analog to digital converter. When a conversion is complete this event occurs.

Event 4 occurs when the synchronising pulse occurs in the screen control circuits. It provides a more complex alternative to OSBYTE 19 for the synchronising of animation in graphics. When OSBYTE 19 is used quite a lot of CPU time is

wasted just waiting for the synchronisation pulse to occur.
It is possible to restructure programs so that screen writing
occurs under the control of the event and the main program is
then free to use the time that would have been spent waiting.

Event 5 is used in conjunction with the interval timer. This
has already partly been described in chapter 8. The interval
timer is incremented every hundredth of a second and maintains
a 5 byte count in binary. When it overflows to 0 event 5 is
caused. To set a delay of say 10 seconds the timer is loaded
with the 5 byte 2s complement of - 10 * 100. The following
program will cause a beep to be made every 10 seconds.

The timer is set by the OSWORD subroutine using a 5 byte data
block and this is done by the subroutine SET. Lines 50 to 60
set up the data block to the required value using BASIC. The
address of ROUT is loaded into &220, &221 in lines 260 and 270
and the event is enabled in line 280. The counter is
incremented every hundredth of a second and overflow occurs
after 10 seconds. The subroutine ROUT is then obeyed and this
first makes a note on the sound generator by sending 7 to the
OSWRCH routine (equivalent to VDU7 in BASIC) and then the
timer is again set up to a delay of 10 seconds in line 130.

```
          NEW
   10     OSBYTE=&FFF4: OSWRCH=&FFEE:
   20     OSWORD=&FFF1
   30     EVECT=&220: EVECTOLD=&70
   40     DIM BLOCK 5, S% 100
   50     !BLOCK=-1000
   60     BLOCK?4=&FF
   70     FOR PASS = 0 TO 2 STEP 2
   80     S%=P%
   90     [OPT PASS
  100     .ROUT: PHP: PHA:
  110     TXA: PHA: TYA PHA
  120     LDA #7: JSR OSWRCH
  130     JSR SET
  140     PLA: TAY: PLA: TAX
  150     PLA: PLP
  160     RTS
  170     .SET
  180     LDX #BLOCK MOD &100
```

```
190    LDY #BLOCK DIV &100
200    LDA #4: JSR OSWORD
210    RTS
220    .PROG
230    LDA EVECT: STA EVECTOLD
240    LDA EVECT+1: STA EVECTOLD+1
250    JSR SET
260    LDA #ROUT MOD &100: STA EVECT
270    LDA #ROUT DIV &100: STA EVECT+1
280    LDA #14: LDX #5: JSR OSBYTE
290    RTS
300    .normal
310    LDA #13: LDA #5: JSR OSBYTE
320    LDA EVECTOLD: STA EVECT
330    LDA EVECTOLD+1: STA EVECT+1
340    RTS: ]
350    NEXT
360    CALL PROG
```

Normal operation can be restored by a CALL normal instruction
which disables the event and resets the vector to its original
value.

Event 6 is used to detect if the ESCAPE key is pressed.

Event 7 is used to detect errors when the RS423 receiver is
being used.

Event 8 is used to detect errors when a network error occurs.

Event 9 is provided so that the event system can be extended
to handle events generated by the user's program. The details
of how to do this have not been documented by ACORN but some
the use of the operating system routine OSEVEN (&FFBF) has
been described in ref 2. Briefly, OSEVEN will generate an
event when called, the event number generated being specified
by Y on entry.

Writing Your Own Interrupt Software

Writing software to deal with interrupts is not an easy task
in the author's experience.   Much detailed knowledge of the

operation of the electronic device causing the interrupt is
needed and the problem should only be tackled if you have the
data sheets of the devices you intend to use and also have
acquired quite a lot of assembly language proficiency.

Events provide an easy method of using the interrupts that are
recognised by the operating system. If an interrupt is not
recognised by the operating system, however, an indirect jump
to locations &206, &207 is made and the user must store the
address of a program to deal with the interrupt in &206, &207.

To show the reader a typical example the use of a timer in the
user VIA will be discussed. The VIA (versatile interface
adapter) is used for the printer and user ports described
above but it also contains two 16 bit timers, a serial data
shifter and powerful interrupt facilities linked to all the
interfaces in the device.   The device is very complex in
operation and is really beyond the scope of the present text
but the operation of one of the timers will be described in
simplified terms for the purposes of illustrating the
interrupts.

The timer in question is known as Timer 1 and it is a 16 bit
timer. The timer has several modes of operation and the mode
which we require is that of counting the system clock,
generating interrupts every time an overflow occurs. To set
the timer in this mode and to enable the interrupt capability
we must write &C0 to a register in the VIA known as ACR and
&C0 to a register knowm as IER. The timer itself is loaded in
two bytes, the lower byte, known as T1C-L followed by the
higher byte, known as T1C-H. The lower order byte is loaded in
first and then, when the higher byte is loaded in, the timer
starts to count. The timer counts the system clock until
overflow occurs and then an interrupt is generated.   The
operating system detects this and, as the timer is not
recognised by the operating system, a jump is made to the
contents of &206, &207, which contains the address of the
section of program which is to deal with the interrupt.

The user's subroutine must reset the interrupt flag register
of the VIA, which it does by performing a read of T1C-L , then
it must perform the operation which the user requires and jump
back to the correct point in the operating system.   The

address of this point is obtained from &206,&207 before these
locations are modified.

The following shows the program:

```
          NEW
    10    IVECT=&206
    20    VIA=&FE60
    30    ACR=VIA+11
    40    IER=VIA+&E
    50    T1CL=VIA+4
    60    T1CH=VIA+5
    70    OSWRCH=&FFEE
    80    DIM S% 100
    90    FOR PASS = 0 TO 2 STEP 2
   100    P%=S%
   110    [OPT PASS
   120    .PROG
   130    LDA IVECT: STA RTN
   140    LDA IVECT+1: STA RTN+1: SEI
   150    LDA #II MOD &100: STA IVECT
   160    LDA #II DIV &100: STA IVECT+1: CLI
   170    LDA #&CO: STA ACR
   180    LDA #&CO: STA IER
   190    LDA #&FF: STA T1CL
   200    LDA #&FF: STA T1CH: CLI
   210    .LOOP: JMP LOOP
   220    .II
   230    LDA T1CL
   240    LDA #ASC"I"
   250    JSR OSWRCH
   260    JMP (RTN)
   270    .RTN
   280    NOP: NOP
   290    ]
   300    NEXT
   320    CALL PROG
```

The VIA registers are located in the memory of the computer
and the addresses are given in lines 20 to 60. The first task
is to save the contents of IVECT (&206) as this is the address
which will later be used to return to the operating system.
This is saved starting at address RTN in lines 130, 140. Next

the address of the user's interrupt program II is put into
IVECT in lines 150, 160. The interrupt system is disabled to
prevent any interrupt being generated until the set up
procedure is finished. Lines 170 to 200 set up the registers
in the VIA so that it will generate an interrupt every &FFFF
machine cycles and the program terminates in an infinite loop
in line 210.

The interrupt software begins at II in line 220 and the
interrupt structure of the VIA is reset by reading the T1C-L
register.

This is typical of way that electronic interface devices are
used with interrupts. They generate an interrupt to the
computer using a flag internal to themselves and this flag
remains set until it is subsequently cleared by the interrupt
software. If it is not cleared the CPU will be continuously
interrupted.

The simple task of writing a letter I on the screen is then
carried out to illustrate that an interrupt has occurred. The
return to the operating system is the through the indirect
jump JMP (RTN) in line 260.

Each time that the interrupt occurs an I is printed on the
screen. The BREAK key is needed to get back to BASIC.

Fortunately the built in software is very adequate for the
majority of assembly language applications and the reader will
only need to consider writing the above type of interrupt
software when using the more advanced features of the user VIA
or when adding extra interrupt driven circuits to the
computer.

If the user has an application that needs an interrupt to be
handled in the maximum possible time the normal interrupt
handling process can be overridden by using the IRQ1 vector
(&204,5) instead of IRQ2 (&206,7). In this case <u>ALL</u> the
interrupts from whatever source will have to be dealt with.
This is definately not for the beginner!

Software Interrupts

The instruction BRK is used to cause a software interrupt to occur. This instruction causes an interrupt which the operating system recognises and treats in a rather special way due to the fact that BASIC uses this instruction to generate its error messages. In the BASIC interpreter the BRK instruction is followed by a byte containing a fault number and also the text of an error message. On encountering a BRK instruction the operating system sets the address of the fault number into store &FD and &FE and then performs an indirect jump to location &202, &203 which contains the address of a subroutine to print the error number and error message.

This system can be used in two ways. Firstly the user can take advantage of the existing system to generate new error numbers and error messages. This is described in the user manual p.446. Alternatively the existing sytem may be replaced by storing the address of the user's own subroutine in &202.

11

Lists and Searches

Lists are an essential part of much important software and examples which the reader may be familiar with include assemblers and disassemblers, compilers and interpreters, word processors, file handling and spread sheets. All these rely quite heavily on the use and manipulation of lists.

Probably the simplest type of list is a data structure consisting of a number of bytes, stored one after the other in the memory and we have, in fact, already met this type of simple list described in the book. For example in graphics, the screen and writing of objects could be regarded in terms of lists and the moving of data blocks may be looked at as copying lists. More complex types of lists are also possible involving items of more than one byte, possibly of varying length, and we can thus have lists of say addresses or lists of strings or numbers. It is even possible to have lists composed of items which are themselves lists or addresses of lists.

The basic operations with all lists are: the addition of items, the removal of items, searching the list to see if a particular item is present and sorting the list into some order.

These operations could be discussed in general terms, not

connected with any particular application but such abstract
considerations are more the province of text books on computer
science and in order to make things a little more interesting
the author has chosen to illustrate the use of lists by
describing the design of a simple word processor. This, of
course, also has the advantage that it gives a good start to
readers who want to write their own more advanced word
processor. The program is described in stages but for those
readers who do not want to type in the quite long programs
involved the tape contains the final version of the program
under the file name "WORD".

Pointers and Separators

In handling a list we need some method of referring to items
in the list and of knowing where the list begins and ends. A
common method is to use 16 bit pointers which contain the
relevant addresses of places in the list and we could
typically have pointers for several functions associated with
the list. The use of a 16 bit address or pointer is one way
of determining the end of a particular item in the list, or
indeed the end of the list itself, but another way is to use a
unique piece of data called a terminator to mark the end of an
item or the list. We have already met this in the discussions
of strings which are terminated with the code &D.

Terminators are often useful where the items are of variable
length or the list is of variable length.

It is also quite common for information on the length of a
list to be included as say the first item in the list.

SIMPLE WORD PROCESSOR

A word processor is a program which can be used to input and
edit text using the computer. Text may be regarded in terms
of lists in various ways depending on what is thought of as
the basic item. This could be taken at almost any level:
book, chapter, page, paragraph, sentence etc down to character
and text could be thought of as lists of any of these. For
the present we shall take the simplest alternative and

consider text to be a list of characters, a terminator being
used to fix the end of the text. The code &80 being chosen as
the terminator as it does not correspond to any of the normal
ASCII characters and thus it can be used to uniquely mark the
end of text. The first item in the list is the first
character and the list contains characters in order as they
are normally written from left to right etc.

The basic operations are inserting and deleting characters at
various positions in the list. A 16 bit zero-page pointer can
be used to hold the current position in the list and this is
known as CUR. The name has been chosen because when the text
is displayed on the screen the flashing CURSOR will be used to
display its position.

The author is a believer in the use of subroutines to
structure complex assembly language programs so some simple
subroutines will be introduced first. These are LCUR, which
decrements CUR by 1 thus moving the cursor left and RCUR,
which increments CUR by 1 thus moving the cursor right.
Another pointer called TXTPNT will be used and the subroutine
PNTINC increments this pointer so that it will point to the
next item.

```
100    .LCUR
110    LDA CUR: SEC: SBC #1: STA CUR
120    BCS LC1: DEC CUR+1
130    .LC1: RTS
140    .RCUR
150    LDA CUR: CLC: ADC#1: STA CUR
160    BCC RC1: INC CUR+1
170    .RC1: RTS
180    .PNTINC
190    LDA TXTPNT: CLC: ADC #1: STA TXTPNT
200    BCC PN1: INC TXTPNT+1
210    .PN1: RTS
```

To insert a character at position CUR all the characters
between CUR and the end of text must be moved up one place in
the list and the character inserted into the hole created.

The following subroutine shows this using CUR to contain the
address at which the byte is to be inserted into the list and

the X register contains the byte to be inserted. The contents
of the pointer needs to be changed during the course of the
subroutine so to preserve the value of CUR it is first copied
into another pointer TXTPNT which is used to carry out the
shifting around of the bytes. The byte currently occupying
the place at which the insert is to be made is first obtained
in line 270 and pushed onto the stack for temporary storage.
Then the byte is obtained from the X register and put into the
list in line 280. Next comes the test to see if the byte
removed was the end of text terminator and if it is a branch
is made to the label INESC. If it is not, the byte that was
removed is placed into the X register and the pointer TXTPNT
is incremented in line 310. A jump is then made back to the
label INLOOP and in this way each byte is moved up a position
in the list until the end of text is reached when the branch
to INESC is made. Then the end of text is put at the end of
the file in 340 and then the cursor incremented by 1 so that
CUR points to the byte inserted.

```
220    .INCHR
230    LDA CUR: STA TXTPNT
240    LDA CUR+1: STA TXTPNT+1
250    .INLOOP
260    LDY #0
270    LDA (TXTPNT),Y: PHA
280    TXA: STA (TXTPNT),Y
290    PLA: CMP #&80: BEQ INESC
300    TAX
310    JSR PNTINC
320    JMP INLOOP
330    .INESC
340    LDY #1: STA (TXTPNT),Y
350    JSR RCUR
360    RTS
```

When inserting characters using this subroutine two simple
modifications help with the display of text on the screen.
Imagine the screen with text written on it and the flashing
cursor underneath the point where the character is to be
inserted. As the character is inserted we would like all the
text to the right of the cursor to move right one place. At
line 280 the A register contains exactly the required sequence
of characters as the loop is repetitivly obeyed and thus the

inclusion of a line to print A at this point will help with
the control of the screen display when inserting.

285   JSR OSASCI

The subroutine OSASCI (&FFE3) is similar to OSWRCH but it
automatically inserts newlines every time that it prints the
RETURN (&D) character.

Line 285 moves the screen cursor from underneath the character
position. It is restored by the subroutine WRCUR, covered a
little later in the text, and a jump to this may be made at
the end of the subroutine.

358   JSR WRCUR

The second modification is to make the subroutine rewrite the
entire text to the screen whenever an end of line &D character
is inserted.   This is a simple way of ensuring that the
displayed text always reflects the characters stored in the
list.

This is done by adding the following lines

```
245    TXA: PHA
355    PLA: CMP #&D: BNE IN1
356    JSR WRTEXT
357    .IN1
```

WRTEXT is the subroutine which will write the entire list to
the screen.

To delete a character the byte pointed to by CUR is removed
from the list and all the bytes up until the end of text are
moved down one place in the list.   The following subroutine
shows the basic method.

```
370    .DELCHR
380    LDA CUR: STA TXTPNT
390    LDA CUR+1: STA TXTPNT+1
400    .DLOOP
410    LDY #1: LDA (TXTPNT),Y
420    DEY: STA (TXTPNT),Y
```

```
430    CMP #&80: BEQ DESC
440    JSR PNTINC
450    JMP DLOOP
460    .DESC
470    RTS
```

Again the cursor is copied into TXTPNT so that its value is preserved and a loop is used to copy each byte down a place in the list.

Just as the insert subroutine was modified to help with the display of text DELCHR may also write text. As each character is moved down one place it can be written to the correct place on the screen. The A register contains the character following line 430 and we can thus add, say,

```
435    JSR OSASCI
```

If a byte has been deleted and all the text, from the cursor to the end, moved one place left then the byte at the end of the text will actually appear twice on the screen. Once in its old position and again in the new postion. To prevent this it can be overwritten with a space.

```
463    LDA #ASC" ": JSR OSWRCH
```

and to reposition the cursor at the end of the subroutine

```
469    JSR WRCUR
```

As done previously when inserting, a test was made for the end of line character, the same thing is done when deleting and if this character is deleted from the list then the entire screen contents are written to the screen. The following lines are added to carry this out.

```
395    LDY #0: LDA (CUR),Y:PHA
465    PLA: CMP #&D: BNE DD1
466    JSR WRTEXT
467    .DD1
```

As this subroutine writes text to the screen there is a possibility that when a newline character is written that a

stray character is left at the end of the line. The following
additions to the program ensure that this does not occur by
writing a blank space before the newline.

```
431   CMP #&D: BNE DD2
432   LDA #ASC" ":JSR OSWRCH
433   LDA #&D
434   .DD2
```

We next come to the subroutine which will write the entire
text to the screen.

```
500   .WRTEXT
510   JSR SETPNT
520   LDA #&C: JSR OSWRCH
530   LDY#0
540   .WRLOOP
550   LDA (TXTPNT),Y: CMP #&80
560   BEQ WRESC
570   JSR OSASCI
580   JSR PNTINC
590   JMP WRLOOP
600   .WRESC
610   RTS
620   .SETPNT
630   LDA #TEXT MOD &100: STA TXTPNT
640   LDA #TEXT DIV &100: STA TXTPNT+1
650   RTS
```

SETPNT is a subroutine which sets TXTPNT to the start of the
text. The screen is cleared in 520 and then a program loop is
used to write each character in turn until the end of text
terminator is reached. The character is written to the screen
in line 570 by the operating system routine OSASCI which also
expands RETURN characters so that a newline is printed.

Cursor

The screen cursor is controlled by sending codes to the
operating system screen writing subroutines OSWRCH and OSASCI.
The code &1E will home the cursor to the top left, &9 will
move the cursor right one place, &8 will move it left a

place. The code &D moves the cursor to the beginning of a
line and &A moves it down a line.

The cursor is written to the correct place on the screen by
first homing it to the top left and then working through the
list issuing commands to the operating system depending on the
characters encountered. If a normal character is found then
the cursor is advanced a position (LDA #9: JSR OSASCI) but if
the end of line character &D is found then the cursor is moved
to the start of a newline by sending &D to OSASCI.

```
700     .WRCUR
710     LDA #&1E: JSR OSWRCH
720     JSR SETPNT
730     .CRLOOP
740     LDA CUR+1: CMP TXTPNT+1
750     BNE CR1
760     LDA CUR: CMP TXTPNT: BEQ ESCUR
770     .CR1
780     LDY #0: LDA (TXTPNT),Y
790     CMP #&D: BEQ CR2
800     LDA #9
810     .CR2
820     JSR OSASCI
830     JSR PNTINC
840     JMP CRLOOP
850     .ESCUR
860     RTS
```

Line 710 homes the cursor to the top left of the screen and
SETPNT in the following line sets TXTPNT to the start of the
text. A check is then made to see if we have reached the item
in the list pointed to by CUR and if so then an exit is made.
If not the item is checked to see if it is the end of line
code and the cursor is either advanced a character or to the
start of a newline as needed.

Command Loop

We need to control the subroutines described to insert, delete
and display text in a suitable fashion. The following system
of control will be used: a character is read from the keyboard

and is checked to see if it is one of three control
characters, the DELETE key, the ← key or the → key. If it is
one of these then a subroutine is called to delete a character
or move the cursor left or right. If the character is not one
of the three control characters then it is inserted into the
text at the current cursor position.

The use of the cursor editing keys to produce ASCII codes must
first be enabled using the OSBYTE equivalent of *FX 4,1 and
this and the setting up of the initial empty list are done in
the following subroutine.

```
1000    .INIT CLD
1010    LDA #TEXT MOD &100: STA CUR
1020    LDA #TEXT DIV &100: STA CUR+1
1030    LDA #&80: LDY #0
1040    STA (CUR),Y
1050    LDA #4: LDX #1: JSR OSBYTE
1060    RTS
```

The command loop of the word processor is given in the section
of program beginning CMD.

Lines 1110 to 1130 perform the initialisation and then the
main command loop begins with a character being read from the
keyboard.

The subroutines RIGHT and LEFT increment and decrement the
cursor pointer using RCUR and LCUR and also move the visible
screen cursor. This is mostly done using the standard cursor
moving codes and OSWRCH as described above but if the byte
pointed to is a &D code corresponding to a newline then the
WRCUR subroutine is called as this correctly places the
cursor, taking account of the newline characters.

```
1100    .CMD
1110    JSR INIT
1120    JSR WRTEXT
1130    JSR WRCUR
1140    .CMDLP
1150    JSR OSWRDCH
1160    CMP #&88: BNE CM1
1170    JSR LEFT: JMP CMDLP
```

```
1180    .CM1
1190    CMP #&89: BNE CM2
1200    JSR RIGHT: JMP CMDLP
1210    .CM2
1220    CMP #&7F: BNE CM3
1230    JSR DELCHR: JMP CMDLP
1240    .CM3
1250    TAX: JSR INCHR
1260    JMP CMDLP
```

Sometimes in this sort of program we would like to be able to
return to BASIC. This can be done using the ESCAPE key.   The
command loop can check if ESCAPE has been pressed and if this
is so then the operating system is informed using OSBYTE &7E,
the ESCAPE acknowledge function. A further call to OSBYTE 4,0
will reset the functions of the cursor control keys to normal
and a return may then be made to BASIC. In fact the last two
functions may be combined with the instruction JMP OSBYTE,
(rather than the sequence JSR OSBYTE: RTS). The required
program lines are:

```
1152   CMP #&1B: BNE NOESC
1154   LDA #&7E: JSR OSBYTE
1156   LDA #4: LDX #0: JSR OSBYTE
1158   JMP OSBYTE
1159   .NOESC
```

The subroutine for moving the both CUR and the screen cursor
left is called LEFT and is as follows

```
1300    .LEFT
1310    JSR LCUR
1320    LDA #8: JSR OSWRCH
1330    LDY #0: LDA (CUR),Y
1340    CMP #&D: BNE LFT1
1350    JSR WRCUR
1360    .LFT1 RTS
```

In line 1310 the subroutine LCUR decrements CUR and then the
screen cursor is moved left by line 1320. If CUR now points to
a newline character then WRCUR is called in line 1350.

A simple test can be added to ensure that the cursor is not
AAL-I

moved to before the start of the text area.

```
1301    LDA CUR: CMP #TEXT MOD &100
1302    BNE LFT2
1303    LDA CUR+1: CMP #TEXT DIV &100
1304    BEQ RT1
1306    .LFT2
```

The subroutine RIGHT moves both CUR and the screen pointer right.

```
1400    .RIGHT
1410    LDY #0: LDA (CUR),Y
1415    CMP #&80: BEQ RT1: PHA
1420    JSR RCUR
1430    LDA #9: JSR OSWRCH
1440    PLA: CMP #&D
1450    BNE RT1
1460    JSR WRCUR
1470    .RT1 RTS
```

The character pointed to on entry is first obtained and checked to see if it is the end of text marker &80. If it is then an exit from the subroutine is made. If it is not then it is pushed on the stack and then CUR is incremented and the screen cursor moved right in 1420, 1430. The byte put on the stack is then recalled and if it was a newline then the WRCUR subroutine is called to correctly locate the screen cursor. The cursor is prevented from moving beyond end of the text in line 1415.

To complete the word processor a few extra program lines are needed:

```
  10    DIM TEXT 3000,WPRO 1000
  20    OSWRCH=&FFEE: OSRDCH=&FFE0
  30    OSASCI=&FFE3: OSBYTE=&FFF4
  40    TXTPNT=&70: CUR=&72
  50    FOR PASS = 0 TO 2 STEP 2
  60    P%=WPRO
  70    [OPT PASS
2000    ]
2010    NEXT
```

2020   CALL CMD

Line 10 reserves 3000 bytes to hold the text.   This is more
than adequate as the word processor really is suitable in this
simple form for text up to 1 screen full (max 80 x 32=2560).

The complete program, including the additions described in the
next section, is listed in APPENDIX E and is also included on
the tape as a program called WORD.

SEARCHES

The basic skeleton of a word processor can be built upon in
all sorts of ways for specific requirements. To illustrate
the searching of lists in the forward and backwards directions
the obvious modification to allow the use of the two unused
cursor control keys will be described. The ↓ key has the
ASCII code &8A and this will be used to search the text from
the current cursor position to the end of text for the next
end of line character. The CUR pointer will be moved to this
position.

The following subroutine will search the text from the current
cursor position comparing each character with the X register
and also checking to see of the end of text has been reached.

```
1500    .SRCHR
1510    LDY #0
1520    .SRLP
1530    LDA (CUR),Y: CMP #&80: BEQ SRR1
1540    JSR RCUR
1550    TXA: CMP (CUR),Y
1560    BNE SRLP
1570    .SRR1
1580    JSR WRCUR: RTS
```

Line 1530 checks for the end of text and if it has been
reached a branch is made to the end of the subroutine. The
cursor is then moved right a place and the X register compared
with the current character.   If a match is obtained then an
exit is made from the subroutine but if there is no match the
loop is repeated.

Similarly a backwards search can be made as shown in the
following subroutine. The command is initiated by the ↑ key
code &8B.

```
1600    .SRCHL
1610    LDY #0
1620    .SLLP
1630    LDA #TEXT MOD &100
1640    CMP CUR: BNE SLL1
1650    LDA #TEXT DIV &100
1660    CMP CUR+1: BEQ SLL2
1670    .SLL1
1680    JSR LCUR
1690    TXA: CMP (CUR),Y
1700    BNE SLLP
1710    .SLL2
1720    JSR WRCUR: RTS
```

Lines 1630 to 1660 check to see if the cursor is already
pointing to the start of the text and if it is an exit is made
from the subroutine. If it is not the cursor is moved left
one place in 1680 and then the contents of the X register are
compared with the current character. A match between the two
finishes the subroutine, a mismatch causes the loop to be
repeated.

The two new commands to search up and down the text may be
added to the command loop by the following lines:

```
1241    CMP #&8A: BNE CM4
1242    LDX #&D: JSR SRCHR
1243    JMP CMDLP
1244    .CM4
1245    CMP #&8B: BNE CM5
1246    LDX #&D: JSR SRCHL
1247    JMP CMDLP
1248    .CM5
```

The searching subroutines provide a powerful method of
extending the word processor. For example, as well as
searching for the end of line character we can also search for
the end of a word (&20 space character) and for given

characters in the text.

Readers looking for some fairly ambitious project on which to
extend their experience might well consider taking this simple
word processor and extend it in various ways.   Some possible
improvements might include adding a printer output (this is
not too difficult just write &2 to OSWRCH to enable the
printer and &3 to disable it), storing and recalling the text
in files (see section on files from assembly language),
handling more   than one screenfull of text (needs more
sophisticated versions of the WRTEXT and insertion and
deletion of characters).

LINKED LISTS

The simple lists studied so far are organised so that items
follow each other in the memory. This is fine if all the
items are the same length and we can set aside a fixed length
of store to contain a given list.   In more complex
applications, however, the items may be of variable length and
in addition the list may have to be stored in several parts of
the memory.

The linked list is one solution to these types of problems.
Each item contains a pointer which indicates where the next
item may be found.   An example which will no doubt be of
interest is the storage of BASIC programs in the   BBC
microcomputer. These are stored as a linked list with each
item in the program being a program line. The item starts
with the RETURN code &D and then follows two bytes which are
the line number in binary, the most significant byte first
followed by the least significant byte. The next byte in the
list contains the link information and it contains a number
which is added to the start address of the item to get the
start of the next item in the list. The rest of the item
contains the actual BASIC program line and consists of ASCII
characters, BASIC tokens and numbers in a special format (for
GOTO and GOSUB instructions).   A BASIC program then consists
of a list of these items terminated with a special item which
is a line with a line number whose first byte is has its most
significant bit set to 1 e.g. &FF or &80.

BASIC uses a single byte for the link and this restricts the distance between the start of items. Linked lists commonly use two bytes for the link information and this means that the next item may be anywhere in the memory.

SORTING A LIST

A common requirement with lists is that they need to be sorted into some specified order. This could be numerical order, chronological order, alphabetical order etc., depending on the list being sorted. A problem with sorting is that even simple sorts require a large number of comparisons to be made and if a long list is to be sorted it can take a very long time using a high level language such as BASIC. This indicates that it is an area of programming where the use of assembly language can give real advantages in terms of speed of operation, although of course it is more difficult to program.

A popular method of sorting is a technique known as the BUBBLE SORT which goes as follows. We first start at the beginning of the list and compare the first two items. If they are in the right order then they are left alone but if the order is wrong then they are swapped over. We next move along the list a position and this time compare the second and third items. If they are in the right order they are left alone but again they are swapped over if the order is wrong. All the list is operated on in this way and at the end of a pass some of the incorrect ordering will have been rectified but not all. Another pass through this revised list will improve the order still further and the process can be repeated as many times as necessary until the list finally settles in the right order. This point is recognised when a pass through the list results in no swaps between items when they are being compared.

An example will be given in sorting the list of numbers: 7, 2, 1, 9, 3 into numerical order, from smallest to greatest. On the first pass through the list we start by comparing 7 and 2, these are in the wrong order and so they are swapped to get: 2, 7, 1, 9, 3. Moving along the list a position we compare 7 and 1 and again swap to get: 2, 1, 7, 9, 3. We next compare 7 and 9 but this time they are in the right order and so the list is left unchanged. The next comparison is between 9 and

3 and these are swapped to get: 2, 1, 7, 3, 9. This completes
the first pass and although the order is better it is still
not right.

The next pass starts by comparing the 2 and 1 and swapping
them to get 1, 2, 7, 3, 9. Next 2 and 7 are compared and the
list left unchanged. A comparison of 7 and 3 is then made and
they are swapped to give 1, 2, 3, 7, 9 and a final comparison
on this pass leaves the 7 and 9 unchanged.

A final pass through the list requires no more changes to be
made and thus the sort is completed.

A demonstration program will consider the sorting of a list of
bytes into simple numerical order as above. The first item in
the list will be taken as the number of following bytes in the
list rather than as an item to be sorted. The list is taken
as starting at, say, &5000 in the memory and is up to 256
bytes in length.

The subroutine PASS does as its name suggests, it makes a
complete pass through the list interchanging items as above.
If an item is interchanged then the location called flag is
incremented and thus if flag contains 0 at then end of the
subroutine then no swaps have been made. In line 90 the X
register is set up to the number of items in the list and then
a loop is used to go through the list comparing bytes, lines
110 to 130, and then interchanging them if they are in the
wrong order, lines 140 to 190. A test of the X register at the
end of the loop is used to finish the subroutine when a
complete pass through the list has been made.

The subroutine SORT does the actual sorting by repeatedly
calling the subroutine PASS until FLAG indicates that a pass
has been made without any swaps being made.

```
        10    DIM S% 100
        20    LST=&70
        30    FLAG=&72
        40    FOR P = 0 TO 2 STEP 2
        50    P%=S%
        60    [ OPT P
        70    .PASS
```

```
 80    LDY #0: STY FLAG
 90    LDA (LST),Y: TAX: DEX: INY
100    .PLOOP
110    LDA (LST),Y: INY
120    CMP (LST),Y
130    BMI SKIP: BEQ SKIP
140    .SWAP
150    PHA: LDA (LST),Y
160    DEY: STA (LST),Y
170    PLA: INY
180    STA (LST),Y
190    INC FLAG
200    .SKIP
210    DEX
220    BNE PLOOP
230    RTS
240    .SORT
250    LDA #0: STA LST
260    LDA #&50: STA LST+1
270    .RPT
280    JSR PASS
290    LDA FLAG
300    BNE RPT
310    RTS
320    ]
330    NEXT
```

Note that the method of comparison treats the numbers as twos complement numbers and thus they are considered to be in the range -128 to +127.

A few lines of BASIC can be added to input a list to &5000.

```
400    PRINT "HOW MANY ITEMS", N%
410    ?&5000=N%
420    FOR M% = 1 TO N%
430    INPUT "NEXT ITEM ", I%
440    &5000?M%=I%
450    NEXT M%
460    CALL SORT
470    FOR M%= 1 TO N%
480    PRINT ~ &5000?M%; "   ";
490    NEXT M%
```

Appendix A

6502 INSTRUCTION CODES

Notes:

Code is first byte of instruction in hex

Cycles is no of clock cycles that the instruction takes to be obeyed.

* means add 1 if a page boundary is crossed,

+ means add 1 if a branch occurs and add 2 if the branch crosses into another page.

Bytes is the total number of bytes in the instruction.

ADC

Add data plus carry to A.

Modes	Code	Cycles	Bytes	Example
immediate	69	2	2	ADC #5
zero-page	65	3	2	ADC &70
absolute	6D	4	3	ADC &5000
zero-page,X	75	4	2	ADC &70,X
absolute,X	7D	4*	3	ADC &5000,X
absolute,Y	79	4*	3	ADC &5000,Y
(indirect),Y	71	5*	2	ADC (&70),Y
(indirect,X)	61	6	2	ADC (&70,X)

Flags affected: N,Z,C,V

AND

The 8 bit data pattern is logically anded with the data already in A.

247

Modes	Code	Cycles	Bytes	Example
immediate	29	2	2	AND #5
zero-page	25	3	2	AND &70
absolute	2D	4	3	AND &5000
zero-page,X	35	4	2	AND &70,X
absolute,X	3D	4*	3	AND &5000,X
absolute,Y	39	4*	3	AND &5000,Y
(indirect),Y	31	5*	2	AND (&70),Y
(indirect,X)	21	6	2	AND (&70,X)

Flags affected: The Z flag is set to 1 if the result is zero. The N flag is a copy of bit 7 of the result.

ASL

The data pattern specified by the addressing mode is shifted left one place. The bit on the right is filled with a 0. The carry flag is set, after the instruction, with the bit that is shifted out of bit 7 of A.

Modes	Code	Cycles	Bytes	Example
zero-page	06	5	2	ASL &70
absolute	0E	6	3	ASL &5000
zero-page,X	16	6	2	ASL &70,X
absolute,X	1E	7	3	ASL &5000,X
accumulator	0A	2	1	ASL A

Flags affected: If the result is zero the Z flag is set to 1. The carry flag contains the bit shifted out. The N flag is set to bit 7 of the result.

BCC

Branch on carry clear.

Mode	Code	Cycles	Bytes	Example
relative	90	2+	2	BCC &5000

Flags affected: none.

BCS

Branch on carry set.

Mode	Code	Cycles	Bytes	Example
relative	B0	2+	2	BCS &5000

Flags affected: none.

BEQ

Branch on the zero flag set (result equal to zero).

Mode	Code	Cycles	Bytes	Example
relative	F0	2+	2	BEQ &5000

Flags affected: none.

BIT

The bit pattern in A is logical anded with the data specified in the addressing mode and the flags are set according to the result.

Mode	Code	Cycles	Bytes	Example
zero-page	24	3	2	BIT &70
absolute	2C	4	3	BIT &5000

Flags affected: Z is set to 1 if the result is zero, 0 otherwise: V is set to bit 6 of the data: N is set to bit 7 of data

BMI

Branch if N flag is 1 (result is negative).

Mode	Code	Cycles	Bytes	Example
relative	30	2+	2	BMI &5000

Flags affected: none

BNE

Branch if the Z flag is 0 (result not equal to zero).

Mode	Code	Cycles	Bytes	Example
relative	D0	2+	2	BNE &5000

Flags affected: none

BPL

Branch if N is zero (result plus)

Mode	Code	Cycles	Bytes	Example
relative	10	2+	2	BPL &5000

Flags affected: none

BRK

Causes a software interrupt. On the BBC microcomputer this is used by BASIC for the handling of errors. The BRK instruction is followed by a byte which is the error number and by a string, delimited by &0D, which is the error message.

Mode	Code	Cycles	Bytes	Example
implied	00	7	1	BRK

Flags affected: B is set to 1: I is set to 1

BVC

Branch if V is 0

Mode	Code	Cycles	Bytes	Example
relative	50	2+	2	BVC &5000

Flags affected: none

BVS

Branch if V is 1

Mode	Code	Cycles	Bytes	Example
relative	70	2+	2	BVS &5000

Flags affected: none

CLC

Clear the carry (C) flag to 0.

Mode	Code	Cycles	Bytes	Example
implied	18	2	1	CLC

CLD

Clear decimal arithmetic mode.

Mode	Code	Cycles	Bytes	Example
implied	D8	2	1	CLD

Flags affected: D is set to 0.

CLI

Enable interrupts.

Mode	Code	Cycles	Bytes	Example
implied	58	2	1	CLI

Flags affected: I is set to 0.

CLV

Clear the V flag (to reset an overflow condition)

Mode	Code	Cycles	Bytes	Example
implied	B8	2	1	CLV

Flags affected: V is set to 0

CMP

The data specified by the addressing mode is subtracted from A in a special internal register. The flags are set according to the result. A is unchanged.

Mode	Code	Cycles	Bytes	Example
immediate	C9	2	2	CMP #5
zero-page	C5	3	2	CMP &70
absolute	CD	4	3	CMP &5000
zero-page,X	D5	4	2	CMP &70,X
absolute,X	DD	4*	3	CMP &5000,X
absolute,Y	D9	4*	3	CMP &5000,Y
(indirect),Y	D1	5*	2	CMP (&70),Y
(indirect,X)	C1	6	2	CMP (&70,X)

Flags affected: If the data is equal to A then Z and C are both set to 1. If the data is less than A then Z is set to 0 and C is set to 1. If the data is greater than A then Z and C are both set to 0. The N flag is made equal to bit 7 of the result.

CPX

The data specified by the addressing mode is subtracted from X in a special internal register. The flags are set according to the result. X is unchanged.

Mode	Code	Cycles	Bytes	Example
immediate	E0	2	2	CPX #5
zero-page	E4	3	2	CPX &70
absolute	EC	4	3	CPX &5000

Flags affected: as for CMP

CPY

As for CPX but using Y instead of X.

Mode	Code	Cycles	Bytes	Example
immediate	C0	2	2	CPY #5
zero-page	C4	3	2	CPY &70
absolute	CC	4	3	CPY &5000

DEC

The contents of the memory specified by the addressing mode are decreased by 1. If the memory contains zero before the instruction then it contains &FF after.

Mode	Code	Cycles	Bytes	Example
zero-page	C6	5	2	DEC &70
absolute	CE	6	3	DEC &5000
absolute,X	DE	7	3	DEC &5000,X
zero-page,X	D6	6	2	DEC &70,X

Flags affected: If the result is decremented to zero the Z flag is set. The N flag is a copy of bit 7 of the result.

DEX

The contents of X are decremented by 1.

Mode	Code	Cycles	Bytes	Example
implied	CA	2	1	DEX

Flags affected: The Z flag is set to 1 if the result is 0. The N flag is a copy of bit 7 of the result.

DEY

The contents of Y are decremented by 1.

Mode	Code	Cycles	Bytes	Example
implied	88	2	1	DEY

Flags affected: As for DEX.

EOR

The data specified by the addressing mode is exclusive ORed with the A register.

Mode	Code	Cycles	Bytes	Example
immediate	49	2	2	EOR #5
zero-page	45	3	2	EOR &70
absolute	5D	4	3	EOR &5000
zero-page,X	55	4	2	EOR &70,X
absolute,X	5D	4*	3	EOR &5000,X
absolute,Y	59	4*	3	EOR &5000,Y
(indirect),Y	51	5*	2	EOR (&70),Y
(indirect,X)	41	6	2	EOR (&70,X)

Flags affected: Z is set to 1 if the result is zero. N is a copy of bit 7 of the result.

INC

The contents of the memory location specified by the addressing mode are incremented by 1.

Mode	Code	Cycles	Bytes	Example
zero-page	E6	5	2	INC &70
absolute	EE	6	3	INC &5000
zero-page,X	F6	6	2	INC &70,X
absolute,X	FE	7	3	INC &5000,X

Flags affected: As for DEC

INX

The X register is incremented by 1.

Mode	Code	Cycles	Bytes	Example
implied	E8	2	1	INX

Flags affected: As for DEX

INY

The Y register is incremented by 1.

Mode	Code	Cycles	Bytes	Example
implied	C8	2	1	INY

Flags affected: As for DEY

JMP

The CPU jumps to the address specified.

Mode	Code	Cycles	Bytes	Example
absolute	4C	3	3	JMP &5000
indirect	6C	5	3	JMP (&5000)

Flags affected: none

JSR

Jump to the subroutine specified storing the return address (-1) on the stack.

Mode	Code	Cycles	Bytes	Example
absolute	20	6	3	JSR &5000

Flags affected: none

LDA

The A register is loaded with the data specified by the addressing mode.

Mode	Code	Cycles	Bytes	Example
immediate	A9	2	2	LDA #5
zero-page	A5	3	2	LDA &70
absolute	AD	4	3	LDA &5000
zero-page,X	B5	4	2	LDA &70,X
absolute,X	BD	4*	3	LDA &5000,X
absolute,Y	B9	4*	3	LDA &5000,Y
(indirect),Y	B1	5*	2	LDA (&70),Y
(indirect,X)	A1	6	2	LDA (&70,X)

Flags affected: The Z flag is 1 if the data is zero. The N flag is a copy of bit 7 of the data.

LDX

The X register is loaded with the data specified by the addressing mode.

Mode	Code	Cycles	Bytes	Example
immediate	A2	2	2	LDX #5
zero-page	A6	3	2	LDX &70
absolute	AE	4	3	LDX &5000
zero-page,Y	B6	4	2	LDX &70,Y
absolute,Y	BE	4*	3	LDX &5000,Y

Flags affected: As for LDA.

LDY

The Y register is loaded with the data specified by the addressing mode.

Mode	Code	Cycles	Bytes	Example
immediate	A0	2	2	LDY #5
zero-page	A4	3	2	LDY &70
absolute	AC	4	3	LDY &5000
zero-page,X	B4	4	2	LDY &70,X
absolute,X	BC	4*	3	LDY &5000,X

Flags affected: As for LDA.

LSR

The data is moved right by 1 position. Bit 0 goes into the carry, 0 goes into the most significant bit.

Mode	Code	Cycles	Bytes	Example
zero-page	46	5	2	LSR &70
absolute	4E	6	3	LSR &5000
zero-page,X	56	6	2	LSR &70,X
absolute,X	5E	7	3	LSR &5000,X
accumulator	4A	2	1	LSR A

Flags affected: The N flag is reset to 0. The Z flag is set to 1 if the result is zero. The carry flag receives the bit shifted out of bit 0.

NOP

No operation. The CPU does nothing. This is a dummy operation which merely takes up a single byte of code and takes 2 cycles to run.

Mode	Code	Cycles	Bytes	Example
implied	EA	2	1	NOP

Flags affected: none

ORA

The data specified by the addressing mode is logic ORed with the A register.

Mode	Code	Cycles	Bytes	Example
immediate	09	2	2	ORA #5
zero-page	05	3	2	ORA &70
absolute	0D	4	3	ORA &5000
zero-page,X	15	4	2	ORA &70,X
absolute,X	1D	4*	3	ORA &5000,X
absolute,Y	19	4*	3	ORA &5000,Y
(indirect),Y	11	5*	2	ORS (&70),Y
(indirect,X)	01	6	2	ORA (&70,X)

Flags affected: as for AND.

PHA

The value in A is pushed onto the stack and the stack pointer is decremented by 1.

Mode	Code	Cycles	Bytes	Example
implied	48	3	1	PHA

Flags affected: none

PHP

The values of the microprocessor status register (the flags organised as a single byte) are pushed onto the stack and the stack pointer decremented by 1.

Mode	Code	Cycles	Bytes	Example
implied	08	3	1	PHP

Flags affected: none

PLA

The value on the top of the stack is pulled off into the A register. The stack pointer is incremented by 1.

Mode	Code	Cycles	Bytes	Example
implied	68	4	1	PLA

Flags affected: If the data pulled off is zero the Z flag is set to 1. The N flag is a copy of bit 7 of the data.

PLP

The value on the top of the stack is pulled off and placed in the status register.

Mode	Code	Cycles	Bytes	Example
implied	28	4	1	PLP

Flags affected: All flags are changed to the values on the top of the stack.

ROL

The data specified is rotated left one place. The least significant bit is set to the old value of the carry flag. The new value of the carry flag is the bit shifted out of bit 7.

Mode	Code	Cycles	Bytes	Example
zero-page	26	5	2	ROL &70
absolute	2E	6	3	ROL &5000
zero-page,X	36	6	2	ROL &70,X
absolute,X	3E	7	3	ROL &5000,X
accumulator	2A	2	1	ROL A

Flags affected: If the result is zero the Z flag is set. The carry contains the bit shifted out. The N flag contains a copy of bit 7 of the result.

ROR

The data specified is rotated right by 1 place. Bit 7 is set to the old value of the carry flag. the new value of the carry flag is the bit shifted out of bit 0.

Mode	Code	Cycles	Bytes	Example
zero-page	66	5	2	ROR &70
absolute	6E	6	3	ROR &5000
zero-page,X	76	6	2	ROR &70,X
absolute,X	7E	7	3	ROR &5000,X
accumulator	6A	2	1	ROR A

Flags affected: If the result is zero the Z flag is set. The C flag contains the bit shifted out. The N flag is a copy of bit 7 of the result.

RTI

Return to the main program from an interrupt servicing routine.

Mode	Code	Cycles	Bytes	Example
implied	40	6	1	RTI

Flags affected: All flags are restored to the values that they had just before the interrupt was serviced.

RTS

Return to the main program from a subroutine.

Mode	Code	Cycles	Bytes	Example
implied	60	6	1	RTS

Flags affected: None.

SBC

Subtract the data specified from the A register together with the inverse of the carry flag.

Mode	Code	Cycles	Bytes	Example
immediate	E9	2	2	SBC #5
zero-page	E5	3	2	SBC &70
absolute	ED	4	3	SBC &5000
zero-page,X	F5	4	2	SBC &70,X
absolute,X	FD	4*	3	SBC &5000,X
absolute,Y	F9	4*	3	SBC &5000,Y
(indirect),Y	F1	5*	2	SBC (&70),Y
(indirect,X)	E1	6	2	SBC (&70,X)

Flags affected: As for ADC

SEC

Set the carry (C) flag to 1

Mode	Code	Cycles	Bytes	Example
implied	38	2	1	SEC

Flags affected: C is set to 1

SED

Set decimal arithmetic mode.

Mode	Code	Cycles	Bytes	Example
implied	F8	2	1	SED

Flags affected: The D flag is set to 1.

SEI

Disable interrupts.

Mode	Code	Cycles	Bytes	Example
implied	78	2	1	SEI

Flags affected: The I flag is set to 1.

STA

Store the value of A in the memory location specified.

Mode	Code	Cycles	Bytes	Example
zero-page	85	3	2	STA &70
absolute	8D	4	3	STA &5000
zero-page,X	95	4	2	STA &70,X
absolute,X	9D	5	3	STA &5000,X
absolute,Y	99	5	3	STA &5000,Y
(indirect),Y	91	6	2	STA (&70),Y
(indirect,X)	81	6	2	STA (&70,X)

Flags affected: None.

STX

Store the value of X into the memory location specified.

Mode	Code	Cycles	Bytes	Example
zero-page	86	3	2	STX &70
absolute	8E	4	3	STX &5000
zero-page,Y	96	4	2	STX &70,Y

Flags affected: None.

STY

Store the value of Y into the memory location specified.

Mode	Code	Cycles	Bytes	Example
zero-page	84	3	2	STY &70
absolute	8C	4	3	STY &5000
zero-page,X	94	4	2	STY &70,X

Flags affected: None.

TAX

Transfer the contents of A to X.

Mode	Code	Cycles	Bytes	Example
implied	AA	2	1	TAX

Flags affected: If the data is zero the Z flag is set to 1. The N flag is a copy of bit 7 of the data.

TAY

Transfer the contents of A to Y.

Mode	Code	Cycles	Bytes	Example
implied	A8	2	1	TAY

Flags affected: As for TAX.

TSX

The contents of the stack pointer are copied into X.

Mode	Code	Cycles	Bytes	Example
implied	BA	2	1	TSX

Flags affected: As for TAX.

TXA

Transfer the contents of X to A.

Mode	Code	Cycles	Bytes	Example
implied	8A	2	1	TXA

Flags affected: As for TAX.

TXS

Transfer the contents of X to the stack pointer.

Mode	Code	Cycles	Bytes	Example
implied	9A	2	1	TXS

Flags affected: None.

TYA

Transfer the contents of Y to A.

Mode	Code	Cycles	Bytes	Example
implied	98	2	1	TYA

Flags affected: As for TAX.

Appendix B

```
    0GOTO10120
    9FOR£Z=0TO3STEP3:P%=££START:[OPT£Z
   10LDX#0
   20.LOOP
   30LDA&5000,X
   40CMP#&D
   50BEQ EXIT
   60JSR OSWRCH
   65 INX
   70JMPLOOP
   80.EXIT
10040]NEXT
10044?P%=&20
10050?(P%+1)=BREAK MOD &100
10060?(P%+2)=BREAK DIV &100
10065?(P%+3)=0
10070£BADDR%=P%
10080£BRK%(1)=&20
10090£BRK%(2)=BREAK MOD &100
10100£BRK%(3)=BREAK DIV &100
10110VDU15:GOTO10750
10120DIM £TAB$(256)
10121MODE7:OSRDCH=&FFE0:OSWRCH=&FFEE
10122OSASCI=&FFE3:OSNEWL=&FFE7
10123OSWORD=&FFF1:OSBYTE=&FFF4
10125DIM ££START 500
10131OSFIND=&FFCE:OSGPB=&FFD1
10132OSBPUT=&FFD4:OSBGET=&FFD7
10133OSARGS=&FFDA
10155£ASS=0
10160*KEY0
10170*KEY1
10180*KEY2
10210*KEY9
10220*KEY10OLD|MMO.7|MRUN|M
10230VDU12
10240DIM £BRK%(3),£TRA%(3)
```

```
10260DIM £MONITOR% 200
10280PRINTCHR$(141);"MONITOR"
10281PRINTCHR$(141);"MONITOR"
10290PRINT',"(C) Prentice Hall Ltd  1984";'
10300 PRINT"COMMANDS AVAILABLE "'
10303PRINT"Display              memory"TAB(20)"Modify
memory";'"Edit              program"TAB(20)"Assemble
program"'"Run program"TAB(20)"Breakpoint"'"U resume
from                 break"TAB(20)"Trace"'"X
Disassemble"TAB(20)"Goto machine code"
10310PRINT"List  memory as text"TAB(20)"N  Renumber
program"
10311PRINT"Calculations"TAB(20)"S Assembler origin"
10312PRINT"HELP"
10330FOR I=1 TO 256
10340READ £TAB$(I)
10350NEXT I
10360FOR£Z=0TO2STEP2
10370P%=£MONITOR%:[OPT Z
10371.STACK:TSX:TXA:JSR PHEX:RTS
10380.PRTA:CLD:AND #&0F
10390CLC:ADC #&30:CMP #&3A:BMI LT1:CLC:ADC #&7
10400 .LT1:JSR &FFEE
10410 RTS
10420.PHEX:PHP:PHA:PHA:LSR A:LSR A:LSR A:LSR A
10430JSR PRTA:PLA:JSR PRTA:PLA:PLP:RTS
10440 .£A:NOP
10450 .£X:NOP
10460 .£Y:NOP
10470 .£H:NOP
10480 .£L:NOP
10490 .£P:NOP
10500.PBIN:LDA#8:STA£CNT
10510.PBINL:ROL£BIN:BCC PBIN0
10520.PBIN1:LDA#ASC"1":JMP PBINC
10530.PBIN0:LDA#ASC"0"
10540.PBINC:JSR&FFEE
10550DEC£CNT:BNE PBINL:RTS
10560.£CNT:NOP
10570.£BIN:NOP
10580.BREAK:PHP:STA £A:PLA:STA £P
10590STY £Y:STX £X:
10600PLA:STA £L:CLD:SEC:SBC #2:STA £RTL:PLA:STA £H:
```

```
SBC#0:STA£RTH
10610RTS
10620 .TRA:PHP:STA £A:PLA:STA £P
10630STY £Y:STX £X
10640PLA:STA £L:CLD:SEC:SBC #2:STA £RTL:PLA:STA £H:
SBC#0:STA£RTH
10650RTS
10670 .£RTL:NOP:.£RTH:NOP
10680.REST:LDX £X:LDY £Y
10690LDA £H:PHA
10700LDA £L:PHA
10710LDA £P:PHA
10720LDA £A
10725PLP
10730RTS
10740 ]:NEXT
10750REM
10770ON ERROR VDU13:GOTO10780
10780PRINT'"COMMAND ?";:£C$=GET$
10785PRINT£C$;
10786IF£C$="S" THEN13750
10790 IF£C$="B" THENVDU15:GOTO 11590
10800 IF£C$="G" THEN PRINT"OTO ":GOTO11680
10830IF £C$<>"A" THEN 10870
10840PRINT"SSEMBLER ":PRINT"ADDR CODE      SOURCE ":
VDU14
10850ON ERROR VDU15:PRINT"ERROR AT LINE ";ERL
:GOTO10780
10855£ASS=1
10860GOTO9
10870IF £C$="R" THEN VDU15:GOTO10970
10875IF£C$="H" THEN VDU12:GOTO10280
10890IF £C$="E" THEN PRINT"DIT MODE  BASIC"
:GOTO11390
10895IF£C$="C"THEN GOTO12990
10900 IF £C$="M" THEN PRINT"EMORY MODE ":GOTO11100
10910 IF £C$="D" THEN PRINT"ISPLAY MODE":GOTO11230
10930 IF £C$="T" THEN PRINT"RACE -SINGLE STEP PROGRAM"
:GOTO11770
10940 IF £C$="X" THEN 12370
10950 IF £C$="L" THEN12620
10952IF£C$="N" THEN PRINT" RENUMBER USERS PROGRAM"
:GOTO12750
```

```
10955IF £C$="U" THEN GOTO12710
10960VDU13:FORX%=0TO20:VDU32:NEXT:VDU13
10965VDU11:GOTO10780
10970REM
10975IFfASS=0THEN VDU127: PRINT"NOT ASSEMBLED YET"
:GOTO10770
10980PRINT"UNNING ASSEMBLY CODE":CALL ffSTART
10990PRINT'"BREAK AT ";
11000PRINT;~?£RTH*&100+?£RTL;
11010PROC£PRSTAT:GOTO10770
11020DEF PROC£PRSTAT
11030PRINTTAB(13)" A   X   Y   NV BDIZC"
11040PRINTTAB(14);~?£A;TAB(17);~?£X;TAB(20);~?£Y;
11050 ?£BIN=?£P:PRINTTAB(23);:CALL PBIN
11060 ?£BADDR%=£BRK%(1)
11070 ?(£BADDR%+1)=£BRK%(2)
11080 ?(£BADDR%+2)=£BRK%(3)
11090 ENDPROC
11100ONERRORIFERR=17THENGOTO10770ELSE
PRINT"NO SUCH NUMBER":GOTO11110
11110 PRINT"START ADDRESS   ";:INPUT£ADDR$
:£ADDR%=EVAL(£ADDR$)
11120 PRINT"ADDR  CONTENTS"
11130 A%=£ADDR%/&100:CALL PHEX
11140 A%=£ADDR%:CALL PHEX
11150PRINT"   ";:A%=?£ADDR%:CALL PHEX:  PRINT"  ";
11160ONERROR IF ERR=17THEN GOTO10770 ELSE
PRINT "NO SUCH NUMBER":GOTO11120
11170INPUT ""£CODE$
11180IF £CODE$="" THEN 11210
11190IF£CODE$="^" THEN £ADDR%=£ADDR%-1:GOTO11130
11191IFMID$(£CODE$,1,1)="$"THEN
$£ADDR%=MID$(£CODE$,2,LEN(£CODE$)-1)
:£ADDR%=£ADDR%+LEN(£CODE$):GOTO11130
11200?£ADDR%=EVAL (£CODE$)
11210£ADDR%=£ADDR%+1:GOTO11130
11220GOTO 11130
11230INPUT"START ADDRESS ",£ADDR$
11240£DSTART%=EVAL(£ADDR$)
11250INPUT"NO OF BYTES ",£ADDR$
11260£TIMES%=EVAL (£ADDR$)
11270 PRINT"ADDR  MEMORY CONTENTS"
11280 £N%=0
```

```
11290 A%=£DSTART%/&100:CALL PHEX
11300 A%=£DSTART%:CALL PHEX:PRINT"   ";
11310FOR £I%=1 TO 8
11320A%=?£DSTART%:CALL PHEX:PRINT" ";
11330 £DSTART%=£DSTART%+1
11340 £N%=£N%+1
11350IF£N%<£TIMES% THEN 11360 ELSE £I%=8
11360NEXT£I%
11370 IF £TIMES%<£N%+1 THENPRINT:GOTO 10770
11380 PRINT:GOTO11290
11390*KEY00.|MDEL.0,9|MOG.10120|M9FOR£Z=0TO3STEP3
:P%=££START:[OPT£Z|MRUN|M
11400*KEY1L.10,10000|L|M
11430*KEY9DEL.10,10000|L|M
11440*KEY2DEL.10,10000|L|MAU.|L|M
11470PRINT"f0 to return to MONITOR"
11480 PRINT"f1 to list your program"
11490PRINT"f2 to enter a program"
11500 PRINT"ESCAPE key to stop entering a program"
11550PRINT"f9 to completely erase your program"
11560 END
11570 IF ERL <=10000 THEN
PRINT"ASSEMBLER ERROR AT LINE ",ERL ELSE
PRINT"ERROR NO ",ERR," AT LINE ",ERL
11580 GOTO10770
11590IF £ASS=0 THEN VDU127:
PRINT"NOT ASSEMBLED YET":GOTO10780
11592PRINT"REAK ADDRESS? ";
11595£ADDR$=GET$ :PRINT£ADDR$;:IF £ADDR$<>"&"
THEN PRINT" NOT HEX ?"'"B";:GOTO11592
11600INPUT ""£ADDR$:£BADDR%=EVAL ("&"+£ADDR$)
11610£BRK%(1)=?£BADDR%
11620 £BRK%(2)=?(£BADDR%+1)
11630£BRK%(3)=?(£BADDR%+2)
11640?£BADDR%=&20
11650?(£BADDR%+1)=BREAK MOD &100
11660?(£BADDR%+2)=BREAK DIV &100
11670 GOTO10770
11680PRINT"MACHINE CODE ADDRESS ";
11690INPUT £A$
11700£ADDR%=EVAL (£A$)
11710PRINT"RUNNING ASSEMBLY CODE "
11720CALL £ADDR%
```

```
11730GOTO 10780
11770VDU15
11771IF£ASS=0THEN PRINT"NOT ASSEMBLED YET":
GOTO10780
11772?£P=0
11775PRINT"SPACE BAR TO MOVE TO NEXT INSTRUCTION"
11776PRINT"S TO SKIP INSTRUCTIONS"
11777£A$=GET$:IF£A$="S"THEN PROC£S ELSE
IF£A$=" "THEN £TADDR%=££START ELSE GOTO11770
11780£TNXT%=££START
11785PROC£T2
11790£LA$=£TAB$((?£TNXT%)+1):£LL$=LEFT$(£LA$,1):
£ADDR%=£TNXT%:PROCPRMN(£LA$)
11791IF£LA$="BBPL " AND (?£P AND &80)=0THEN
PROC£T1:GOTO11840
11792IF£LA$="BBMI " AND (?£P AND &80)<>0THEN
PROC£T1:GOTO11840
11793IF£LA$="BBVS " AND (?£P AND &40)<>0THEN
PROC£T1:GOTO11840
11794IF£LA$="BBVC " AND (?£P AND &40)=0THEN
PROC£T1:GOTO11840
11795IF£LA$="CJMP "THEN
£TADDR%=?(£TNXT%+1)+&100*?(£TADDR%+2):GOTO11840
11796IF£LA$="BBNE " AND (?£P AND &02)=0 THEN
PROC£T1:GOTO11840
11797IF£LA$="BBEQ " AND (?£P AND &02)<>0 THEN
PROC£T1:GOTO11840
11798IF£LA$="BBCC " AND (?£P AND &01)=0 THEN
PROC£T1:GOTO11840
11799IF£LA$="BBCS " AND (?£P AND &01)<>0 THEN
PROC£T1:GOTO11840
11800 ON ASC£LL$-&40 GOTO11810,11820,11830,11820
      ,11820,11820,11820,11830,11830,11830,11810
11810£TADDR%=£TNXT%+1:GOTO11840
11820£TADDR%=£TNXT%+2:GOTO11840
11830£TADDR%=£TNXT%+3
11840REM
11845PROC£T2
11950£A$=GET$:IF£A$=" "THEN 11790 ELSE IF£A$="S"
THEN PROC£S:PROC£T2:GOTO11790:ELSE11950
11960GOTO10770
11970DEF PROCPRMN(£A$)
11980PRINT
```

```
11990PRINT;~£ADDR%;
12000 PRINT" " ;
12010££A$=MID$(£A$,2,7)
12020 PRINT££A$;:£ADDR%=£ADDR%+1
12030ON ASC (£A$)-&40 GOTO 12040,12050,12070,12110
        ,12140,12170,12190,12210,12250,12280,12320
12040GOTO12350
12050PRINT;~?£ADDR%;:£ADDR%=£ADDR%+1
12060GOTO12350
12070REM
12080A%=?£ADDR%+&100*?(£ADDR%+1)
12090PRINT;~A%;
12100£ADDR%=£ADDR%+2:GOTO12350
12110PRINT;~?£ADDR%;",X";
12120 £ADDR%=£ADDR%+1
12130GOTO12350
12140PRINT;~?£ADDR%;",Y";
12150 £ADDR%=£ADDR%+1
12160GOTO12350
12170PRINT;~?£ADDR%;",X)";
12180£ADDR%=£ADDR%+1:GOTO12350
12190PRINT;~?£ADDR%;"),Y";
12200£ADDR%=£ADDR%+1:GOTO12350
12210A%=?£ADDR%+&100*?(£ADDR%+1)
12220PRINT;~A%;
12230£ADDR%=£ADDR%+2
12240PRINT",X";:GOTO12350
12250A%=?£ADDR%+&100*?(£ADDR%+1)
12260PRINT;~A%;:£ADDR%=£ADDR%+2
12270PRINT",Y";:GOTO12350
12280A%=?£ADDR%+&100*?(£ADDR%+1)
12290PRINT;~A%;
12300£ADDR%=£ADDR%+2
12310 PRINT")";:GOTO12350
12320A%=?(£ADDR%-1):PRINT~;A%;
12330 PRINT"                ";
12340 IF A% >&20 AND A% <ASC ("x") THEN
PRINTCHR$(A%);
12350ENDPROC
12360 END
12370 ON ERROR GOTO 10770
12380DATA ABRK,FORA (,K,K,K,BORA ,BASL ,K,APHP
,BORA #,AASL A,K,K,CORA ,CASL ,K
```

AAL-J

```
12390DATA BBPL ,GORA (,K,K,K,DORA ,DASL ,K,ACLC
,IORA ,K,K,K,HORA ,HASL ,K
12400DATACJSR ,FAND (,K,K,BBIT ,BAND ,BROL ,K
,APLP ,BAND #,AROL A,K,CBIT ,CAND ,CROL ,K
12410DATABBMI ,GAND (,K,K,K,DAND ,DROL ,K
,ASEC ,IAND ,K,K,K,HAND ,HROL ,K
12420DATAARTI ,FEOR (,K,K,K,BEOR ,BLSR ,K,APHA
,BEOR #,ALSR A,K,CJMP ,CEOR ,CLSR ,K
12430DATABBVC ,GEOR (,K,K,K,DEOR ,DLSR ,K,ACLI
,IEOR ,K,K,K,HEOR ,HLSR ,K
12440DATAARTS,FADC (,K,K,K,BADC ,BROR ,K,APLA,BADC #
,AROR A,K,JJMP (,CADC ,CROR ,K
12450DATABBVS ,GADC (,K,K,K,DADC ,DROR ,K,ASEI ,IADC
,K,K,K,HADC ,HROR ,K
12460DATAK,FSTA (,K,K,BSTY ,BSTA ,BSTX ,K,ADEY ,K
,ATXA ,K,CSTY ,CSTA ,CSTX ,K
12470DATABBCC ,GSTA (,K,K,DSTY ,DSTA ,ESTX ,K,ATYA
,ISTA ,ATXS ,K,K,HSTA ,K,K
12480DATABLDY #,FLDA (,BLDX #,BLDY ,K,BLDA ,BLDX ,K
,ATAY,BLDA #,ATAX ,K,CLDY ,CLDA ,CLDX ,K
12490DATABBCS ,GLDA (,K,DLDY,K,DLDA ,ELDX ,K,ACLV
,ILDA ,ATSX,K,HLDY ,HLDA ,ILDX ,K
12500DATA BCPY #,FCMP (,K,K,BCPY ,BCMP ,BDEC ,K
,AINY,BCMP #,ADEX,K,CCPY ,CCMP ,CDEC ,K
12510DATABBNE ,GCMP (,K,K,K,DCMP ,DDEC ,K,ACLD,ICMP
,K,K,K,HCMP ,HDEC ,K
12520DATABCPX #,FSBC (,K,K,BCPX ,BSBC ,BINC ,K,AINX
,BSBC #,ANOP,K,CCPX ,CSBC ,CINC ,K
12530 DATABBEQ ,GSBC (,K,K,K,DSBC ,DINC ,K,ASED,ISBC
,K,K,K,HSBC ,HINC ,K
12540 INPUT" DISSASSEMBLER ADDRESS ",XT$:
£ADDR%=EVAL(XT$)
12550 INPUT"NO OF INSTR ",XT$
12560 VDU 14
12570£N=EVAL(XT$)
12580 FOR £I=1 TO £N
12590PROCPRMN(£TAB$(?(£ADDR%)+1))
12600NEXT £I
12610GOTO 10770
12620 ON ERROR VDU15:GOTO 10770
12630VDU 14:INPUT"IST START ",£A$
12640£A%=EVAL(£A$)
12650IF £A% MOD &100 =0 THEN PRINT:A%=£A% DIV &100:
```

```
CALL PHEX:A%=£A%MOD &100: CALL PHEX:PRINT
12660 IF ?£A%>&1F AND ?£A%<ASC("z")+1THEN
PRINTCHR$(?£A%);  ELSE PRINT "~";
12670£A%=£A%+1:GOTO12650
12680DEFPROC£T1
12690IF ?(£TNXT%+1)>127 THEN
£TADDR%=£TNXT%+?(£TNXT%+1)+2-256ELSE
£TADDR%=£TNXT%+?(£TNXT%+1)+2
12700ENDPROC
12710PRINT" RESUME AT ";~&100*?£RTH+?£RTL
12715£RTN=&100*?£RTH+?£RTL-1
12720?£H=£RTN DIV &100:?£L=£RTN MOD&100
12730CALL REST
12740GOTO10990
12750£L%=PAGE
12760£N%=20
12770REPEAT
12775£L%=£L%+?(£L%+3)
12780UNTIL (?(£L%+1)*&100+?(£L%+2))>9
12800REPEAT
12810?(£L%+1)=£N%/&100
12820?(£L%+2)=£N%
12830£L%=£L%+?(£L%+3)
12835£N%=£N%+10
12840UNTIL ?(£L%+1)*&100+?(£L%+2) >10000
12850GOTO10770
12860DEF PROC£T2
12870£TRA%(1)=?£TADDR%
12880£TRA%(2)=?(£TADDR%+1)
12890£TRA%(3)=?(£TADDR%+2)
12900?£TADDR%=&20
12910?(£TADDR%+1)=TRA MOD &100
12920?(£TADDR%+2)=TRA DIV &100
12930?£L=(£TNXT%-1) MOD &100:
?£H=(£TNXT%-1) DIV &100: CALL REST
12940PROC£PRSTAT
12950?£TADDR%=£TRA%(1):?(£TADDR%+1)=£TRA%(2)
12960?(£TADDR%+2)=£TRA%(3)
12970£TNXT%=£TADDR%
12980ENDPROC
12990PRINT"ALCULATIONS"
12995ON ERROR PRINT"ERROR": GOTO10770
13000PRINT"Hex or Decimal Result ? ";
```

```
13010£A$=GET$
13015PRINT
13020 IF £A$="H" THEN PRINT"HEX RESULT OF ";:
INPUT£A$:PRINT" = ";~EVAL£A$;
13030 IF £A$="D" THENPRINT"DECIMAL RESULT OF ";:
INPUT£A$:PRINT" = ";EVAL£A$
13040GOTO10780
13050DEF PROC£S
13060PRINT'"SKIP TRACING UP TO ADDRESS ? ";
13070£A$=GET$:PRINT£A$;:IF £A$<>"&"THEN
PRINT"NOT HEX":GOTO13060
13080INPUT""£A$:£TADDR%=EVAL("&"+£A$)
13090ENDPROC
13750PRINT'"INPUT NEW ASSEMBLY START ADDRESS"'
"(MUST BE GREATER THAN &";~(TOP+&F00);") ";:INPUT""A$
13760IF EVAL A$<TOP+&F00 THEN13750
13770££START=EVAL A$
13780GOTO10780
```

Appendix C

HEX CODE	CHAR
20	
21	!
22	"
23	#
24	$
25	%
26	&
27	'
28	(
29	)
2A	*
2B	+
2C	,
2D	-
2E	.
2F	/
30	0
31	1
32	2
33	3
34	4
35	5
36	6
37	7
38	8
39	9
3A	:
3B	;
3C	<
3D	=
3E	>
3F	?
40	@
41	A
42	B
43	C
44	D

HEX CODE	CHAR
45	E
46	F
47	G
48	H
49	I
4A	J
4B	K
4C	L
4D	M
4E	N
4F	O
50	P
51	Q
52	R
53	S
54	T
55	U
56	V
57	W
58	X
59	Y
5A	Z
5B	[
5C	\
5D	]
5E	^
5F	_
60	£
61	a
62	b
63	c
64	d
65	e
66	f
67	g
68	h
69	i
6A	j
6B	k
6C	l

HEX CODE	CHAR
6D	m
6E	n
6F	o
70	p
71	q
72	r
73	s
74	t
75	u
76	v
77	w
78	x
79	y
7A	z
7B	{
7C	¦
7D	}
7E	~

Appendix D

BIBLIOGRAPHY

1. The BBC Microcomputer USER GUIDE, John Coll, British Broadcasting Corporation.

2. THE ADVANCED USER GUIDE FOR THE BBC MICRO, BRAY, DICKENS & HOLMES, Cambridge Microcomputer Centre

3. 6502 Assembly Language Subroutines, Leventhal

Appendix E

LISTING OF PLANE4 - CHAPTER 9

```
  10 MODE 4
 900 XC=&70: YC=&72: ADDR=&74
 910 YADD=&76: XADD=&78
 920 BYTE=&7A:XSHIFT=&7C
 930 DIM S% 600
 935 DIM ST 128
 940 FOR PASS=0 TO 2 STEP 2
 945 OBJ=&7E: OBJIND=&80
 946 XL=&81:YL=&82:YCT=&83
 947 XP=8
 948 STP =&84
 950 P%=S%
 960[ OPT PASS
 970 .PUT
 980 CLD
1000.YCALC
1010LDA YC:AND#&F8: STA YADD
1020LDA #0: STA YADD+1
1030ASL YADD: ROL YADD+1
1040ASL YADD: ROL YADD+1
1050LDA YC: AND #&F8
1060CLC: ADC YADD: STA YADD
1070BCC Y1: INC YADD+1
1080.Y1
1090ASL YADD: ROL YADD+1
1100ASL YADD: ROL YADD+1
1110ASL YADD: ROL YADD+1
1120LDA YC: AND #7:CLC
1130ADC YADD: STA YADD
1140BCC Y2: INC YADD+1
1150.Y2
1500.XCALC
1510LDA XC: AND #7: STA XSHIFT
1520LDA XC: AND #&F8: STA XADD
1530LDA XC+1: STA XADD+1
1550LDA #HIMEM MOD &100
1560CLC: ADC YADD: STA ADDR
```

```
1570LDA #HIMEM DIV &100: ADC YADD+1
1580STA ADDR+1
1590LDA ADDR: CLC
1600ADC XADD: STA ADDR
1610LDA ADDR+1: ADC XADD+1
1620STA ADDR+1
1650LDA #0: STA BYTE+1
1660LDA XSHIFT: BEQ WR1
1670.XLOOP
1680LSR BYTE: ROR BYTE+1
1690DEC XSHIFT
1700BNE XLOOP
1710.WR1
1720LDY #0: LDA (ADDR),Y: PHA
1730ORA BYTE: STA (ADDR),Y
1740PLA: STA BYTE: LDY #8
1750LDA (ADDR),Y: PHA
1760ORA BYTE+1: STA (ADDR),Y
1770PLA: STA BYTE+1
1800 RTS
1900.PUT8
1910LDA #0:STA OBJIND
1920LDX #8
1930.OBLP
1940LDY OBJIND
1950LDA (OBJ),Y: STA BYTE
1960JSR PUT
1970INC OBJIND: INC YC
1980DEX: BNE OBLP
1990RTS
2110.PUTOBJ
2111 LDX#0
2120LDA XL: PHA
2130LDA #0: STA OBJIND
2140.PU1
2150LDA YL: STA YCT
2160.PU2
2170LDY OBJIND
2180LDA (OBJ),Y: STA BYTE
2190JSR PUT
2191 LDA ADDR: STA ST,X:INX
2192 LDA ADDR+1:STA ST,X: INX
2193 LDA BYTE: STA ST,X: INX
```

```
2194 LDA BYTE+1: STA ST,X: INX
2200INC OBJIND:INC YC
2210DEC YCT:BNE PU2
2220LDA XC:CLC:ADC #XP:STA XC
2230BCC PU3: INC XC+1
2240.PU3 LDA YC:SEC:SBC YL:STA YC
2250DEC XL:BNE PU1
2260PLA: STA XL
2270.PU4
2280LDA XC:SEC:SBC #XP:STA XC:BCS PU5
2290DEC XC+1: .PU5
2300DEC XL: BNE PU4
2310RTS
2400.REST
2410LDX STP
2420.RSTLP
2430LDY#0
2440LDA ST,X: STA ADDR: INX
2450LDA ST,X:STA ADDR+1: INX
2460LDA ST,X: STA (ADDR),Y: INX
2470LDA ST,X: LDY #8
2480STA (ADDR),Y
2490TXA: SEC: SBC #7: TAX
2500BPL RSTLP
2510RTS
2600.SYNC
2610LDA#19
2620JSR &FFF4
2630RTS
2650.TESTKEY
2660LDY #&FF
2670LDA #&81
2680JSR &FFF4
2690TXA: RTS
5000.fly
5010LDA #PLANE MOD &100: STA OBJ
5020LDA #PLANE DIV &100: STA OBJ+1
5030LDA #0: STA XC:STA XC+1:LDA#100:STA YC
5040.SPLP
5050LDA #2: STA XL: LDA #8: STA YL
5060LDA #60: STA STP
5070JSR PUTOBJ
5075 JSR SYNC
```

```
5080JSR REST
5085LDX#(-54 AND &FF):JSR TESTKEY
5086BEQ NTU:SEC :LDA YC: SBC#2: STA YC
5087JMP SPLP
5088.NTU LDX #(-51 AND &FF): JSR TESTKEY
5089BEQ NTD: CLC: LDA YC:ADC #2:STA YC
5090JMP SPLP
5091.NTD LDX #(-87 AND &FF): JSR TESTKEY
5092BEQ NTL: SEC: LDA XC:SBC #2:STA XC
5093BCS SPLP: DEC XC+1:JMP SPLP
5094.NTL LDX #(-52 AND &FF):JSR TESTKEY
5095BEQ SPLP: CLC:LDA XC: ADC #2: STA XC
5096BCC SPLP: INC XC+1:JMP SPLP
5100JMP SPLP
6000 .PLANE
6010]
6015 NEXT
6020FOR Z=P% TO P%+15
6030READ A$
6040?Z=EVAL A$
6050NEXT
6060DATA &0,&80,&C0,&E0,&F0,&FF,&C0,&FF
6070DATA &0,&0,&0,&0,&1C,&F4,&FE,&FF
6080CALL fly
```

LISTING OF ARROW5 - CHAPTER 9

```
  10 MODE5
 900 XC=&70: YC=&72: ADDR=&74
 910 YADD=&76: XADD=&78
 920 BYTE=&7A:XSHIFT=&7C
 930 DIM S% 600
 935 DIM ST 128
 940 FOR PASS=0 TO 2 STEP 2
 945 OBJ=&7E: OBJIND=&80
 946 XL=&81:YL=&82:YCT=&83
 947 XP=4
 948 STP =&84
 950 P%=S%
 960[ OPT PASS
 970 .PUT
 980 CLD
```

```
1000.YCALC
1010LDA YC:AND#&F8: STA YADD
1020LDA #0: STA YADD+1
1030ASL YADD: ROL YADD+1
1040ASL YADD: ROL YADD+1
1050LDA YC: AND #&F8
1060CLC: ADC YADD: STA YADD
1070BCC Y1: INC YADD+1
1080.Y1
1090ASL YADD: ROL YADD+1
1100ASL YADD: ROL YADD+1
1110ASL YADD: ROL YADD+1
1120LDA YC: AND #7:CLC
1130ADC YADD: STA YADD
1140BCC Y2: INC YADD+1
1150.Y2
1500.XCALC
1510 LDA XC: AND #3:STA XSHIFT
1520 LDA XC: AND #&FC: STA XADD
1530LDA XC+1: STA XADD+1
1535 CLC: ASL XADD: ROL XADD+1
1550LDA #HIMEM MOD &100
1560CLC: ADC YADD: STA ADDR
1570LDA #HIMEM DIV &100: ADC YADD+1
1580STA ADDR+1
1590LDA ADDR: CLC
1600ADC XADD: STA ADDR
1610LDA ADDR+1: ADC XADD+1
1620STA ADDR+1
1650LDA #0: STA BYTE+1
1660LDA XSHIFT: BEQ WR1
1670.XLOOP
1680 JSR SHIFT5
1690DEC XSHIFT
1700BNE XLOOP
1710.WR1
1720LDY #0: LDA (ADDR),Y: PHA
1730ORA BYTE: STA (ADDR),Y
1740PLA: STA BYTE: LDY #8
1750LDA (ADDR),Y: PHA
1760ORA BYTE+1: STA (ADDR),Y
1770PLA: STA BYTE+1
1800 RTS
```

```
1900.PUT8
1910LDA #0:STA OBJIND
1920LDX #8
1930.OBLP
1940LDY OBJIND
1950LDA (OBJ),Y: STA BYTE
1960JSR PUT
1970INC OBJIND: INC YC
1980DEX: BNE OBLP
1990RTS
2110.PUTOBJ
2111 LDX#0
2120LDA XL: PHA
2130LDA #0: STA OBJIND
2140.PU1
2150LDA YL: STA YCT
2160.PU2
2170LDY OBJIND
2180LDA (OBJ),Y: STA BYTE
2190JSR PUT
2191 LDA ADDR: STA ST,X:INX
2192 LDA ADDR+1:STA ST,X: INX
2193 LDA BYTE: STA ST,X: INX
2194 LDA BYTE+1: STA ST,X: INX
2200INC OBJIND:INC YC
2210DEC YCT:BNE PU2
2220LDA XC:CLC:ADC #XP:STA XC
2230BCC PU3: INC XC+1
2240.PU3 LDA YC:SEC:SBC YL:STA YC
2250DEC XL:BNE PU1
2260PLA: STA XL
2270.PU4
2280LDA XC:SEC:SBC #XP:STA XC:BCS PU5
2290DEC XC+1: .PU5
2300DEC XL: BNE PU4
2310RTS
2400.REST
2410LDX STP
2420.RSTLP
2430LDY#0
2440LDA ST,X: STA ADDR: INX
2450LDA ST,X:STA ADDR+1: INX
2460LDA ST,X: STA (ADDR),Y: INX
```

```
2470LDA ST,X: LDY #8
2480STA (ADDR),Y
2490TXA: SEC: SBC #7: TAX
2500BPL RSTLP
2510RTS
2600.SYNC
2610LDA#19
2620JSR &FFF4
2630RTS
2650.TESTKEY
2660LDY #&FF
2670LDA #&81
2680JSR &FFF4
2690TXA: RTS
2700.SHIFT5
2710ROR BYTE+1: LDA #&77: AND BYTE+1
2720STA BYTE+1
2730LDA BYTE:AND #&11
2740ASL A: ASL A: ASL A
2750ORA BYTE+1: STA BYTE+1
2760LDA BYTE: LSR A
2770AND #&77: STA BYTE
2780RTS
5000.fly
5010LDA #PLANE MOD &100: STA OBJ
5020LDA #PLANE DIV &100: STA OBJ+1
5030LDA #0: STA XC:STA XC+1:LDA#100:STA YC
5040.SPLP
5050LDA #2: STA XL: LDA #8: STA YL
5060LDA #60: STA STP
5070JSR PUTOBJ
5075 JSR SYNC
5080JSR REST
5085LDX#(-54 AND &FF):JSR TESTKEY
5086BEQ NTU:SEC :LDA YC: SBC#2: STA YC
5087JMP SPLP
5088.NTU LDX #(-51 AND &FF): JSR TESTKEY
5089BEQ NTD: CLC: LDA YC:ADC #2:STA YC
5090JMP SPLP
5091.NTD LDX #(-87 AND &FF): JSR TESTKEY
5092BEQ NTL: SEC: LDA XC:SBC #2:STA XC
5093BCS SPLP: DEC XC+1:JMP SPLP
5094.NTL LDX #(-52 AND &FF):JSR TESTKEY
```

```
5095BEQ SPLP: CLC:LDA XC: ADC #2: STA XC
5096BCC SPLP: INC XC+1:JMP SPLP
5100JMP SPLP
6000 .PLANE
6010]
6015 NEXT
6020FOR Z=P% TO P%+15
6030READ A$
6040?Z=EVAL A$
6050NEXT
6060 DATA &80,&40,&20,&0F,&0F,&20,&40,&80
6070 DATA &88,&44,&22,&0F,&0F,&22,&44,&88
6080CALL fly
```

LISTING OF THING2.TXT - CHAPTER 9

```
  10 MODE 2
 900 XC=&70: YC=&72: ADDR=&74
 910 YADD=&76: XADD=&78
 920 BYTE=&7A:XSHIFT=&7C
 930 DIM S% 600
 935 DIM ST 128
 940 FOR PASS=0 TO 2 STEP 2
 945 OBJ=&7E: OBJIND=&80
 946 XL=&81:YL=&82:YCT=&83
 947 XP=2
 948 STP =&84
 950 P%=S%
 960[ OPT PASS
 970 .PUT
 980 CLD
1000.YCALC
1010LDA YC:AND#&F8: STA YADD
1020LDA #0: STA YADD+1
1030ASL YADD: ROL YADD+1
1040ASL YADD: ROL YADD+1
1050LDA YC: AND #&F8
1060CLC: ADC YADD: STA YADD
1070BCC Y1: INC YADD+1
1080.Y1
1090ASL YADD: ROL YADD+1
1100ASL YADD: ROL YADD+1
```

```
1110ASL YADD: ROL YADD+1
1115 ASL YADD:ROL YADD+1
1120LDA YC: AND #7:CLC
1130ADC YADD: STA YADD
1140BCC Y2: INC YADD+1
1150.Y2
1500.XCALC
1510 LDA XC: AND #1:STA XSHIFT
1520 LDA XC: AND #&FE: STA XADD
1530LDA XC+1: STA XADD+1
1535 ASL XADD: ROL XADD+1
1536 ASL XADD: ROL XADD+1
1550LDA #HIMEM MOD &100
1560CLC: ADC YADD: STA ADDR
1570LDA #HIMEM DIV &100: ADC YADD+1
1580STA ADDR+1
1590LDA ADDR: CLC
1600ADC XADD: STA ADDR
1610LDA ADDR+1: ADC XADD+1
1620STA ADDR+1
1650LDA #0: STA BYTE+1
1660LDA XSHIFT: BEQ WR1
1670.XLOOP
1680 JSR SHIFT2
1690DEC XSHIFT
1700BNE XLOOP
1710.WR1
1720LDY #0: LDA (ADDR),Y: PHA
1730ORA BYTE: STA (ADDR),Y
1740PLA: STA BYTE: LDY #8
1750LDA (ADDR),Y: PHA
1760ORA BYTE+1: STA (ADDR),Y
1770PLA: STA BYTE+1
1800 RTS
1900.PUT8
1910LDA #0:STA OBJIND
1920LDX #8
1930.OBLP
1940LDY OBJIND
1950LDA (OBJ),Y: STA BYTE
1960JSR PUT
1970INC OBJIND: INC YC
1980DEX: BNE OBLP
```

```
1990RTS
2110.PUTOBJ
2111 LDX#0
2120LDA XL: PHA
2130LDA #0: STA OBJIND
2140.PU1
2150LDA YL: STA YCT
2160.PU2
2170LDY OBJIND
2180LDA (OBJ),Y: STA BYTE
2190JSR PUT
2191 LDA ADDR: STA ST,X:INX
2192 LDA ADDR+1:STA ST,X: INX
2193 LDA BYTE: STA ST,X: INX
2194 LDA BYTE+1: STA ST,X: INX
2200INC OBJIND:INC YC
2210DEC YCT:BNE PU2
2220LDA XC:CLC:ADC #XP:STA XC
2230BCC PU3: INC XC+1
2240.PU3 LDA YC:SEC:SBC YL:STA YC
2250DEC XL:BNE PU1
2260PLA: STA XL
2270.PU4
2280LDA XC:SEC:SBC #XP:STA XC:BCS PU5
2290DEC XC+1: .PU5
2300DEC XL: BNE PU4
2310RTS
2400.REST
2410LDX STP
2420.RSTLP
2430LDY#0
2440LDA ST,X: STA ADDR: INX
2450LDA ST,X:STA ADDR+1: INX
2460LDA ST,X: STA (ADDR),Y: INX
2470LDA ST,X: LDY #8
2480STA (ADDR),Y
2490TXA: SEC: SBC #7: TAX
2500BPL RSTLP
2510RTS
2600.SYNC
2610LDA#19
2620JSR &FFF4
2630RTS
```

```
2650.TESTKEY
2660LDY #&FF
2670LDA #&81
2680JSR &FFF4
2690TXA: RTS
2700.SHIFT5
2710ROR BYTE+1: LDA #&77: AND BYTE+1
2720STA BYTE+1
2730LDA BYTE:AND #&11
2740ASL A: ASL A: ASL A
2750ORA BYTE+1: STA BYTE+1
2760LDA BYTE: LSR A
2770AND #&77: STA BYTE
2780RTS
2800.SHIFT2
2810ROR BYTE+1:LDA#&55:AND BYTE+1
2820STA BYTE+1
2830LDA #&55: AND BYTE: ASL A
2840ORA BYTE+1: STA BYTE+1
2850LDA BYTE: AND #&AA
2860LSR A: STA BYTE
2870RTS
5000.fly
5010LDA #PLANE MOD &100: STA OBJ
5020LDA #PLANE DIV &100: STA OBJ+1
5030LDA #0: STA XC:STA XC+1:LDA#100:STA YC
5040.SPLP
5050 LDA#4:STA XL:LDA#8: STA YL
5060 LDA#124: STA STP
5070JSR PUTOBJ
5075 JSR SYNC
5080JSR REST
5085LDX#(-54 AND &FF):JSR TESTKEY
5086BEQ NTU:SEC :LDA YC: SBC#2: STA YC
5087JMP SPLP
5088.NTU LDX #(-51 AND &FF): JSR TESTKEY
5089BEQ NTD: CLC: LDA YC:ADC #2:STA YC
5090JMP SPLP
5091.NTD LDX #(-87 AND &FF): JSR TESTKEY
5092BEQ NTL: SEC: LDA XC:SBC #2:STA XC
5093BCS SPLP: DEC XC+1:JMP SPLP
5094.NTL LDX #(-52 AND &FF):JSR TESTKEY
5095BEQ SPLP: CLC:LDA XC: ADC #2: STA XC
```

```
5096BCC SPLP: INC XC+1:JMP SPLP
5100JMP SPLP
6000 .PLANE
6010]
6015 NEXT
6020FOR Z=P% TO P%+31
6030READ A$
6040?Z=EVAL A$
6050NEXT
6060DATA &00,&00,&00,&10,&30,&20,&20,&00
6065DATA &04,&0D,&0D,&0D,&0D,&0D,&41,&D6
6070DATA &00,&08,&08,&18,&18,&08,&00,&82
6075DATA &00,&00,&00,&00,&20,&20,&20,&00
6080CALL fly
```

LISTING OF WORD PROCESSOR WPRO - CHAPTER 11

```
 10 DIM TEXT 3000, WPRO 1000
 20 OSWRCH=&FFEE:OSRDCH=&FFE0:OSBYTE=&FFF4
 30 OSASCI=&FFE3
 40 TXTPNT=&70: CUR=&72
 50 FOR PASS=0 TO 2 STEP 2
 60 P%=WPRO
 70 [OPT PASS
100.LCUR
110LDA CUR:SEC:SBC #1:STA CUR
120BCS LC1:DEC CUR+1
130.LC1:RTS
140.RCUR
150LDA CUR:CLC:ADC#1:STA CUR
160BCC RC1:INC CUR+1
170.RC1:RTS
180.PNTINC
190LDA TXTPNT:CLC:ADC#1:STA TXTPNT
200BCC PN1:INC TXTPNT+1
210.PN1 RTS
220.INCHR
230LDA CUR: STA TXTPNT
240LDA CUR+1:STA TXTPNT+1
245 TXA:PHA
250.INLOOP
260LDY#0
```

```
270LDA (TXTPNT),Y:PHA
280TXA:STA (TXTPNT),Y
285 JSR OSASCI
290PLA :CMP#&80:BEQ INESC
300TAX
310JSR PNTINC
320JMP INLOOP
330.INESC
340LDY#1:STA (TXTPNT),Y
350JSR RCUR
355PLA:CMP#&D:BNE IN1
356JSR WRTEXT
357.IN1
358 JSR WRCUR
360RTS
370.DELCHR
380LDA CUR:STA TXTPNT
390LDA CUR+1:STA TXTPNT+1
395 LDY#0:LDA(CUR),Y:PHA
400.DLOOP
410LDY#1:LDA (TXTPNT),Y
420DEY: STA (TXTPNT),Y
430CMP#&80:BEQ DESC
431CMP#&D:BNE DD7
432LDA#&20:JSR OSWRCH
433LDA#&D
434.DD7
435 JSR OSASCI
440JSR PNTINC
450JMP DLOOP
460.DESC
463 LDA #ASC" ":JSR OSWRCH
465 PLA: CMP #&D:BNE DD1
466 JSR WRTEXT
467 .DD1
469 JSR WRCUR
470RTS
500.WRTEXT
510JSR SETPNT
520LDA#&C:JSR OSWRCH
530LDY#0
540.WRLOOP
550LDA(TXTPNT),Y:CMP#&80
```

```
560BEQ WRESC
570JSR OSASCI
580JSR PNTINC
590JMP WRLOOP
600.WRESC
610RTS
620.SETPNT
630LDA #TEXT MOD &100:STA TXTPNT
640LDA #TEXT DIV &100:STA TXTPNT+1
650RTS
700.WRCUR
710LDA#&1E:JSR OSWRCH
720JSR SETPNT
730.CRLOOP
740LDA CUR+1: CMP TXTPNT+1
750BNE CR1
760LDA CUR: CMP TXTPNT: BEQ ESCUR
770.CR1
780LDY#0:LDA(TXTPNT),Y
790CMP#&D:BEQ CR2
800LDA#9
810.CR2
820JSR OSASCI
830JSR PNTINC
840JMP CRLOOP
850.ESCUR
860RTS
1000.INIT CLD
1010LDA#TEXT MOD&100:STA CUR
1020LDA#TEXT DIV &100:STA CUR+1
1030LDA#&80:LDY#0:STA(CUR),Y
1040LDA#4:LDX#1:JSR OSBYTE
1050RTS
1100.CMD
1110JSR INIT
1120JSR WRTEXT
1130 JSR WRCUR
1140.CMDLP
1150JSR OSRDCH
1152CMP#&1B:BNE NOESC
1154LDA#&7E:JSR OSBYTE
1156LDA#4:LDX#0:JSR OSBYTE
1158JMP&FFE7
```

```
1159.NOESC
1160CMP#&88:BNE CM1
1170JSR LEFT:JMP CMDLP
1180.CM1
1190CMP#&89:BNE CM2
1200JSR RIGHT:JMP CMDLP
1210.CM2
1220CMP#&7F:BNE CM3
1230JSR DELCHR:JMP CMDLP
1240.CM3
1241 CMP#&8A:BNE CM4
1242 LDX#&D:JSR SRCHR
1243JMP CMDLP
1244.CM4
1245 CMP#&8B:BNE CM5
1246 LDX#&D:JSR SRCHL
1247JMP CMDLP
1248 .CM5
1250TAX:JSR INCHR
1260JMP CMDLP
1300.LEFT
1301LDA CUR: CMP #TEXT MOD &100
1302 BNE LFT2
1303 LDA CUR+1:CMP #TEXT DIV &100
1304 BEQ RT1
1306.LFT2
1310JSR LCUR
1320LDA#8:JSR OSWRCH
1330LDY#0:LDA(CUR),Y
1340CMP #&D: BNE LFT1
1350JSR WRCUR
1360.LFT1 RTS
1400.RIGHT
1410LDY#0:LDA (CUR),Y
1415CMP#&80:BEQ RT1:PHA
1420JSR RCUR
1430LDA#9:JSR OSWRCH
1440PLA:CMP#&D
1450BNE RT1
1460JSR WRCUR
1470.RT1 RTS
1500.SRCHR
1510LDY#0
```

```
1520.SRLP
1530LDA(CUR),Y:CMP#&80:BEQ SRR1
1540JSR RCUR
1550TXA:CMP (CUR),Y
1560BNE SRLP
1570.SRR1
1580 JSR WRCUR:RTS
1600.SRCHL
1610LDY#0
1620.SLLP
1630LDA#TEXT MOD&100
1640CMP CUR:BNE SLL1
1650LDA #TEXT DIV &100
1660CMP CUR+1: BEQ SLL2
1670.SLL1
1680JSR LCUR
1690TXA: CMP(CUR),Y
1700BNE SLLP
1710.SLL2
1720 JSR WRCUR:RTS
2000 ]
2010 NEXT
2020 CALL CMD
```

Index